Urban Encounters

Urban Encounters

Helen Liggett

Minneapolis   London

University of Minnesota Press

Published by the University of Minnesota Press
111 Third Avenue South, Suite 290
Minneapolis, MN 55401-2520
http://www.upress.umn.edu

Printed in the United States of America on acid-free paper

The University of Minnesota is an equal-opportunity educator and employer.

Library of Congress Cataloging-in-Publication Data

Liggett, Helen.
    Urban encounters / Helen Liggett.
        p. cm.
Includes bibliographical references and index.
    ISBN 0-8166-4126-9 (HC : alk. paper) — ISBN 0-8166-4127-7 (PB : alk. paper)
    1. Cities and towns—United States. 2. Cities and towns—United States—
Pictorial works. 3. City and town life—United States—Pictorial works.
4. Urban geography—United States. I. Title.

    HT123 .L44 2003

                                                                    2002153622

12 11 10 09 08 07 06 05 04 03   10 9 8 7 6 5 4 3 2 1

Contents

Preface
vii

Introduction
ix

Urban
1

Space
37

City
75

Streets
117

Acknowledgments
161

Notes
165

Index
183

Preface

This is a book of images and text written for people who read on the way to work instead of looking at the city around them. The text is arranged into four sections: "Urban," "Space," "City," "Streets." They present an argument for approaching urban experience as a situation of indebtedness rather than as a site for enacting prior narratives.

There is play between images and text. Each is meant to be read with attention to the other. Both images and text function as instruments of thought; neither merely illustrates the other. The images are also independent of the text, arranged in sequences designed as "constellations" of city life. Each individual image also stands alone as testimony to life in the city.

The book encourages participatory reading in a way not different from reading in general but perhaps more self-conscious about the reading process. I wish to invite attention to how the processes of attracting meanings is indebted to situations in which readers find themselves as well as to the circumstances that make street photography possible.

Photography is not confined to arresting time as a holding back; it also uses the light to provoke a letting go—a tribute to the art of life. A bow to the city.

Introduction

You have to have situation awareness.

> —LT. COL. SHINGLES, U.S. Marine Corps, during a National Public Radio
> interview on training for urban warfare

This book enters the battle for situation awareness. In a way that differs from how I imagine the U.S. Marine Corps approaching the issue, it is not about the truth of the urban situation, or power over it, or control of its contingencies. Instead, I come to terms with the city by presenting "urban encounters." These encounters are based in urban experience without pretending to tell the truth or even to construct a narrative about the city. Rather than assessing the city as a site of economic production or as an object of governance, this work seeks out cities as places of life.

The following sections are arranged as sequences of images and text. They are montages, or encounters, in which the joys of looking around are combined with the deep pleasures of making connections. This entails recognizing irony and beauty as well as fear and danger. One of the mysteries explored in this book is why cultural conventions lead us to expect the latter from urban space while on city streets the former is so often the case.

The analytic component of each section focuses on how prejudices presented in discussions of public issues and embodied in cultural codes either remove us or bring us into relationship with the city as lived space. The images in each section retain a visible relation to that lived space; sometimes complementing the text, sometimes contradicting it. Thus the book as a whole brings Urban Space and City Streets together as instruments of engagement.

Urban

American urban studies and planning education are heavily empirical. When and where theory does appear, it tends to be highly Americacentric in ways that highlight current public issues as they are understood from within the perspective of traditional cognitive conundrums. This blurs the distinction between "the city" and "urban culture." There are thoughts on Los Angeles and Disneyland; there are hopes for urban neighborhoods and the fate of democracy at large; there are concerns about past industrial cities in need and reports on the failure of urban policy in general.

Such tendencies favor the cognitive over the felt. They are organized around issues of economic production and political governance and do not problematize overlapping issues of cultural presentation except as critique. Partly as a result of these intellectual habits, class is rarely an issue and it's hard to notice the extent to which the custom of buying ourselves out of our longing is taken for granted. The language of the loyal Marxist opposition is too often contained by being accepted merely as the house critique. Similarly, desire finds its most ordinary expression within the territory of the still somewhat titillating but safely cordoned-off realm of erotic potential, real and imagined.

European thinkers such as Walter Benjamin and Henri Lefebvre employed more integrative approaches, bringing issues of production, governance, and desire together at the center of cultural analysis. They interrogated the function of desire within the context of the modernist preoccupation with constructing and maintaining ordered space. In a related vein, Michel Foucault placed concerns with normalization at the center of social order in contemporary life. He theorized this in relationship to more open-ended processes in real space that he called heterotopic. One of the themes of this book is to draw attention to the cohabitation of heterotopic space and the larger normalizing spatial order. To say this metaphorically, I explore why we agree that it is both so nice and so necessary to honor the illusion of being slightly out of control.

Space

In early modernist theory the city and the culture of industrialization were often conflated. To read the city was to write about modernity. At the same time the city was accepted unproblematically as bounded physical and social space. Today, in contrast, the city is better understood as a subset of contemporary urban practices.[1] Compared with the bounded challenges understood as traditional issues of modernity, we wander through an age without borders or boundaries. Rather than moving between clearly defined urban life and a nostalgically rendered rural existence, we are

part of a global urban culture. Rather than relying on the need to explain continued growth and development, we experience alternative processes of assembly and disassembly. Rather than growing roots we are rewarded for developing the capacity to navigate.

As it becomes useful to analyze the built environment in terms of contemporary urban processes, it also becomes necessary to reconceptualize "the city." In this country the city itself is beside the point of a suburban ideal identified with educational opportunity, material success, and the good life enacted within privatized family space and without public conflict. Yet, not only do most of the world's people live in cities, but even in societies such as America, where the suburban life style is the modal and ideal form, the city continues to play a role in the field of the urban. The city persists, operating in fact and fiction as part of the imagination of conventional culture. As a subset of contemporary urban processes in America, the city functions, among other things, to define not-city. That is to suggest the city has moved from the paradigmatic status accorded it in modernist theory to a necessary but supporting role. When the city is no longer understood as the site of civilization at the center of culture, it becomes a site for the performance of a number of border maintenance functions: dystopic space that supports the places of moralized normality.

In this context the most vocal voices heard from and about the city express what suburban life strives not to be: the city and crime; the city and exotic entertainment; the city and danger; and, most particularly, the city in need. This is to say, when presentations of the city are based on the most readily available cultural codes, these accounts are debilitating. At the very least it is difficult to hear the daily life of the city and more difficult to see city spaces as meaningful in their own right.

City

If it appears necessary to make a case for the city, this is partly because of the disjunctures between representations of urban space and spatial practices within cities. Within conventional systems of valuation certain aspects of daily life are reduced and/or become invisible, sometimes even to those who enact them. My purpose here is to present another approach: to use the city as a site where the daily patterns that involve ongoing negotiation with existence within it can be made to surface.

This search for life in the city provokes a return to modernist theory to search for conceptual and concrete tools. In American social thought cultural critique is well developed. We are familiar with carefully articulated accounts of what is lacking in everyday life but have an impoverished sense of what is or could be there. The politics of assimilation is part of a long history of subtracting heterogeneous possibilities from the American Dream. The sameness, security, and comfort of what we might call the moral order of the suburbs exclude difference as difference beyond control. Fordist spaces of suburban consumption and the decadent transformation of Jefferson's yeoman farmer into a homeowner with multiple vehicles and a home entertainment center reduce the potential for engaged human experience. Buying into this critique, cultural producers seeking sites of presentation often move outside the boundaries of respectable containment. The edge becomes the only place to stand. But neither political correctness nor the ability to shock upsets the spaces of order so much as reaffirms them and makes certain people feel litigious.

Over half a century ago, Walter Benjamin understood modernity in a more complex way, as a source of tools with which to explore the possibility for experience within its confines.[2] Rather than reject modernity completely and settle in for thoroughgoing critique, no matter how well taken, he immersed himself in modernity. Returning to the center of material culture, he asked how it might be activated. By conceptualizing desire at the base of bourgeois comfort, he sought to invigorate those elements that usually promise comfort without uncertainty. Benjamin's images of urban life were meant to attract meanings in which one has some purchasing power—identity by addition. Henri Lefebvre also saw the potential of the city as the space of life. Contemporary urban processes have made the city heterotopic space. It remains available for "urban encounters," moments that sidestep the dominance of the abstract spaces of late capitalism.

Streets

Like many other artists and writers of his time, Walter Benjamin reacted to, used, and transformed the fragmentation of life in modernity in his experiments with montage. Although Benjamin wrote about photography, his own experiments were literary, not photographic. But they were image based in the sense that he was interested in producing meanings from the juxtaposition of glimpses of worlds we might think we already know. This mode can be deployed merely to reinforce a familiar world, as in advertising, but in his hands the literary montage became an instrument of experience.

By being a tool of engagement in the first instance, the camera provides the possibility for a new kind of seeing for the photographer. This is particularly true now when the venues for writing and reading images are vastly expanded from those of the 1930s, when artists such as John Heartfield deployed photographic montages as weapons against fascism in Europe and Walker Evans invented the photographic as a form of cultural presentation in America. The technological innovations of our age facilitate making, reproducing, mixing, remixing, and manipulating images with speed and ease but not with an intelligence undreamed of before. This has occurred in a context where two generations have now been raised on the screen and so are visually receptive. The train window has morphed into the computer screen, but the terms of engagement are not necessarily altered unless we make it our political business to do so.

Every expansion of photographer/reader, viewer/writer relations can open the field for attracting meaning. Both the arrest entailed in making images and the movements required to combine and read images encourage reflection, which is to say consciousness—the production of viewers as cultural producers in their own right. Combinations of images and text presented here are cultural spaces, making the case for the life out of which they came. The images "think" and the text "shows," both testifying on behalf of the city.

If contemporary ethics must be situational, forcing us to consider what it means to be worthy of where we are,[3] using the camera heterotopically is an ethical activity.

To form linkages among images made of encounters among the camera, the city, and experience can reengage the city for the viewer while enacting an ethics of participation. From this perspective, a constitutive overlap exists between how we present cities and how we present ourselves.

Urban Encounters testifies on behalf of the city by approaching the city as a place where material and experience come together.[4] It presents urban life as both social production and cultural imaginary playing in real space. It uses the tools of this complex reality to construct an engaged art. Testifying on behalf of the city *is* situation awareness—a series of movements that promote the city as a construction site open to the public and as space where, increasingly, we find ourselves.

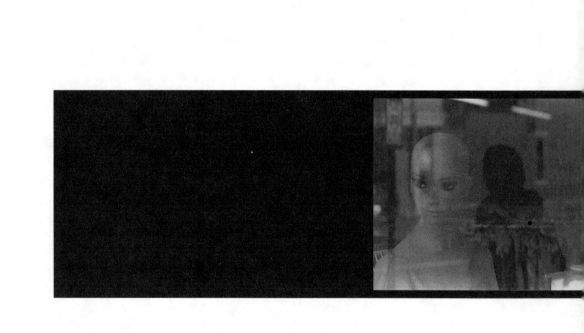

Urban

A recent Harry and David's sale catalog included an advertisement for a "New 'Everlasting Crocus Bowl.'" The copy read: "We emphasize the fact that this is an 'everlasting' arrangement, because from the photo—and even up close— it's nearly impossible to distinguish from the real thing."[1]

This information, designed to attract new and old customers alike, is wonderfully evocative of the inconsistencies that are contained in the notions of the real and the representational, in the complicity of image making in claims to truth, and also in our tendency not to be disturbed by certain bouts of logical inconsistency.

The crocuses in question were "handcrafted of polyester fabric" and were "botanically correct, down to the bulbs and their rootlets." The rootlets were obviously required for true appearance rather than the health of the flowers. Being polyester, and so forth, they were not in particular need of nourishment or connection to the "natural pebbles and clear acrylic" below.[2] Everything was in order here, albeit at the expense of what we might think of as a more organic relation between bulbs and their context.

Harry and David are known as the mail order source of the most delicious real pears available anywhere, so these crocuses represent quite a lapse. Or maybe we should rethink pears.

From the perspective of active theories of language that have helped define contemporary social theory, meaning is constructed within contexts of deployment and use. From minor retail issues, such as mail order pears, to major public issues, such as urban policy, presentations of situations are understood as somewhat open-ended processes involving relays and connections that are both theoretical and practical.[3] Theory does not operate outside of and is not abstracted from the politics of representation in everyday practice: it is an integral part of politics. Practical politics does not occur in cultural vacuums but requires systems of mediation that are sites of negotiation between approved methods and authorized values.[4]

It follows from this that any notion that is found in so many verbal and visual venues, as the city is, would have a versatile existence. To present a very short list, cities appear, with great variation in meaning, in academic discourses, in policy discussions, in advertisements for harmful and helpful substances, as part of entertainments ranging from the edifying and/or lucrative to the costly and/or forbidden. Many presentations of the city obscure the relation between how images of urban life function in the larger culture and the contexts out of which these images are taken. The extent to which our ideas of the city exclude daily life within it and at the same time play fully integrated roles in the larger culture leaves us strangely unheeding of the dailiness of city existence. As Harry and David's ad people might say, it's nearly impossible to distinguish the real thing.

Common presentations of the city are both abstract and real at the same time. From this perspective various conventional approaches to studying urban life are different strategies for taking account of the difficulties entailed in encountering the city. Three approaches are explored below for the purposes of illustrating how each works to highlight some elements of urban life while submerging others.

Of all the familiar defining notions attached to cities, "urban decline" is one of the most unproblematic. It is such an ordinary phrase that it functions almost automatically as a descriptor of city life in our times. Within discussions of public policy, debate about urban decline deals less with what we mean by this term and more with how and why cities are in decline.[5] Assumptions about urban decline also function as an unexamined foil for a great deal of the publicity surrounding "comeback" cities, such as Cleveland. This booster activity has been known to leave exactly what is meant by "the city" up to the imagination of the reader (at the same time as it is taking an active role in shaping that imagination). For example, some of the material promoting Cleveland employs photographs from the nearby suburbs when discussing residential opportunities. Technically, Cleveland and its suburbs are different cities, but they are presented as part of the greater metropolitan experience (lessons from Harry and David).

As soon as these conventions are interrogated, the slippage in usage that makes room for this kind of politics of representation becomes apparent. We can begin by asking what exactly is being talked about when the words *city* and *urban* are used. Long before urban theory shifted from addressing issues raised by the modernist city to analyzing urban processes more generally, observers of the American scene described a blurring of cultural and physical space in this country that throws notions of the city and urban space into question. Tocqueville himself noted an American tendency towards homogeneous culture that was decidedly "urban," no matter if it appeared in urban or in rural space. In his history of American cities, Rybczynski agrees: "Americans were rural but that did not mean that they were rustic. Rather, they were, at least culturally speaking, urban."[6] Thus, notwithstanding the sociological categories of rural and urban and the assumptions about the shift from a primitive

peasant life to a cosmopolitan city life as Europeans understand it, American culture was about the development of itself. Rybczynski suggests that, "as a result, the United States is the first example of a society in which the process of urbanization began, paradoxically, not by building towns, but by spreading an urban culture."[7] By many accounts, this development has been accompanied by both rampant boosterism in cities and decidedly antiurban biases within and without city limits.[8] A primary spatial manifestation of these biases is, of course, the transformation of the countryside into residential suburbs. Rybczynski presents a typology of city types in the European context: "The continental model, dense, communal, and oriented to life in the square and in the street; and the Anglo-Dutch model, more spread out, more private and socially focused on the family house."[9] But rather than a neat typology of city types to which American urban development might add a form or two, we continue to conceptualize and experience a way of life that is both urban and constituted against the city. The culture of urbanism and the physical space of the city might not cover the same ground, but they aren't totally discrete either.

In the following discussion, notions of the city and their connection to representations of urban decline are examined to show how urban images are linked to cities. I argue that presenting cities is not different from constructing cities. The discussion is organized by looking at presentations of urban decline from the perspective of three different but overlapping approaches to the city. Each framework is discussed and illustrated below with an example (out of the many possible) from the urban literature. Approved methods for approaching the city are shown to be intertwined with culturally authorized valuations of the city and urban life. Each approach uses conceptual tools well-known to urban scholars. Each example discussed below produces "new knowledge," constructing urban space that reinforces general cultural understandings of the city as dystopic space.

In the most conventional of the three approaches, the city appears as an entity existing in a particular place. This is the kind of approach that is often used in empirical research. For example, place-based data such as the census and similar sources of quantitative data that are collected in terms of geographic boundaries are common bases for analysis. In the example discussed below, this place-based approach is one in which the city is available for a prior narrative about the city as a central place. Ironically, notions of central place have come to function in the marginalization of the city. The city is presented as a site to be investigated, but a narrative precedes that investigation and could easily be lodged elsewhere, in someone else's grant proposal.

The second approach discussed below is one in which the city and urban life are objects to be interpreted. Crudely put, from this general perspective there is a hermeneutic in them there streets, and the task at hand is one of presenting the best insight into the meaning of some aspect of urban experience. Text-trekking is the realm of semiotics and often of literature. If the narrative doesn't come first, a quest or search for a "deep" understanding of the city does. A successful interpretation is one in which we "learn" or "understand" or come to "know" something about urban life by investing the city with meaning. The interpretation discussed here presents an understanding of urban decline in relation to democratic ideology and ideals of social justice in this country.

Exploring these two approaches suggests an informal intellectual division of labor between research on city places and interpretations of urban culture. Each mode of analysis is part of the presentation of the object of inquiry. The city as place is available for empirical research. Urban culture is a subject for interpretation, an instrument of both imagination and code.

In the third approach discussed in this section, the city is the raw material for production. In this approach, a recognizable totality called the city is no longer the primary focus. Here, place and culture are both present, but not only as abstractions of data or interpretation. Spatial and imaginary practices play a role. There are fewer prior claims and less pressure for coherence. This approach is closer to making it up as you go along. Using the city as material for production is not a marginal approach or an approach that appears only in the arts or academe. Rather, this approach is shared by such diverse operators as real estate developers, designated civic visionaries, urban researchers, artists, and people on the street, even if they don't articulate their work in these terms. Using the city as the raw material for production can lead to the redeployment of narratives of the city and free the play of interpretation to move across the claims of accepted convention. At the same time, the politics of this approach varies in practice. Sometimes existing power relations are reproduced, and sometimes alternative articulations of urban processes occur. The final part of this section focuses on the politics of using the city as the raw material for production. There I am interested in explaining how the material of the city can be used to make the city a place of life.[10]

The city is not an elusive reality behind one or the other of these approaches, any more than a complete analysis of a city can be achieved from the perspective of a single approach or from using all three in combination. At the same time, each approach is implicated in the others. A study of a city as a particular kind of place is also always an interpretation of urban space and, by so being, is necessarily active: it produces the urban as we know it. Because of this constitutive force, it is possible to interrogate approaches to the city as modes of "making space" and, hence, as part of the cultural work the city does.[11]

Urban Decline and the City as a Particular Kind of Place

Tax Base Disparity: Development of Greater Cleveland's Sapphire Necklace is an example of empirical research into the city as a place.[12] This report presents various types of information related to the residential tax bases of the communities that compose the Greater Cleveland region. The introduction to the report presents the subjects of the inquiry:

> The seven-county Greater Cleveland region has 226 cities, villages and townships. For all units of government, tax base is lifeblood. Growth in tax base is life itself; decline (or little growth) portends trouble—trouble in providing services, financing schools, and meeting special needs such as rebuilding deteriorating sewers.
>
> This report documents the status of tax bases across the region and relates tax-based change to real estate development, population movement and public policy.[13]

Obviously, as this quotation illustrates, the research presented in this report is about a particular place. It also presents the city as a particular *kind* of place. These two are related. The particular place includes the various political entities referred to above. The particular kind of place is a model of the city surrounded by outward movement and growth. These two levels of presentation are intertwined throughout the report in both the images and the text, producing not only an idea of what is happening in Cleveland but also information about cities in general, that is, information that is implicitly generalizable to any city. This general city is especially important to the policy recommendations that are major raisons d'être for the analysis.

In the body of the report, shifts in concentrations of wealth as measured by analysis of residential data are presented centrifugally. The city, in this case Cleveland, is assumed to be the center, surrounded by inner suburbs, outer suburbs, and outlying rural areas. Information is displayed graphically and textually in terms of a series of concentric circles around the central place, the city. Because Cleveland is bordered by Lake Erie on the north, these are actually half circles,[14] but figures in the report incorporate the notion of concentric zones to present the data.

The language of the text reports data about specific places that are also organized "around" the central city, even though the city of Cleveland itself is rarely referred to directly in the study. Examples of this framework are visible in the following information taken from the report: Residential housing permits in the outlying areas vastly exceed those issued in Cleveland. Property tax rates are highest in the inner areas and lowest in outlying areas; at the same time, the most valuable property is farther out from the city, and the least valuable is closest to the center of Cleveland. The very low value of nearby rural land is mentioned as an exception. This same comparative pattern is used to organize data about variations in the income tax base "across the region," but (in terms of its form) it is presented from the city center.

Direct indicators of urban decline are derived from data about particular places and interpreted in terms of movement and/or predicted movement out from the center. Thus, having established reason to believe in the specter of decline, further data on particular places function to substantiate the same overall picture. Additional indicators of decline or potential decline are presented in the same format as the primary fiscal data. For example, the tax base is lowest per student in the inner areas; the market value of property is increasing in outer areas; property tax delinquency is highest in inner areas; the percentage of families receiving ADC in school districts is highest in inner areas;[15] a higher percentage of blacks reside in inner areas; and the racial mix is the most changeable in the so-called inner suburbs. From this viewpoint, the inner suburbs become an endangered area, in part because the central city is assumed already gone. The outer areas are presented, in contrast, as places of growth and fiscal well-being and, hence, of general well-being, implicitly implying they are better places.

What Bier calls a "sapphire necklace" of relatively affluent, growing development now surrounds the city of Cleveland and its inner suburbs. Bier is concerned to point out that tax and transportation policy at all levels of government favor development in outlying areas at the expense of city neighborhoods and inner suburbs, where two-thirds of the region's population resides. As a brake on current trends, he recommends policy solutions that move towards regionalization. Sharing property tax revenues and attempting to "achieve balanced tax base growth across the region" are two suggestions that flow from the framework of the study and from the data organized in terms of that framework.[16]

The politics of this study of a particular place takes the position that there is ample reason to be concerned about places being left behind. Movement out from the center, fiscal stress, phrases such as "vulnerable to tax base erosion," and frequent use of the word *decline* are all indicative of warnings issued from a viewpoint that values the center. Recognition that life is nevertheless growing elsewhere is clear in the "sapphire necklace" metaphor that is used throughout the report.

The data in the report are recent and newly interpreted, but the narrative that is used to give them coherence is well within venerable traditions of conventional American urban theory. Urbanists have been studying cities as particular places using variations on models of central place since the founding of the "Chicago School" by Park, Burgess, McKenzie, and their colleagues in the 1920s.

A rough enumeration of some of the basic tenets of this general narrative of the city includes the following: The city exists as a place. It is natural that cities grow and develop from the center outward. Zones divided by function and class form outward from the central productive core of the city. The inhabitants of zones may change and/or the placement of zones may shift, but the basic structure remains. The physical boundaries of sections of the city and assumptions about the viability of community life in those places are combined. Thus geographic units of analysis (political borders at the regional level and census tracts at the local level) also carry assumptions about "neighborhood" or "community."[17] Growth is unexamined, taken as natural, good, and inevitable, and identified with economic expansion. Negative effects are present, of course, but they are temporary and deviate from the norm at the same time as they are a "natural" outcome of development. Thus temporary social disorganization and deviate individuals are part of city life. While disorganization is considered to be outside the norm (in both the statistical and moral senses), it is also thought to accompany growth.

In contemporary discussions of cities, both lay and academic, growth still has a positive valence, as it did in the 1920s, and outward movement is still recognized as the modal pattern. But the kind of pressure that comes from the center is conceptualized now differently from the early days of the central place models. Then, the pressure was brought about by what was thought of as inevitable growth. Today urbanists often write about pressure to escape the center as an emptying out. Similarly to the way in which central business districts (CBDs) were thought to occasion outward expansion, decline is implicitly presented as "increasing" and putting pressure on the city to move outward. Decline is an implicit replacement for the pressures from the central business district in which the Chicago School theorists put so much stock. As suggested above, race (nee ethnicity) is used as a supporting indicator of health (or lack of it), as are income-related measures. Decline in the city (or region) is a matter for concern, but at the same time there are reminders of the Chicago School belief that disruption of the equilibrium of homogeneous zones is an aspect of growth that eventually contributes to the health of a larger system. This is the context in terms of which the desirability of returning to the city becomes a public issue. One indicator of the legacy of belief in the long-term benefits of growth is the relative lack of serious discussion of alternative conceptualizations of the city. Policies such as urban in-filling, the promotion of stable heterogeneous neighborhoods, and studies of successful heterogeneous communities not defined by place, wealth, or race in predictable directions do not fit comfortably within many unexamined conventions of urban studies. This is partly because they do not contribute to the way the central city (gone bad) functions as part of cultural narratives that reinforce various suburban ideals while marginalizing the city.

"Tax Base Disparity" deviates from the Chicago School framework in one important respect, that of emphasizing the role of public policy in promoting outlying growth, but most of the other aspects of the social ecology narrative are used without comment. The policy initiatives Bier recommends are based on restoring equilibrium to the area by making it a bigger place. This is in opposition to current public policy that allows the multiplication of a number of separate places whose governance is linked only minimally and that encourages growth by providing infrastructure development. The idea of city as place, as a geographically bounded entity, remains constant. Bier's policy recommendations follow from this: enlarge the place to a region in the interests of more equable distribution of the benefits of growth.

Although any report must mobilize cultural preferences in order to make sense at all, interrogating these is not always included. Usually the purpose of empirical research is delineated clearly in the beginning of the work. This kind of research is likely to use authorized values rather than interrogate them at length. Bier does not take up what he does not claim to cover. As a result there is no critique of the assumptions that help produce such narrowly defined, albeit conventional, notions of health and decline. For example, such possibilities as fostering sustainability, the value of unique aspects of urban life, the cultural advantages of living near a large city, and the development of urban culture unbound to place are beyond the scope of the study because of what it is. Most of the aspects of the organizing framework of the study seem obvious or self-evident, because approaching the city as place and as failing at the center is one of the most recognizable ways of talking about cities. The report is not concerned with reorienting our thinking about the cultural prejudices regarding urban and suburban life at the constitutive level. Except, of course, that is exactly the implication of the policy recommendations that Bier makes—to reorganize our thinking about what cities are and how they work.

Approaching the city as place provides the framework for a variety of inquiries into city places in addition to research into tax bases. Other research into cities as places focuses on the agglomerate effects of a city; on the city as entrepôt for goods, services and people; on the presence of high culture in urban places; and on the kind of daily interactions that constitute spatial practices in urban settings. These topics, as well as studying tax bases, also open the possibility of unlinking oneself from the city as a declining place. To do this is to invent alternative city narratives, as some studies of global cities have done. Thus, when studies of the city as place are pushed, they reveal how they actively construct "the city" at just about every stage of their formulation and implementation, including defining research projects, interpreting findings, and making recommendations for further work. Elements of interpretative work are woven into the research, enabling it. And rethinking these, as Bier's conclusions suggest, is one way to participate in remaking cities. This suggests considering studies that approach the city as a place as themselves active components of culture. They produce urban space, whether the authors and readers are conscious of it or not.

Urban Decline as a Component of Culture

In *Voices of Decline: The Postwar Fate of U.S. Cities*, Robert Beauregard interprets the city as a component of culture. He begins with what he sees as "the failure of [American] urban theory to confront in any meaningful way the issue of representation."[18] His response is an extensive study of representations of urban decline in popular periodical literature during the era after the Second World War. Beyond merely summarizing, Beauregard includes sections of popular texts that give the flavor of the rhetoric of each period and places these in the context of the current events of the time.[19] Following these "data" chapters, he writes final interpretative chapters that take up the issue of the meaning of urban decline in American cities. In this section, I look at Beauregard's selections from the literature, his historical summaries, and his interpretations as an interwoven project. As his work illustrates, approaching the city as a component of culture is not an inductive process but one underwritten by certain prior concerns. Just as in the example above, in which the city was approached as a place, a politics of presentation is an unavoidable component of interpretative work.

Voices of Decline begins by discussing the importance of interrogating notions of urban decline that are usually taken for granted. "Despite the notoriety of urban decline and despite the pervasiveness of talk about it, the discussion itself has not been closely scrutinized. It is as if the topic is so familiar that it neither deserves nor requires special attention.... My ... primary goal is to give meaning to the discourse."[20]

Beginning with the observation that decline has been a constant theme in popular and academic venues since the Second World War, Beauregard shows how the rhetoric of decline initially takes shape against idealizations of a fully operative, culturally active industrial city assumed to be (even if never experienced as) the norm. He traces cycles of economic decline, demographic shifts, and rising indications of social disintegration, of which urban riots were only the most vivid example, in chapters that chronicle the modernist city in America.[21]

During the period studied, the very notion of what constitutes urban space changes. The city is always the place where decline is sited, but what the city is thought to be shifts from the robust identifications of the total city with growth, progress, permanence, and civilization that characterized the prewar era (1890s–1920s). Eventually, the central city becomes a separate place, partitioned off from the rest of the metropolis. At a later stage there is a burgeoning of the urban to include strip cities, and then a period in which the viability of the city is in doubt. Finally, a recent celebratory notion of the city as the site of economic development and festive consumption emerges. These shifts are useful for Beauregard in interpreting the relationship between how decline and the city are understood and how (or whether) urban policy is formulated, or unlikely to be formulated, to attend to decline in any meaningful way.

To introduce how his interpretation of the rhetoric of decline is framed, Beauregard uses Forester's wonderful phrase describing this country as "precariously democratic but strongly capitalistic."[22] How we live with the contradictions between capitalism and democracy organizes his interpretation of representations of urban decline. Urban decline is one site where contradictions between a political ideology of equality and a political economy based on hierarchy and competition are played out. In the end, Beauregard constructs an interpretation in which the conventional cultural understandings are seen as being a legitimating force in the symbolic economy of advanced capitalism: situating decline at a distance, justifying it, and assuring the middle class of their spatial and moral position in society.

The conditions that legitimate the middle class's disengagement from urban life are related to the political economy that has chosen to disengage from the city for reasons of capitalist logic. The success of the home building industry and the proliferation of a consumer society after the Second World War is a historical example of that logic. The concomitant emptying out of the cities by citizens for whom suburban housing was affordable was a matter of both choice and the opportunity structure. It was also the creation of a new kind of middle class.[23]

Beauregard points out that popular treatments of decline do not link the successes of capital and the comforts of the middle class with urban decline and suffering of remaining residents. Economic restructuring in the 1970s and 1980s, which included the abandonment of northern industrial cities and factory towns and the growth of the service industry and Sun Belt cities, is another example of the logic of capital reorganizing the identity of the middle class. Again, links are not made in the popular literature between decline and success within the system as a whole. Instead, Beauregard suggests, the literature helps substantiate the reassuring notion that citizens are the cause of their own well-being and position in life. Political commentary could point out that the political economy that provides a computer in every home is the same system that employs workers at various levels of exploitation to make computers. Instead of illuminating these kinds of linkages, however, the conventional understandings and popular representations of suburban life are as more or less self-contained, amenity-ridden, and (increasingly) safe places separated from the dangers of the city.

Beauregard notes that ideas of racial difference were used to contribute to notions of decline. The popular literature treated the influx of American blacks into northern industrial cities the way previous generations treated the influx of foreigners—as detached from the needs of capital and threatening to the "middle class" (i.e., American) way of life. But these similarities between the two immigrations were not discussed in the popular literature or in Beauregard's interpretation. Black migration is treated as a singular experience.

Nevertheless, the use of race in the rhetoric of urban decline in the postwar period can be seen as part of the politics of forming an American identity. It also draws on the antiurbanism that has been a part of American cultural consciousness since the days of Jefferson's yeoman farmer.[24] If the Progressive Era antiurban nativism was a way of expressing disapproval and fear of the values of an industrializing North, the racism in the rhetoric of urban decline is a expression that helps illuminate fear and loathing of an emerging postindustrial world. The use of race in the rhetoric of decline also illustrates the dynamics of how reduced discursive space precludes certain topics of discussion. Race is a central concern in discussions of decline where class might be a more apt category to use. This pushes consideration of structural inequality further off the agenda.

It is against the background of rhetoric about the emptying out of the center that Beauregard gives meaning to the societal disinclination to tend to cities. He suggests that to argue for any kind of restructuring that would seriously threaten existing spatial categories of life would be to argue for taking apart a middle-class world. In seeking to explain why the urban areas endure cycles of decline, Beauregard implies that urban decline is a working part of the culture. Not only can urban space be awful and bad as long as it is other; it is also useful for it to be that way.

There is a tendency to link certain unsavory urban themes together in the popular literature. "Slums, poverty, unemployment, welfare, massive public housing projects, illegal drugs, crime—have become associated with their urban concentration."[25] These themes are tied to racial minorities, usually blacks, sometimes Hispanics. As a result, we have the culturally handy constitution of a problem with one name. It is called race. When race becomes a stand-in for accusations of personal irresponsibility, the price we agree to pay for our way of life is the existence of this inexplicable remnant of uncivilized life at the heart of the city. The wages we reap are a removal of involvement or responsibility for involvement.

Most among the audience for the rhetoric of decline don't actually have much to do with literal (within the geographic boundaries of) urban places these days.[26] Urban decline is outside various middle-class worlds; it helps form the boundaries of those worlds. The urban functions as a liminal place—at the edge of civilization, to use Edward Said's phrase, but still central to it. Stallybrass and White explore the liminal urban places of modernity, arguing that in the modern Europe, the top *includes* the low symbolically, as a primary eroticized constituent of its own fantasy life.... It is for this reason that what is socially peripheral is so frequently *symbolically* central (like long hair in the 1960s). The low-Other is despised and denied at the level of political organization and social being whilst it is instrumentally constitutive of the shared imaginary repertoires of the dominant culture.[27]

"The urban" has come to function as this kind of liminal place in the urban culture of postmodern America. Escape from the moral squalor and danger of urban space is a marker of success in America. Not escaping from the city has become a sign of individual moral ineptitude and worse. Collective responsibility for cities more or less drowns in so much righteousness and detachment.

The meanings Beauregard gives to popular discourse on urban decline are framed by his intellectual and ethical concern with the relationship between the promise of a democratic vision based on social responsibility for a more equitable society and the functional inequalities of capitalism. The city, he argues, is very much a component of the culture where capitalism and democracy as we know them reside together. Looking at the material on urban decline thematically, he sees a redemption narrative. The familiar plot is a repetition of "ascension, dominance, degeneration, and redemption."[28] Decline is the degeneration stage before redemption, which is identified with new growth. Redemption can be connected to a particular savior in the form of a dynamic mayoral figure, of which Mayor Lee of *Who Governs?* fame is only a paradigmatic case,[29] or to a particular program, of which the War on Poverty was a similarly paradigmatic case. But it is also a moral tale that functions for Beauregard to justify the political economy as a whole. Like the Chicago School narrative, which made peace with deviance, the redemption narrative makes intellectual peace with poverty and suffering in the city.

One of the things demonstrated in *Voices of Decline* is how interpretation leads to insights into urban space not just as a component of culture but as an active component of culture.[30] An interpretation may be structured as a hermeneutic, but it is also itself a functioning, constitutive project. For example, staying within the framework of decline, we can imagine urban space (as material for constructing decline) playing a number of cultural roles. The urban can be a liminal site: it can appear as an icon of marginality for youth in transition from indulgent childhoods to worker bee adulthoods. The urban can be a place of charitable attentions among the good-hearted, particularly in times of crisis. Beauregard suggests in his interpretation that, during the postwar period, "the city" (implicitly meaning urban decline) was needed because of how decline functioned as an active component of a culture. This interpretation itself highlights certain aspects of urban life that reinforce its marginalization. The city was, in effect, represented by popular media discussions of it. With friends such as these . . .

Interpreting urban decline as a component of culture is an approach to urban space that produces an understanding of why decline has continued to have such a strong presence in American discussions of urbanism. Cities as declining places and the idea of decline contribute to forging an American whole on a daily basis. The identification of urban space with decline has been so complete that what the city can not be in the context of popular forms of representation is a place with which "the average American" identifies, where active life continues, where one goes to work, shop, eat, or wants to make friends. Urban space can and has, as discussed below, become a place of leisure, sport, and excitement, but this has been negotiated in the context of widespread understanding of the urban as liminal space.

Urban decline interpreted as a component of culture differs from the city as a particular place in that the frame of analysis is less troubled by slippage among particular cities, cities in general, and cities as cultural space. The city is still regarded as a whole, but less attention is paid to the details tied to the location of a particular place. Speaking of the city as a whole is one way to avoid issues of selectivity inherent in interpretation, or at least speaking so pushes these issues to the background. So, for example, the popular literature on decline is mostly about northeastern, industrial cities. This comes to stand for "city" in a way that ignores the history and spatial differences between industrial urban areas in the North and cities in the South and West. To say "the urban space functions" is to help construct some entity as a whole. In discussions of urban decline as a component of culture, use of this phrase is justified only because the discussion makes it so.

Another way to say this is to point out that research that approaches the city as a particular place and interpretations of urban space as components of culture are themselves productions. In research and in interpretation, a (thing called a) city or urban space is being crafted. The truth and nothing but the truth is more or less a nonissue. The truth as known is known because of how it was generated. An observer of the city as a particular place is at the same time watching urban space being made and participating in that making. An inquiry into the meaning of urban space is at the same time looking inward and constructing an external reality.

The urban space Beauregard constructed was crafted from the literature he studied and from his commitment to participatory democracy. This combination is what gives his production its political edge. Recognizing the performative aspects of interpretative work leads to discussion of a third approach to urban space, the city as raw material for production.

Urban Space as the Raw Material for Production

The City of Collective Memory: Its Historical Imagery and Architectural Entertainments, by M. Christine Boyer, is based on an approach to urban space that uses the city as raw material for production.[31] Her interest is in the active role images of the city play in economic development and urban design. She explores festive market places and self-contained areas such as South Street Seaport and Battery Park City in New York City as instances of what she calls nodes of development in the city. They ignore the city as a whole while trading on images of the city as a complete environment.

Boyer conceptualizes the link between urban images and the production of urban space in terms of what she calls "collective memory." This puts the current historic preservation fad in the much larger context of the ascent of the modern city in western Europe. She explores collective memory as a cultural construction, no more diachronically correct than it is synchronically correct. The city of collective memory is not accurate about history, nor is it a total representation of the city at any one time. But it comes to stand for both by creating what Boyer calls an "aesthetics of distinction."[32]

One way to understand Boyer's conceptualization of how urban spaces are produced according to the aesthetics of distinction is to compare two projects from roughly the same period: Engels's famous book on the condition of the working class in Manchester, England, and the participation of European powers in the restoration of Athens. In the former, engagement with the city of Manchester undergirded Engels's presentation of the industrial city of modernity. In the latter, a European ideal of Greek civilization shaped the rebuilding of the city of Athens.

In 1842, when Engels was twenty-three he was sent by his family to learn the family business in Manchester. The family did not have in mind the kind of learning he set himself to. Instead of concentrating on the mechanics of business production and administration, he turned to a broader inquiry into the generative relation between industrial production and the city of Manchester. Steven Marcus's article on Engels's *Condition of the Working Class* shows how Engels's exhaustive description of the working-class districts of Manchester is also a systemic analysis of the industrial city.[33] Several distinguishing features of Engles's work are relevant to understanding Boyer's conceptualization of "the city of collective memory."

To begin, there is Engels's thoroughness. Engels explored Manchester, bit by bit. Dividing the city into wedges like hours on a clock, he walked each section and took extensive notes on what he saw. This reading of the city, as Marcus calls it, was a direct engagement with the city and an attempt to come to terms with the city by participating in its daily spatial practices. A complimentary way to characterize Engels's method is to say that, rather than fitting Manchester into a preexisting narrative, he used his eye as a camera. From this point of view a camera operates as an opening to the light reflecting off objects before it. Engels worked similarly, using the same kind of openness to experience the city. Marcus notes that Engels struggled, not only to directly engage the space of the city, but also to present it. It is as part of this struggle, in the gap between what he experienced and the ability of language to articulate it, that Engels produced a description of the condition of the working class that is also an analysis of how the industrial city functions as a whole. As an example we can look at how Engels describes the "normal separations" in what Marcus calls "one of the most enduring and important statements ever written about the modern city":

The town itself is peculiarly built, so that someone can live in it for years and travel into it and out of it daily without ever coming into contact with a working-call quarter or even with workers—so long, that is to say, as one confines himself to his business affairs or to strolling about for pleasure. This comes about mainly in the circumstances that through an unconscious, tacit agreement as much as through conscious, explicit intention the working-class districts are most sharply separated from the parts of the city reserved for the middle class. Or, if this does not succeed, they are concealed with the cloak of charity.[34]

The spatial layout of the city and its customary spatial practices function as shields that obscure the political economy of the city as a whole. Similarly, conventional language about cities leads away from explaining how the classes are linked to each other. The image of the city and urban space itself is different for members of different classes because of the spatial patterns that they reproduce in their routine movements. Thus class distinction and spatial separation are part of the same societal symptoms. Engels's method was to use his experience of the city to produce a framework for seeing it. As Marcus suggests, "If one follows Engels in thinking of the city as a systematic, dynamic whole, the inherent course of its development brings that which has been pressed away and hidden into sight; it exposes itself by its own movement, the exposure being understood in a double sense."[35]

Marcus goes on to say this exposure is not the result of the diligence of the young Hegelian, applying a philosophical system, nor is it "immediately victories of language, since social reality, on this side, expresses itself first in the concrete language of the nose, the eyes, and the feet." The stuff of the city as experienced is the raw material that Engels "must meet, follow, and transform into the language of conceptualization."[36]

In relating Engels's harrowing description of the conditions of the life of one man he found, Marcus comments, "It is quite impossible to know whether this is an image or a reality; that is its point."[37] In other words, it is impossible to differentiate between whether Engels wants readers to see an image of this particular situation or whether Engels wants readers to see that the lives of the working class are so horrible that there is no difference between them and the filth they occupy. The space and the identities that occupy the space collapse into each other. Engels found that language failed him, not being adequate to the task of describing what the very structure of urban space so carefully puts out of sight. The city is used in two ways in Engels's work—as the basis for particular descriptions and as raw material for producing a mode of understanding the generative forces of the industrial city.

Marcus shows how Engels willfully committed the act of presenting overwhelming amounts of detail in order to interpret how the city worked as an active, structurally coherent system. The city was both a particular place, Manchester, and a presentation of the workings of the economic system by which industrial cities produced wealth. Engels overcame the separations that city dwellers normally experience both by his more complete explorations of the material space of the city and by learning how to write descriptions that link the various parts of the city together as parts of the working machinery of industrial capitalism.

Engels produced an image of how urban industrial space works, an image that he hoped no right-thinking person could ignore. The urban space Engels made is both in *The Condition of the Working Class in England* in 1844 and came to be all across Europe to Moscow into the next century.

Engles's concern with immediate experience, his attempt to present a new way of seeing, his struggle to overcome the moral aesthetics of distinction are all quite different from the way in which European restorers approached Athens at roughly the same time period in European history. In contrast with Engels's direct experience of the streets of Manchester, Boyer reports that the city of Athens was somewhat incidental to attempts to restore it. Engels was explicitly concerned with "more than an abstract knowledge of [his] subject."[38] Athens was restored according to Europe's wishes for it—as a collective memory of the birthplace of democracy.

Collective memory is first of all selective. But the pretense is to wholeness: it stands in for a totality. In contrast with Engels's walking the whole of Manchester and attempting to come to terms with it, "collective memory" works by boring into only the most presentable. And rather than struggling with the relation between image and reality, it happily promotes a blurring of the two in the interests of foregrounding the force of a prior narrative in shaping an image of reality. The image as contained, controlled, and deployable are all defining traits of collective memory. Engels struggles with the tension between experience and articulation in the interests of forming the conceptual tools for showing how urban space is active. The restorers of Athens projected an image of Greek antiquities in the interests of the ascendant social order they represented. The processes are similar only because both actively construct urban space. They differ in the logic of production. For Engels the city as experience plays a major role. Boyer suggests that in Athens, the city was secondary to its restoration.

The disorder of early nineteenth-century Greek society was somewhat embarrassing, from the viewpoint of western Europe, because Greece, and particularly Athens, was identified with an apex in Western civilization. Europe, and England of course, claimed direct descent from, not to say improvement and refinement of, ancient Greek civilization. But this Greece was an ideal place, an invention of the European mind.[39] The contemporary Greeks living in the early nineteenth century were viewed as primitive, politically backward, and not at all to be trusted with their own history. From the viewpoint of western Europeans, "the ideal of neoclassical purity remained unattainable by the Greeks except through European translation."[40]

Hence, when the war to overthrow Turk rule resulted in the destruction of Athens and many antiquities, plans to restore the city weren't oriented towards fostering an emerging democracy among the Greeks. Planning for the city was oriented toward representing the image of democracy in antiquity. The point was to preserve as much as possible of the Acropolis, to enhance it, to make it into the first city of democracy—available for visit, contemplation, and edification. The narrative of the glories of Greek civilization so overrode the idiosyncrasies of the particular place that there was no particular need to mention them. The polyglot city that had grown up though years of successive colonizations from both western and eastern neighbors and was then partly destroyed in wars against the Turks was not of interest; rather than focusing on the city as lived, the restoration of Athens was about the city as "symbolic heritage of the West."[41]

Boyer describes the plan drawn up by Stamatis Cleanthes and Eduard Schauber in 1832:

> In accordance with the glory and beauty of the ancient city of Athens, they developed a triangular plan that turned all perspectives towards the Acropolis yet refrained from encircling its girth. The base of the triangle, named Ermou, was drawn across the old Turkish town, placing what would become the new bourgeois city to its north and leaving the so-called polluting place isolated to its south.[42]

Neoclassical forms became the measure in European architecture and the rage among educated Greeks. "Architecture was another area in which Greeks could attempt to recover their classical past, for every neoclassical facade visually conveyed itself to be a symbol of Hellenism."[43] The first among the symbols of Hellenism was the pure white marble Doric column. We are indebted to Gottfried Semper, a nineteenth-century architect, for a broader understanding of this marble and of the purity of those white columns. Semper attempted to overcome the reigning conventional imagery of his time by pointing out that the Greek temples were brightly painted. The symbolically loaded pure white marble was a later cultural invention. Among the original users of the Acropolis, ornamentation was central to their experience of these public places. Marble made a good base on which to paint. "The marble is transformed from the traditional paradigm of authenticity and exposure of truth into a 'natural stucco,' a smooth surface on which to paint."[44] Nevertheless, white-columned buildings, so called neoclassical architecture, became as ubiquitous as markers of democracy (and of the dominant world order) in Europe and in the colonies as the staging of elections is today.

So whereas we might have fantasies of urban spaces as solid, irrefutable physical carriers of memory, Boyer introduces an alternative viewpoint that problematizes the city as a totality and foregrounds images in its production. The coherence of the city can no longer be counted upon to be "beyond" political representations of it. She follows Walter Benjamin in detaching memory from the realm of natural forces and placing it within the realm of human activity.

Abetted by photography, the concept of an organic city totality—one that gave rise to involuntary memory—died and in its place rose a new visual perception, an archival consciousness that focused on details.... From the camera's viewpoint, the past was a pile of rubble and the present a chaos of information; both offered a thousand views to be appropriated and recorded.[45]

From this perspective, Engels's work on Manchester was a modernist construction as much as the plans for restoring Athens were. But Engels's project was not just to record all of Manchester; it was to develop conceptual tools that would organize "a chaos of information" into a communicable articulation. In the restoration of Athens, the preexisting idea of the Greek city-state as interpreted by the European mind dominated at every stage. Like the panoramas and other urban entertainments developed in cities of modernity, in the restoration of Athens a selective image of the whole came first. This was to represent the whole and successfully edify, excite (in the case of Athens), amuse, and celebrate (in the case of European urban entertainments) the middle and upper classes while shielding them from the mechanisms that produce the city. Boyer notes that for Walter Benjamin, mechanical forms of reproduction, such as the camera, can support or change the meaning of these activities in modernity: "Thus it was from out of the debris produced in the wake of modernity that the collector of photographs appeared like a ragpicker rummaging among fragments."[46] Just as the camera can be used to support or critique the modernist myth of progress, constructions that remake the city from selected fragments of city life can be either closed or open. Boyer is concerned with the extent to which uncritical support for the status quo has prevailed: the completed (partial) Athens over the generative (total) Manchester.

Historical examples of the role of collective memory in constructing urban space are background for Boyer's analysis of contemporary urban development. Here she sees developed nodes, based in the "aesthetics of distinction," creating "the figured city." In contrast with this, large areas of untracked territory that she calls "disfigured" continue to exist in cities.[47] Rather than being held together as a functional whole, albeit one based on more or less exploitation, the figured city is an image of the city that functions to obscure the existence of the disfigured city. This larger urban area remains, but it is as if it weren't there.

One of the most popular motifs for the development of figured nodes is the "historical." Here historical is meant not in the sense of historic preservation but in the sense that the plans to restore Athens were historical. These motifs guide the reproduction of elements of city life that can be appropriated to current uses of urban space. It is not that empty space is filled or that old space is restored; it is that various possible elements of urbanism are assembled into new space. The newly made urban nodes are often spaces of consumption. One of the principal supporting activities in them is the buying and selling of consumer goods, and in addition the space itself is "consumed" as city space.

Boyer presents several case studies of this form of redevelopment in New York during the 1980s. Both South Street Seaport and Battery Park City are stunning examples of urban consumption that use motifs taken from New York's past.

Boyer's detailed case study of South Street Seaport is called "Producing the Show."[48] This title is a wonderful description of the processes she describes: the detailed negotiations involved in assembling all the pieces that eventually became South Street Seaport, a linked historical, educational, and shopping experience for all who can afford to come. All aspects of the design use imagery that evokes the sea and sea-related activities. With sweet irony, she reports that in spite of the developers' best efforts, the Fulton Fish Market has refused to be moved from the area. As a result the spectacle of New York's seagoing past has had to contend with the daily distribution of more than 350,000 pounds of fresh fish to the city's restaurants and fish markets.[49]

Battery Park City is another example of a carefully constructed development assembled from bits and pieces of urban design details derived from other times, other spaces, and other images of New York City. At the same time, the area is not easily accessible to pedestrians from the "real" city.

Boyer does not just argue that these developments are ways to sell things; she argues at the level of what the city is: an illusion of the city itself is being sold and bought. One aspect of this is the design "montages" assembled from the city's past in the service of consumption. Another aspect is the kind of participation or spatial practices that they make possible. Both are illustrated in this paragraph:

> A well-composed city tableau is itself an incomplete and impoverished picture that can be sustained only by inventing traditions and narrative stories that it calls to its support. Its real value is that of display, enabling the spectator—at South Street Seaport, for example—to travel vicariously and imaginatively into the mercantile past through its architectural traces, its exhibitions, and its commodities for sale. This distilled and composed picture, actually estranged and removed from the contemporary city, can be considered a collective souvenir drawn from the city's historical past. As a possession on display, every souvenir generates a travel narrative.[50]

We are very far away from the young Engels tramping around Manchester. Not only are the productions of city space that Boyer looks at "deliberately" partial and selective; she notes that they themselves become the raw material for the production of urban experiences. The city of collective memory is an assembly that requires three active components in order to work: physical space, selective images of the city, and ongoing use. The kind of use required is not tied to reflection and certainly not tied to the kind of public debate idealized as the product of the modern city. "Battery Park City teaches us how to feel, not think, about the past. . . ."[51] These feelings are not based on the sights and smells of ongoing urban life. They are more self-contained, having been based on developers', educators', and retailers' appropriations of available cultural images of the urban.

In her second case study Boyer looks at a series of advertisements called "City Tales," which celebrate New York. Well-known public figures in the literary arts were asked to write something characteristic and special about everyday life in New York.

These pieces served less as complete narratives of the city that could be interpreted in a systematic way than as short instruction sheets on how to feel about the city. In one there is a fond recollection of New York as the city where you can get fresh fruit at any hour of the night because of ever-present street vendors. The point of Boyer's mentioning this kind of media presentation is to show how it works analogously to the development of urban nodes: both construct urban space selectively. She shares with Beauregard a commitment to rationality and democratic governance based on widespread participation. The fruit vendor's tale shows how pieces of urban life are assembled for the use of the privileged. It excludes mention of the bifurcated service economy that puts such conveniences at the fingertips of some because of the conditions of life of others. In Boyer's words: "Architectural expansionism employed against isolated fragments of the city, the better able to normalize its aesthetics of distinction, set up boundaries that maintained a distance from the unemployed, impoverished and outmoded."[52]

These are very similar to the separations that Engels talked about, albeit by different means. The aesthetics of distinction fosters social and democratic relations among only some of the population and only within a narrow range of activities. (Will it be the Nature Company or Banana Republic?) Much as in the separations with which Engels was familiar, visible, developed areas become "the city" for many users; they participate, as nineteenth-century bourgeois citizens did, in making useful images into believable realities. The city as a whole, for which we would be responsible—both figured and disfigured parts (to use Boyer's terms)—disappears behind an idealization. Disconnected from the material of the city, the daily spatial practices of developed nodes make it possible to produce another kind of lived experience that trains users (who could also be potential citizens) into knowledgeable consumers.

If figured urban space (nodes of development) is successful, it fills with people. This is a kind of urban space Boyer sees contemporary city builders committed to producing. Other urban narratives, such as the city of neighborhoods, may exist as objects in public policy debates, the realm where remnants of concern about decline still operate. But again, as the young Engels might have predicted, those images circulate in separate discursive realms.

Learning how to feel about urban space is to make urban space. That this making is so disregarding and destructive of the potential for widespread democratic participation disturbs Boyer. She is critical of how the practice of urban planning contributes to the production of renewed urban spaces that require not citizens but healthy consumers, and she is critical of the forms of renewal that remove users from direct experience of urban life. For them and theirs it works as American spatial arrangements often do: well for those who can afford them, not at all for the rest of the invisible world. As coconspirators, the design professions have neglected "to challenge the process of colonization that has appropriated the image and representations of the city for private concerns."[53]

Using Buck-Morss's reading of Benjamin's Arcades project, Boyer points to the similarities between today's illusions and the illusions that produced the urban world for the nineteenth-century bourgeois. Nobody is particularly surprised about the extent to which image making becomes real in venues such as *Vogue* magazine. But it is central to Boyer's work that the same approach is used to construct developments that become "the city."

Each of Boyer's case studies is rich in the details of planning, political bargaining, and physical construction. In each, urban space becomes a process of ongoing construction. The urban is not approached as only a particular place or a preexisting site to be interpreted. Instead Boyer approaches urban space as the raw material for production. One of the values of her work is how inclusive it is of the various practices involved in producing urban space; she recognizes many of the various physical and social arenas in which city building occurs. For example, Boyer includes not only design but also the physical construction of space, as well as policy negotiation and the rearticulation of cultural codes.

To cite an example from another urban arena, approaching urban space as the raw material for production is useful for understanding the operation of business improvement districts (BIDs) that attempt to make safe space.[54] BIDs began in New York in the wake of low confidence in the ability of city government to secure and "clean up" major areas of the city for business. These organizations are private but operate as quasi governments, implementing "taxing" and police powers. Here physical construction is not the main tool of production, but rather overseeing the daily workings of the spaces of urban capital is. The activities of BIDs cut across various discursive borders with private and public activities that produce safe urban space. When Boyer talks about Benjamin's belief in the revolutionary potential of the camera, she relates his optimism to the ability to "make" new realities. "Film cut 'reality' like a surgeon's knife into a series of images that mimicked the fragmentary perceptions of modern existence and blew apart an absorbed or concentrated gaze. Subsequently the camera liberated these fragments, allowing them, through editing procedures, to be recontextualized into new constellations."[55] BIDs and all of Boyer's examples of the figured city operate in this way, assembling new constellations of urban space. But BIDs are also conservative productions. They preserve and reinforce existing power relations. To construct alternative constellations from the raw material of the city, one needs to redeploy the tools of modernity to notice the other urban space. The "city of collective memory" can, like "urban decline" take up most of the space we see. Beyond the boosterism of the figured city, an immense image repertoire of urban life exists. This is usually mobilized to support the aesthetics of distinction. The image of urban space as disfigured includes many readily available images, such as "the city and crime," "the city and minorities," "the city and unemployment, drugs, and a failed education system," and, when charity is desirable, "the city in need." Urban space is both figured and disfigured, except when it is useful that it be disfigured or dystopic space to help maintain the border between normal and deviant.

Alternatively we can imagine urban space as a construction site with all those fragments lying around available for use. Boyer makes it clear how selective we have been in constructing programmatic constellations that ignore our own democratic ideology. But it is not necessary to mobilize democratic ideology to make this critique.

One can take a page from Engels and address the problem by engaging urban space directly. This entails not just deselecting the city of collective memory or avoiding the destructive aspects of the disfigured city or ignoring fears that help support the suburban ideal. It means becoming more open to the spatial practices that construct urban life. As overdetermined as the cities of collective memory may be from the viewpoint of political economy, these constructions do not constitute all the possibilities. The potential for Benjamin's seductive notion of "fragments . . . to be recontextualized into new constellations" remains alive.

Testimony on Behalf of Urban Life

The three approaches presented above, the city as a particular place, urban space as a component of culture, and urban life as the raw material for production, can be defined and discussed as if they were mutually exclusive. But to follow any approach in practice is to see how each uses urban space as the raw material for production. This is usually not acknowledged. For example, once a research agenda is established it is not useful to dwell on the extent to which the framework for research is a social construction. Similarly, if the goal of inquiry is an interpretation, the productive aspects of that quest are usually not given much emphasis. If the goals of research and interpretation are clearly defined, this undercuts one's own epistemological ground to think of the work as performance. These are local blindnesses resulting from the constitutive customs lodged in the professional lenses we wear to take care of the business of approaching urban space.

There is obvious political force operating in conventional modes of approaching the city, in assuming the city exists as an entity (a particular place) and in assuming that urban space has meaning (a component of culture), as well as in assuming that the city should be remade in the image of its most potentially profitable parts. Yet as Foucault points out, the tyranny of conventional representational forms is not complete. Instead one aspect of what he calls "the dangers of discourse" is the constant social labor conventional forms require.[56] The unpredictability that comes with use is never quite contained with cultural preferences for completeness and closure. Wholeness implies closure and closure promises to provide all the reassurances of a known reality, of moral rectitude, and of no surprises coming in from the outside and leading god-knows-where. Cultural preferences for settled representational forms reduce the likelihood of highlighting the selectivity inherent in any form of production. The city seems more total and more totally under control than it is. It is politically more reassuring to deal with cities in terms of preexisting frameworks than to take up "fragments," as Benjamin called them, of urban life for the purpose of recontextualizing them "into new constellations."[57]

To say that any approach to the city constructs it anew and selectively, albeit in line with preexisting rules of formation, threatens to heighten awareness of the dangers of discourse and undercut social order by implying that several constructions are possible. This highlights the unpredictability of use. For instance, the specter of relativism can arise. From this perspective each presentation is neither true nor false but convincing only within its own frame. That is, it is not right or wrong except within a set of expectations. Even then it is more appropriate to say that it is well or poorly done: a good example of its type. The danger to any canon is usually articulated as the disaster to be expected from opening the flood gates to "just anything." From another viewpoint this is the fear of having to justify privilege. So the likelihood of experience beyond conventional forms of representation is tied to the cultural pull to produce certitude and reduce the dangers of discourse.

Each of the studies reviewed above participates in the play between the normative preference for wholeness and the possibilities inherent in recognizing fragmentation. Each is important to urbanists because of how it operates within well-known rules of formulation while also bringing some aspect of the cultural prejudices they reproduce into question.

The data Bier gathered were based on the existence of separate but complete political entities: the cities, villages, and townships of the Cleveland metropolitan area. The research design of his study reinforces that view. At the same time the policy recommendations he makes favor public policy that would recognize and foster regional interdependencies. In this way Bier jumps categories, introducing a danger and opening up a realm of new possibilities—literally reorganizing urban space. The difficulties of institutionalizing regionalism attest to widespread perception of the dangers of letting go of current relations of dominance. This is often articulated as a threat to "local sovereignty" and discussed also as a matter of local fiscal responsibility. There is also a threat of unknown possibilities, usually figured as bad and vaguely attached to the spread of the city like a virus.

The popular literature Beauregard reviews evaluates the condition of the city, assumed to be whole even though what is meant by *city* alters through time. His search for meaning reveals our implicit cultural reliance on maintaining separation from urban space. Beauregard's work is "dangerous" because he applies a participatory democratic ethic to the city. This would lead to shared responsibility for urban spatial practices. Maintaining barriers against the danger of having to change a way of life that many citizens experience as beneficial is more important culturally than confronting the conditions of urban life.

In the design projects that Boyer discusses, the image of wholeness has become more convincing than an incoherent or fractured reality. Boyer, like Beauregard, judges from the perspective of an idealized whole, hypothesizing the city from the viewpoint of a democratic ideal. She continues to critique the collapse of the distinction between image and reality in urban development, because she sees them leading to the creation and reinforcement of modes of life that are by tacit agreement complete or, if not, are so pleasurably plausible that the responsibilities connected to an unfragmented existence become very remote. In this case, the dangers of discourse are already upon the city, and the possibilities for finding gaps in conventional representations are reduced.

If she is right in this, that the fragmented constellations of urban processes have superseded the "real" city in the cultural imagination, then approaching urban space as the raw material for production is both an intellectual method and a mode of existence. The politics of American urbanism—that is, using the city as the raw material for production—is shared by professional, aesthetic, and everyday practices.

Yet, from another viewpoint, the "danger" of approaching urban space as the raw material for production is the opportunity to break down a privileged view that sustains the illusion of wholeness. As Benjamin's logic suggests, in a world of fragments, the potential exists to admit (let in) and admit to (testify) alternative realities. Showing what has lately been invisible is to testify on its behalf.

Two sections of Néstor García Canclini's essay "Hybrid Cultures, Oblique Powers" illustrate some possibilities.[58] Instead of showing how collective memory is imposed on the city, as Boyer has done, García Canclini looks at the continual construction of memory in the context of daily experience. First, his case study of border life in Tijuana is a nice counterpoint to the limitations of the presentation of decline in the North American popular print media that Beauregard studied. If Beauregard interprets a discursive practice that leaves the city behind and is silent on the position of immigrants to the city, then García Canclini writes description from within the city center and gives a voice to so-called minorities and recent immigrants to the city. Second, his discussion of monuments in Mexico makes a nice counterpoint to the history of the restoration of Athens. Here rather than a monument's dominating and defining urban space, a monument becomes an active site for attracting layers of new meaning.

The two examples of active urban space that García Canclini presents illustrate the difference between the aesthetics of distinction Boyer critiques and what García Canclini sees as active urban culture. García Canclini argues that, in general, it makes less sense to study "popular culture" than to study "urban culture." The concept of popular culture implies an oppositional "high culture," or some similar term, falling in with other familiar oppositional sets such as subaltern/hegemonic, traditional/modern, and so forth. In each, *popular* is the devalued term, and *high* functions to reinforce hierarchies based on categorical distinctions in the society. Another reason for turning to "urban culture" is that in Latin America, the area of his concern, 60 to 70 percent of the population lives in urban agglomerations. Furthermore, those who don't live in cities are often closely tied to them. García Canclini cites a study by Rouse of Aguililla, a rural Mexican community where almost all the residents have relatives who live abroad. Rouse points out that the relations with distant relatives are as actively maintained as those with neighbors who live nearby. So it is no longer very informative to refer to Aguililla as a self-contained community. Nor do conventional notions of center and periphery make the same kind of sense as they used to. Instead, Rouse suggests, and García Canclini concurs, the utilization of "an alternative cartography of social space" based on notions of "circuit and border."[59] As terms such as *rural* and *urban* become less applicable throughout the world, it is useful to turn to questions about urban culture, asking about circuits (or flows) and borders (or boundaries) rather than looking at just the city or the culture of a particular national place.[60]

The raw material for García Canclini's Tijuana case study is the experiences presented by "border" people who live there part of the time. García Canclini found his interviewees' most prevalent characterizations of the city to be ones in which the composite aspects of life there are illuminated. Many of the residents' daily lives are split by the national border between the United States and Mexico. He found constant ongoing negotiation with these conditions of life. The people he talked to did not identify themselves in terms of categories such as citizen and immigrant. They understand their lives in terms of a flow across borders, and they made up new categories to articulate their fluid identities. The conventional terms continue to shape mainstream media presentations and, more tellingly, the rhetoric of public policy, but they do not provide good descriptions of the spatial practices that have become the norm in this border city.

García Canclini found himself instructed by the various ways in which the people he talked to combined parts of coherent identities into who they are. He also reports an air of celebration. Being not one thing or the other is fine with many people. The porousnesses of boundaries provides spaces of opportunity. To repeat the phrasing I used at the beginning of this "Urban" section: Making it up as they go along becomes a way of life.

The permeable border between Mexico and the United States is a central symbol for García Canclini: "In arriving at the beach 'the line' falls and leaves a transit zone, used at times by undocumented migrants. Every Sunday the fragmented families on both sides of the border gather for picnics."[61] García Canclini puts it in metaphorical terms, arguing that "at every border there are rigid wires and fallen wires."[62] Following Deleuze, he conceptualizes patterns of this new way of life as various deterritorializations and reterritorializations. Examples of deterritorialization are strategies that escape the conventional categories that threaten to split people's lives in reductive ways. García Canclini found patterns of movement through a number of inconsistent and unmoored situations that made use of the best of each. Examples of reterritorialization are attempts to shore up identities by attaching them more firmly to a conventional or nostalgic cultural base.

He calls deterritorializations "performances" rather than "actions." They are not "effective interventions"; instead, they are the exercise of "oblique power." From this point of view, commitment to a shared community of values is less the basis for making decisions about how to act than a series of situated acts of appropriation is. In one example he talks about how a person would consider both Western and traditional medicine before deciding what to do about an illness. It would depend on the circumstances, a matter of what is likely to work best. What to take as one's own and what to let go of or reject entail neither acceptance nor critique of a whole set of medical practices. Instead by exercising this "oblique power," workable lives are constructed as they are performed. García Canclini suggests the dailiness of creating urban life occurs without insisting on stable totalizing contexts of either understanding or action.

Life becomes a series of decisions made within the political and symbolic economies that condition the lives of these city people, but not without constant alteration and amendment to these economies. Things grow, but not into coherent stable wholes. Instead, hybrid identities and situations become the material for the propagation of impure genres and the stage for testimony to the life of the city. Psychological, social, and experiential boundaries are neither determinate nor irrelevant.

The most obvious difference between García Canclini's study and conventional studies of urban decline, discussed above, is where the studies are situated. Foucault would say that the site of enunciation differs.[63] In more conventional presentations, the rhetoric of decline quickly and completely takes its distance from urban life by making decline an object of analysis. Even if the purpose of the analysis is benign, it is still from a distance, producing urban decline according to the requirements and continuation of the larger society. In contrast, García Canclini, like Engels, situates himself inside a working culture. Value is allocated differently in the rhetoric of decline and in hybrid cultures. The details of life in the cities of decline provide human interest material for the larger public so long as they substantiate the bigger picture. The details of life of the border people of Tijuana are the life of the city, are pieces of a mosaic rather than a big picture. "Everyday the spectacular invention of the city itself is renewed and expanded."[64] The kind of power that operates in hybrid situations, oblique power, is a constitutive aspect of urban culture.

So rather than as the image of the unmitigated suffering of the invisible disfigured city, city life is presented as mixed and terribly ingenious. To return to the question of the dangers of discourse, the most obvious danger to pious thinking in the kind of study García Canclini presents is that it validates life as lived rather than planned—life as cobbled together. And it validates those who make themselves central to urban culture rather than external to it.

Oblique powers don't directly challenge ruling ideologies. The threat is not of revolution in a society based on class and ethnic distinctions and capitalist exploitation. The "voices" of urban culture that García Canclini presents don't compete with these issues; they sidestep them. Urban culture in Tijuana is an example of what Foucault calls being "off the table,"[65] but without the negative political implications of exclusion. Life goes on as it is. Oblique powers are simply that.

García Canclini's discussion of monuments is an apt example of the flow of life as lived in the city, particularly fun after considering the restoration of Athens. The restoration of Athens aimed at restoring both the space and the idea of Athens. The "original" was laid over what already existed in order to get it in proper order. The physical manifestation of European idealization of ancient Greece became a monument that gave glory and support to power structures in western Europe. García Canclini begins by pointing out that this approach to monuments is not unusual. He points out that the role of monuments in supporting state power is aided by the ways in which they are removed from the flow of everyday life. At least this is the case if they are viewed as just monuments. They are completed, they are displayed some height from the bustle of the city and sometimes even reside in museums. Monuments in public places are usually designed to make statements. García Canclini offers this concise summary: "'Why are there no statues in short sleeves?' the Argentine television program *La noticia rebelde* asked the architect Osvaldo Giesso, director of the Cultural Center of the city of Buenos Aires."[66]

There is nothing contested in the conventional idea of monuments. They exist in all their administrative and military grandeur. Perhaps this is why revolutionary celebrations when regimes fall include pulling down the monuments of the recently deposed. After the revolution they are hopeless. They are not so much out of place as they have no place.

When García Canclini examines actual monuments in Mexico, he reveals more complex situations. As the photographs he reproduces show,[67] the monuments convey different meanings when portrayed in their everyday surroundings, in relation to daily events. Of an image of Emiliano Zapata photographed in situ, that is, against modern buildings covered with billboards, he asks: "Against what is Emiliano Zapata battling now, at the entrance to the city of Cuernavaca? Against the advertising of hotels, beverages, and other urban messages?"[68]

In another example he shows the Hemiciclo Juárez in the Alameda of Mexico City: "First, a demonstration of parents protesting for their disappeared children. Later, feminists struggling in favor of abortion choose the father of anticlericalism to support their defense of voluntary maternity. The central banner partially obscures the images put up earlier, and between them all they propose various levels of resignification of the monument."[69]

Monuments, advertising, graffiti, modern buildings, and social movements are joint tenants of the space they make. So although the idea of the monument continues to exist, "urban life transgresses this order all the time."[70] And of course contemporary photographs of the Acropolis also show multilayered and competing spaces.

The recoding of monuments is part of the everyday flow of urban culture. As such, it testifies on behalf of the city as lived, not according to an idea of it, but as process. García Canclini does not approach the recoding of the space of monuments as confrontation, as an oppositional stance against the forces of order.[71] His approach is to present recoding and multiple use as urban life: processes of deterritorialization and reterriorialization are what urban space is. This is not to trivialize the issues at hand or to forget the courage of oppositional political activists in Latin American countries during the reign of various totalitarian regimes. It is to say that, regardless of the state (of the moment), the space of monuments is best understood in terms of reutilization. For the observer who approaches monuments in terms of their larger context and for people who use them, the space is active and available. If a feature of a monument is convenient for the hanging of banners and a group has banners, it will be done. In the image of the Hemiciclo Juárez reproduced in García Canclini's essay, there are three visible layers of meaning. All are active productions of city space, using it to make works of life.

Compared with the studies discussed above, the case studies in García Canclini's work appear rather without agenda. They are not linked to public policy affecting particular cities. They do not confront intellectual or ethical concerns about the lack of civic consciousness in American political culture. They do not critique city building from the perspective of an ideal of urban life. Instead they describe. But in contrast with conventional representations that largely ignore the city as lived, and in contrast with the way the restorers of Athens found the actual city troublesome, García Canclini's descriptions are revelatory. They testify on behalf of life as lived: in favor of recognizing urban culture and cities as places of life. They suggest not only that new constellations are possible but also that they are being constructed all the time.

Returning to the city is a large step when we consider how far away from lived experience most presentations of urban space are. These case studies are not meant to be prescriptions for the city as a whole. Their power is in the implications of what they show. We become better observers of urban space and at the same time learn to see differently. It is not that more conventional presentations take a position against life in the city; it is that they make that life irrelevant. García Canclini's work makes a contribution to theorizing the urban by throwing urban processes in the face of their "representatives." His work raises the crucial issue of how urban theory can contribute to "keeping up with" what is already happening in the streets.

As for the matter of the case studies themselves—hybrid identities invented by border people and the images of monuments in use—García Canclini is not making claims to substantive generalizability. His work is testimony to the existence of life in particular cities. Complete and incomplete at the same time, the case studies serve as openings to further speculation. Further, the examples of urban life that García Canclini presents do not attempt to ward off the dangers of discourse. City dwellers would not wish to do that. They live in that space.

It is not necessary to experience urban space by defining it according to preexisting narratives, or to understand it in terms of the logic of a system, or to create it in the image of capital. It is true that these approaches are culturally available and easy and in some instances useful—as are the forms of subjectivity that follow from them. To approach urban space through an aesthetics of distinction and to have the kinds of urban experiences that follow from that is to position ourselves where we already are. García Canclini's work reopens the question of what urban experience can become.

The problem that opened this section, the interweaving of image and reality, dissolves when various representations of urban decline in the city are examined. This is because representations, in whatever framework is employed, are also presentations. That is, images and realities are inseparable generative forces. In contemporary America, presentations of the urban we know best are removed from the daily life of the city. Nevertheless, something remains. As marginalized space, urban spatial practices offer the possibility for exploring an "aesthetics of existence"[72]—an opening to articulating the desire for life in the city.

Space

The morning traffic report is a ubiquitous part of many Americans' morning routines whether or not they themselves commute. We may barely notice, because it is so familiar, that each morning's report is constructed completely in terms of "flows." For example, "traffic is moving well over the such and such merge, and there is little slowdown at Dead Man's Curve." If an accident has been reported, it is presented in terms of information about whether the flow has been impeded or, worse yet, stopped. Helpful alternative routes to reorient the flow are often suggested.

One morning, maybe because there actually is a Dead Man's Curve in the city where I live, I started to consider information about morning traffic accidents in terms that are more common in regular news reports. I wondered if any people were hurt and if the ambulance would get there in time. Were there bodies all over the road stopping "the flow," or had they been thrown neatly onto the median strip so the flow could continue unimpeded?

This rift in my thinking exposed the extent to which the morning traffic report is a highly selective mode of seeing. Morning traffic is about getting to work: the emptying out of hearth and home and the stoking up of the fires of industry and the booting up of the information superhighway. We tend not to do a morning body count because there is only one relevant question: How are we doing in terms of getting there?

We make single-minded distinctions between what to pay attention to and what to ignore all the time. The ability to make distinctions and to navigate among them makes human society possible. Yet as the discussion of conventional approaches to urban decline and urban space in the "Urban" section suggested, systems of meanings that organize our lives do not provide complete coverage, cannot be a finished picture of human existence. In this section, I discuss conceptualizations of space in terms of the play between the desire for order and the need to reach what escapes it. I begin with what Michel Foucault calls heterotopic space, because he suggests that this kind of spatial activity both supports and exceeds life firmly rooted in the political, symbolic, and economic aesthetics of distinction. Although many American theorists have not emphasized this aspect of Foucault's work, his search for an aesthetics of existence speaks directly to questions of engagement in the city and, by extension, to participation in the formation of self.

In the work of both Foucault and Henri Lefebvre, the reach to escape the limitations of linear and abstract thought is conceptualized in spatial terms. The two share and repeat in various ways three themes: space as a process, the porousness of spatial boundaries, and mutually constitutive relations between space and selves. "Space" becomes the site where the production of conventional lives, the politics of exclusion, and the impossible inevitabilities of alternatives are interwoven. Neither Foucault nor Lefebvre theorizes or advocates escape from the material and social space of everyday life. Quite the contrary, both understand the human situation in the context of a concrete, constructed, *occupied* world. The aesthetics that concern them is a capacity to engage the material of the world in which we find ourselves—what Deleuze calls "life as a work of art."[1]

This section considers Foucault's spatial thinking by looking at how he ties the production of memory (what he calls "the history of the present") to experience. Instead of understanding the world from the perspective of a history that is a total and totally secure picture of the past representing the rightness of the reigning order, memory can activate the past in a selective self-conscious relation with current practice. From this way of thinking, memory is a bringing into the present.[2] Thus, rather than removing himself from the world to observe it, Foucault immerses himself in it. He says, "I aim at having an experience myself—by passing through a determinate historical content—an experience of what we are today of what is not only our past but also our present."[3]

The experience of being in and moving through while constituting a space is very evident in the style of Foucault's writing. De Certeau and other writers have written about Foucault's writing as rhetorical or visual.[4] I discuss it here as spatial.[5] Foucault interweaves discursive and nondiscursive modes of presentation; both are construction sites for experience. He puts fiction, not discovery, at the core of this work—memory and experience being made, not found. In his words, "... people who read me, even those who appreciate what I do, often say to me, laughing: 'but in the end you realize that the things you say are nothing but fiction!' I always reply: who ever thought he was writing anything but fiction?"[6]

A major concern of this section is to show how Foucault's spatial approach moves away from abstract discussion of truth and fiction and towards presentations that use real spaces as the basis of experience. Spatial theory builds on the limitations of modernity by seducing thinkers to forgo them.

Heterotopic Space and the Terms of Existence

Gilles Deleuze points out that Michel Foucault was arrested by such examples of daily routine as the one that opens this section. Foucault saw such incidents as an opening to speculation about the larger scheme of things, what Deleuze calls "visibilities."[7] Visibilities include the material world as part of the cultural frames that shape what can be seen. Foucault's interest in systems of visibilities was not that of the contemplative philosopher. The notion of visibilities is more precisely oriented towards recognizing the regularities that organize everyday life within both discursive and nondiscursive realms of life. Foucault interrogated, to refer again to my opening example, the orderly flows we concern ourselves with maintaining. He developed forms of spatial analyses that can be used to link what can be said and analyzed with what can be seen and done. He also explored systems of visibilities as spaces that bring us back to ourselves.

We can approach the daily traffic report, or any other report on contemporary life, unproblematically. Foucault's work expands this unconscious approach in three ways. He looks at the productive force of conventional systems of meaning, at exclusions from conventional spaces, and at the kinds of spatial processes that attract meanings. It is the last that is of the most concern here. The morning traffic report, like the morning news, may provide information about the world. But that is not enough. What the intellect can call up on its own—information—is suspect in modernity among theorists who think that conventional cognitive forms limit imaginative productivity. Foucault's work is interpreted below in light of this tradition within modernity of searching for alternative modes of presentation. If, as Walter Benjamin suggests, the myths of rationality and progress are selective histories, reducing experience of the world, abstract thought can be a barrier to experience in modernity. We can become very smart inside conventional forms of meaning and live reduced existences at the same time.[8] Marx was not the first or the last to suggest that civilization is both savior and drug.

My French and English dictionary presents *mémoire* first as a masculine noun. It means "memorandum, statement, account. . . ." Then the dictionary lists the word as a feminine noun. As such, it means "memory" in English, as in *de mémoire*, "from memory."[9] This is a nice shorthand summary of the critique of contemporary social order formulated in critical social theory. The memorandum and accounts have standing; memories are less important. Foucault's conceptualizations of space are understandable as part of this critique. In another context he has noted that modernity demands a sex.[10] This is not his demand. His approach is to disobey this order of gender. In the place of familiar spaces of information, material goods, and themed existences, Foucault is interested in finding spaces in which to engage.

In the famous opening to *The Order of Things*, Foucault repeats Borges's passage quoting a "certain Chinese encyclopedia" dividing animals into those "a) belonging to the Emperor, b) embalmed, c) tame, d)suckling pigs, e) sirens, f) fabulous, g) stray dogs, h) included in the present classification, i) frenzied, j) innumerable, k) drawn with a fine camel hair brush, l) et cetera, m) having just broken the water pitcher, n) that from a long way off look like flies."[11]

The actual truth of the existence of this encyclopedia and its meaning as a document in the Western sense of a comprehensive compilation of knowledge are not important here. Like the tired Eskimo with twenty-three words for snow who has illustrated the wisdom of cultural relativism for countless undergraduates, the importance of the example is in the use Foucault makes of it. He says he laughed but also that he was uneasy.[12]

This uneasiness came from the absence of space, or, in the figures he uses, a table or site, where all these categories might be arranged together. "[Borges] simply dispenses with the least obvious, but most compelling, of necessities, he does away with the *site*, the mute ground upon which it is possible for entities to be juxtaposed."[13]

Using a spatial term, *site*, to identify social order expands thinking about order from the confines of linear thought to include notions of space. *Space* ties together the idea of area with the idea of domain or regime. It also links the discursive to the material and makes both sites of politics. It expands the way in which we can think about the boundaries of society as well as where we stand in relationship to those boundaries.

Underlying the dis-ease Foucault says he felt is a clear preference for order. As discussed below, there is a tendency in this country to emphasize the implications of Foucault's work on discursive practices for understanding how social order works. There is less attention to how his arguments about order are spatial and how this leads him to implicate nondiscursive elements of experience.[14]

The notion that the familiar sequential presentation of history, the linear form, is confining is one aspect of Foucault's remark that "the anxiety of our era has fundamentally to do with space."[15] Another aspect of this remark is the desire to articulate the complex relationship between discursive and nondiscursive elements of social order and individual experience. For Deleuze, the relationship between the articulable (discursive) and the visible (nondiscursive) occupies Foucault from the time of the publication of *Discipline and Punish* through his later work.[16] The two are never collapsed into each other, in spite of their close relationship. Deleuze argues that the indeterminate relation between the discursive and nondiscursive provides opportunities for "unfore-seeable" events to occur—for "the light to get in."[17] If a totally determinate relationship between the two were to exist, then the question of the Chinese encyclopedia could be solved in one of two ways. Number one: learning how the Chinese organize space. Number two: discovering that the Chinese are crazy.

Foucault appears to begin with the first approach. That is, he asks to what kind of space Borges's quotation might be referring. This is an important question in the context of the total project of his book, because it is also speculation about what space is. Foucault's answer to the question he poses is not at the level of merely understanding why the listed items appear together; it is at the level of how to conceptualize space. The possibilities he presents are organized around discussing how various kinds of space stand in relation to social order. In moving through the possibilities, Foucault moves closer to the second approach—that the Chinese are crazy. And he also entertains the notion that existence is tied to crazy, or at least outside totally articulable organized worlds.

For Foucault the most obvious analogous situation to the Chinese encyclopedia, at least to Europeans, appears to be surrealism. But as he points out, placing the umbrella and the typewriter together on the space of the operating table, one of the best-known surrealistic images, works only because the viewer recognizes the juxtaposition as improbable. It is disconcerting only because it violates a commonly acknowledged social order in which these objects do not occupy the same space. This in turn raises questions about the kind of order the surrealists saw beyond order. One surrealist position privileges the personal unconscious meaning that would be exposed (or composed, depending on your point of view) by those willing to play the game. In the heyday of surrealism, what with Freud and all, the pressures to reorder order from a psychological perspective were as strong among cultural producers as were the forces of passive compliance they saw influencing society in general. So this kind of surrealistic space doesn't dismiss the site of order as Borges's list does. It requires order and asks for more.

Utopias (no spaces) are unusual spaces that don't exist. This kind of space does not provide a welcome for the Chinese animals either: from a utopian perspective, it is perhaps their great misfortune not to be lined up waiting two by two. But utopian space does provide insight into the uneasiness Foucault says he felt. Utopias "afford consolation,"[18] because they are linked directly to our fondest cultural memories and most hopeful dreams in ways that reinstate, without opposition and confusion, a home space. Utopias not only promote order; they also make it accessible. The coherence of the utopian vision that promotes accessibility suggests that there is cultural comfort in them there hills. Thomas More, Edward Bellamy, Le Corbusier, and Disney Corporation all deal from the same deck.

Foucault's initial dis-ease then comes, he suggests, from the lack of coherence and closure. His subsequent laughter, a burst of emotion, comes from a glimpse of life outside the spaces constructed within systems of visibilities. This is what Deleuze refers to as Foucault's "flash of light." Foucault names this kind of incoherent space heterotopias, saying, "They destroy 'syntax' in advance."[19] This suggests a very different function from that of utopias, one that deals not with reaffirming coherence but with violating it. This is not the violation of simple opposition: it is the violation of mixed use that sidesteps the societal common ground while standing in it. One is reminded here of the oblique power exercised by residents of Tijuana, referred to in the last section, "Urban." Heterotopias aren't alternative "free zones" of excess and carnival. They are related in complicated ways to the play of visible and invisible spaces in society.

In a more systematic (but still brief) discussion of heterotopias than the one that opens *The Order of Things*, Foucault hypothesizes that heterotopias take different forms in different societies and that they are connected to the problematics of the society in question.[20] For Foucault, the problematics of space refer to the terms in which social practices and individual identities are constructed and put into play. Space is both arena and domain. That is, spatial activities are ongoing productions that are related to the possibilities for human existence. Heterotopic activities can produce life at the center, where it otherwise would not be authorized or recognized.

Because Foucault sees contemporary Western society in terms of the problematics of normalization, it is not surprising that he proposes that our heterotopias are spaces of deviation.[21] Given the marginalization of cities in this country, we can also expect to find heterotopic activities attached to the urban. García Canclini's work on urban culture is written from this perspective. In looking at life in the city, he looks at cities as heterotopic space.

Foucault lists retirement homes among the more obvious heterotopic spaces of deviation in contemporary life.[22] Examining this example more closely illustrates how the space of normalization and the space of deviation can be linked to one another. Society makes complex use of "the lack of syntax," resolving some of the contradictions order imposes. Retirement homes are just one kind of site where multiple contradictions and interlocking spatial practices make space for life.

On the one hand, retirement homes are about care, but they also have to be productive in the larger economic system in order to survive. Normality is about productivity, among other things. In America, state support handles part of the problem of the economic productivity of retirement homes, but it is not to be counted on entirely. The issue is more complicated because, in addition to the requirements for productivity, retirement "homes" are not homes at all. They are institutions. Yet in order to send your relatives there, they must, at some level, exactly meet some generally recognized standards for care. There is an idealized notion of care in play here that is best evoked by the phrase "like one would get at home." Some approaches are obvious. Depending on the income level, these include clean facilities, good to excellent medical care, well-kept grounds, tasteful decorating in a traditional style, stimulating activities, good food, and professional support. But we also require some of these things of prisons and schools.[23] Retirement homes have an additional task. Their existence is tied to the mission to give care that "the family can no longer provide." It would be more accurate to say that, given how tightly we link notions of responsible adulthood to productive economic activity and given the highly individualized spatial requirements of our lives, there is no actual place in this world for elders after they are no longer self-sufficient.[24] They regain some of their worth by being paying customers at retirement homes. This doesn't handle all the facets of the care issue. Care, particularly for demented and otherwise disabled adults, is very time consuming and expensive in terms of the expenditure of human energy. The labor of care is divided, and the spaces of care are many layered in ways that mollify the dilemma that would be produced by having highly valued people devoting all their energy to the care of those who are not highly valued. So we can imagine separate circuits operating in different but related spaces. In order to organize these circuits there is some play between what is "on the table" and what is off. It depends on where you stand.

The political economy of retirement homes includes payments, either from the savings of the old or from younger relatives. These are discreetly handled in the spaces of accounting. These offices and circuits are quite separate from the spaces of daily care.

The concerns of the relatives, and particularly their awareness that they are not involved in the daily care, nor would they be good at it, nor would they really want to be, is managed within the domain of social work. Here, in better homes, there are periodic meetings with resident helping-professionals in which the state of health of elders is reported, problems that occurred and have been solved are explained, and everyone reasserts his or her commitment to attending to what cannot be any different. Like the economic space, this domain does not involve the concrete presence of the elder in question.

The daily bodily involvement, what becomes the functional equivalent of parents tucking their children in at night, is handled in yet another space. This involves caretakers who are the ones with their hands on the actual recalcitrant bodies of the elders. They do not meet with the professional care group, nor are they connected to the accounting function except to receive a paycheck. They are practical nurses or "custodians," often with very different cultural origins and class backgrounds from those of the more visible caretakers and of the people for whom they provide the most frequent human contact.

The "home" is everything but a home in this minute division of space and domain. Care, in the sense of what is happening at this moment to this person, is in the hands of people who no doubt have official procedures to follow, but who, in the end, provide care in terms of their own modes of being, their personal resources, and their capacity to give. In the best of circumstances, these relations of care produce a kind of human connection where the unseen and the unseeable devise a humanity that reaches beyond the regular spaces that place them there. The societal problem of care is solved, ironically, in part because the actual caregivers are not totally bound by site. They operate in more syntaxless realms of existence. Retirement homes are heterotopias not just because they are for the "not-normalizable." They also function heterotopically, beyond carefully constructed visible spaces, in places off the table, where we can't reach, don't control, and are reduced to hoping for the best.

Heterotopias in this example are real spaces; they are just not noticed. They are not simply spaces in or outside what Foucault calls the regularities that form the recognizable surfaces of our daily lives. One of the "principles" of heterotopias "is that they have a function in relation to all the space that remains."[25] Oblique power also uses cultural conventions as natural resources. Using the language Deleuze introduces, we would say that the spaces of articulation and the spaces of visibility are interwoven in ways that shape the possibility of existence within them. This is why, for example, we can stand to have our parents living in retirement homes. The distance between what is articulable and what is visible is connected to processes that make life sustainable within certain social problematics. The two forms function in society as they do because of their irreconcilability to each other. Deleuze explains that the functional units in discursive space are "statements"; the operative mode of being in nondiscursive realms is "visibility." He summarizes that they are related to each other but are never the same.

The primacy of the statement will never impede the historical irreducibility of the visible—quite the contrary, in fact. The statement has primacy only because the visible has its own laws, an autonomy that links it to the dominant, the heautonomy of the statement. It is because the articulable has primacy that the visible contests it with its own form, which allows itself to be determined without being reduced. In Foucault, the places of visibility will never have the same rhythm, history or form in the fields of statements, and the primacy of the statement will be valuable only in this way, to the extent that it brings itself to bear on something irreducible.[26]

Deleuze suggests a machine to explain the relationship of the articulable and the visible—assemblages of word and deed that are never completely closed off to each other. Within these nonisomorphic elements in social order, Foucault sees possibilities for existence. He ends "Of Other Spaces" by moving this possibility to the center: "The ship is the heterotopia *par excellence.* In civilizations without boats, dreams dry up, espionage takes the place of adventure, and the police take the place of pirates."[27]

Local Politics and the Development of an American Foucault

In the main, the implications of Foucault's spatial theory for questions dealing with "having an experience" have been underexplored in this country, because issues related to spaces off the table, boats, dreams, adventure, and pirates have been less compelling to American intellectuals than the application of Foucault's work to social critique.

American social critics have been concerned about exclusions from American political culture in part because of the promise for inclusion it contains. A moral drama formulated in terms of issues of membership and the right to belong shapes American political consciousness. There have been less obviously compelling reasons for speculations about experience beyond what democratic ideology promises.

Mary Douglas's study of ancient Jewish culture illuminates how aspirations to membership can organize political and moral space. In a discursive analysis of the abominations of Leviticus, in the Old Testament, she explains how the logic in Leviticus creates a world that makes membership a moral imperative.[28]

On first reading, the list of dietary rules in the books of Leviticus and Deuteronomy seems as confusing as Borges's Chinese encyclopedia. Each list raises analogous questions about the system of meanings that makes them possible. The dietary rules make the following distinctions:

2) These are the living things which you may eat among all the beasts that are on the earth. 3) Whatever parts the hoof and is cloven-footed and chews the cud, among the animals you may eat. 4) Nevertheless among those that

chew the cud or part the hoof, you shall not eat these: The camel, because it chews the cud but does not part the hoof, is unclean to you. . . . 7) And the swine, because it parts the hoof and is cloven-footed but does not chew the cud, is unclean to you. . . . 9) These you may eat of all that are in the waters. Everything in the waters that has fins and scales, whether in the sea or in the rivers, you may eat. 10) But anything in the seas or the rivers that has not fins and scales, of the swarming creatures in the waters and of the living creatures that are in the waters, is an abomination to you. 11) They shall remain an abomination their flesh you shall not eat, and their carcasses you shall have in abomination. 12) Everything in the waters that has not fins and scales is an abomination to you. . . . 29) And these are unclean to you among the swarming things that swarm upon the earth; the weasel, the mouse, the great lizard according to its kind. . . . These are unclean to you among all that swarm: whoever touches them when they are dead shall be unclean until evening. . . . 42) Whatever goes on its belly, and whatever goes on all fours, or whatever has many feet, all the swarming things that swarm upon the earth, you shall not eat, for they are an abomination.[29]

Douglas is interested in the kind of interpretation of this list that would connect it to the routines of everyday life. In other words, she asks what kind of visibilities are related to such a set of rules. She feels that most existing interpretations remain at the level of abstract systems of meaning and don't consider the abominations as active components of a living culture. In one kind of abstract interpretation, for instance, the substance of the abominations is considered to be arbitrary, and what is important is that they establish a set of rules for the devout to follow. They are "ethical" or "disciplinary."[30] The rules could apply to any time and place. Another kind of interpretation is what Douglas calls "pious commentaries."[31] Here there is an attempt to assign a religious meaning to the list. She finds this approach weak, because it is more informative about the interpreter's reference system than about the way of life that the rules help organize. Further, "a different explanation has to be developed for each animal and there is no end to the number of possible explanations."[32] Two brief examples illustrate these problems: (1) "Fish with fins and scales, admitted by the law, symbolize endurance and self control, whilst the forbidden ones are swept away by the current, unable to resist the force of the stream." And (2) ". . . Fishes were reputed unclean that had not fins and scales: that is, souls that did not raise themselves up by prayer and cover themselves with the scales of virtue."[33] This threatens to put Leviticus on the operating table with the umbrella, the typewriter, and animals drawn with a fine camel hair brush.

Douglas herself proposes contextualizing the dietary rules in terms of how the ancient Jews lived out their relationship with God. God's blessing was understood to be visible as an orderly prosperous society. The blessing of God is/brings "fertility of women, livestock and fields"; the withdrawal of God's blessing is associated with "barrenness, pestilence and confusion."[34] Being blessed is to live a whole and complete life, not in any abstract sense, but in the material matters of existence.

To organize the world in this way—that is, to understand the state of being in God's grace in terms of fruitfulness and wholeness—is to argue for aligning oneself as much as possible with what can be considered to be whole. Membership announces itself at the levels of material well-being and moral worthiness. A life that identifies membership with an identity and with both worldly prosperity and its visible material signs bodes ill for whatever is deemed incomplete, partial, or mixed.

The dietary rules in Leviticus are part of the enactment of a full and complete life. They carefully separate the incomplete and mixed (that which cannot be blessed) from the whole and good (that which shows the visible presence of God's blessing).

So we can see how the unfortunate "swarming animals" (to take one example) come to be an abomination. "Swarming" is not a mode of propulsion proper to any particular element; it cuts across the basic classification system.[35] Land animals should walk—they were created that way as related in Genesis. Air animals should fly. Water animals should swim. "Swarming" is neither (as they say) fish nor fowl and, hence, is reprehensible. That the Jews lived in a particular climate and cultivated particular crops and livestock is not incidental to this system of evaluation. Douglas's major point is exactly *not* to reconcile the system with an essential reality but rather to identify it with a concrete set of spatial practices, to see it as a system of visibilities. It is a highly selective system that also carries great moral force. To follow the dietary rules is to participate in producing and reproducing an orderly and coherent world. This is a process that is itself an ongoing worship of God. The world is made to appear blessed, and people act to make it so. It is misleading to see the identities of the people separate from their efforts to maintain membership. The narrative is one in which God gives or takes away: the spatial practices require constant activities to make that world come true. The moral success of the individual and active participation in making a world are not separate. In this respect, Job is an exception: his trials are even greater than simple bodily discomforts insofar as the things that show him to be blessed are taken away.

Douglas's analysis explains Foucault's dis-ease at his inability to organize Borges's list. To classify the Chinese animals in terms of a coherent arrangement would identify a system and signal the opportunity to have one's identity shaped by belonging to that system. But at the same time, when Foucault realizes certain failure to make the list into a coherent cosmology, he laughs. His laughter is a sign that he also recognizes the potential for experience in different spaces and for escaping the wages that are extracted from every single one of us by what Mary Douglas calls structures of purity.[36]

In the American context the advantages of problematic membership are less likely to surface. Instead we are more likely to treat exclusion as an unmitigated social ill. Further, we are in the habit of covering up exclusions under a cloak of polite talk and reasonable behavior—the politics of civility. A recent example occurred as part of an interview on National Public Radio with Edward Ball.[37] Ball is a Caucasian man who had been raised in the North but moved to the South to write about the plantation his family had owned before the Civil War. His purpose was to write about what life had been like there. The radio presentation included an excerpt from one of Ball's interviews with an elderly African American woman. Her great-grandparents had lived as slaves on the plantation until her great-grandfather was sold to a nearby landowner. After she told the story, the writer prompted her to go on by saying, "And so after your great-grandfather left, what happened next?" The woman responded, "He didn't leave. He was *sold*."

There is a difference that makes all the assignment of moral difference in whether we understand that the man left or that he was sold. At the very least, it is a stunning historical slip loaded with the kind of polite forgetfulness revisionist historians rail against and the rest of us get by on. To set this sort of forgetfulness in the context of the bias of American political culture, one has only to point out that fathers who leave may be physically elusive, but their moral reprehensibleness is clear. The delinquent father plays a major role in the moral dramas that are public debates about the role of the state in social welfare, the "breakdown" of the family, and the suspect character of the poor. To relate this directly to the previous discussion: a family without a father is a partial family; it is not blessed; it does not belong to or participate in the arena of responsible adulthood and full citizenship. We may not use this kind of language, but we are not that far from the kind of consciousness it articulates.

One of the most commonly used measures of urban decline is the percentage of female-headed households. The bias of this exclusionary principle is particularly clear when one takes another perspective. To see differently could mean taking the position that accepting responsibility for raising the child you helped create is a good thing to do, and it is not easy. This reality of everyday life notwithstanding, the principles of construction that organize the visible objects of public policy continue to enforce an American moral drama that predates and extends beyond the current move to workfare and is somewhat tangential to the demographics of family life in this country.

The fact that the radio interview was referring to an African American father plays handily, albeit implicitly, into the dynamics of racial construction and the barriers to full membership and citizenship that racialization implements. The fact that it is so normal and so *civil* to say "after he left" plays into the continued injuries of race in this country and is especially noticeable in this context of trying to set the record straight. How we make absence problematic is so present here that it is almost redundant to point out the moral implications of the fact that a family without a father is not complete. Again, there are two main choices in the spaces of articulation allocated by the cultural codes that admit only families having two parents of different sexes to full membership in the moral community of respectable adults: (1) It is not their fault that they are not whole and they are eligible to become objects of charity. (2) It is their fault that their existence is partial and they become objects against which the blessed can define themselves.[38] Or both.

This brief analysis suggests that the deep cosmology Douglas discusses is informative about how we organize our own spatial practices. Even the civilities of everyday life harbor a politics of exclusion not only alive but also fully at work. American interpreters of Foucault have been particularly sensitive to the extent to which his work provides analytic tools for exposing such exclusions in all their inescapable everyday ordinariness.

Not only do we make a deep connection between membership and righteousness, but also American political ideology fails to focus on the contexts that make membership (that is to say, success within categories of membership) possible. Our politics begins with the proposition that "all men are created equal." We can trace this, if not literally, at least genealogically, to Locke's *Second Treatise on Government*. Here Locke presents an origin myth that differs in some respects, but not all, from the creation story in Genesis. It functions similarly; that is, it claims to cover everything, while it is in fact the presentation of a highly selective social order. The language is just as stirring as biblical language:

> To understand Political Power right, and derive it from its Original, we must consider what State all Men are naturally in, and that is, a *State of perfect Freedom* to order their Actions, and dispose of their possessions, and Persons

as they think fit within the bounds of the Law of Nature. . . . A *State* also of *Equality*, wherein all the Power and Jurisdiction is reciprocal, no one having more than another: there being nothing more evident, than that Creatures of the same species and rank promiscuously born to all the same advantages of Nature, and the use of the same faculties, should also be equal one amongst another. . . .

The *State of Nature* has a Law of Nature to govern it, which obliges every one; and Reason, which is that Law, teaches all Mankind, who will but consult it, that being all equal and independent, no one ought to harm another in his Life, Health, Liberty, or Possessions.[39]

Laslett reminds readers in his introduction to Locke's *Two Treatises of Government* that these were political documents in the direct sense of providing the rationale for restoring the monarchy. This is a cue to the selectivity used in constructing them. That men consent to be governed is an important principle enabling political empowerment, but nobody entertained the idea that this meant *all* actual living people. A close reading of the introductory sections reproduced above show how reliant on inequality Locke's arguments for equality are. Men are equal, but this means "within their rank." They are free to dispose of their possessions. This naturalizes the notion that citizens are free men of certain rank who have possessions. Similarly, when putting forth the origins of property and labor, Locke makes universal claims in a way that radically narrows their application:

Thus the Grass my Horse has bit; the Turfs my Servant has cut: and the Ore I have diff'd in any place where I have a right to them in common with others, become my *Property*, without the assignation or consent of anybody. The *labour* that was mine, removing them out of that common state they were in, hath *fixed* my *Property* in them.[40]

Obviously, there are certain assumptions about having horses and servants that modify the meaning of equality. Echoes of "become my *Property*, without the assignation or consent of anybody" appeared in recent memory as part of the presidential campaign rhetoric in reference to tax reform, where the logic was basically, "It's your money; you earned it; you have a right to keep it." This makes the kind of sense it does because certain conventions of citizenship, property, and labor are combined into indicators of full membership. To identify this way of life with "America" as candidates tend to do is to reestablish the country's Blessed State for its blessed citizens.

Locke's "state of nature" has also been used to fight for membership. Claims to equality based in reason and shared humanity have been used to contest and expand prevailing notions of citizenship. In American politics this has been a struggle on the surface for the vote and underground for conditions of life that make voting a worthwhile activity. There is a commonly articulated linear history of citizenship in America that tells the story in terms of continual expansion of the rules of membership: it begins with removing barriers of property, then of race, then of gender, and then of race again. This story becomes more complicated when it is joined with practices that limit what citizenship means. The issue of membership resurfaced in the 2000 presidential election at the basic level of the mechanisms of voting. The gap between promise and practice is the space of struggle and possibility in which both the language and practice of citizenship are deployed.[41]

The political rhetoric of social movements expanding the boundaries of citizenship has been shaped by notions of equality that are based in the idea that reason is a universal measure of humanity and in Judeo-Christian ideals of human justice. This struggle for membership appears in the tracts of populism, the labor movement, the women's movement, the civil rights movement, and the anti–Vietnam War movement. The reformist and radical traditions in the social sciences have parallel oppositional practices. In sociology, when the conventional wisdom looked to the functioning of groups in a whole society, the critical opposition focused on the dynamics of exclusion. In political science, studies of democracy, citizen rule, and all the rest are celebrated in the mainstream. The limitations of these in practice have been central to oppositional concerns. Public policy rhetoric, including such phrases as "equal opportunity" and even "affirmative action," draws from the origin myth of equality and membership. These phrases become more palatable, although not uncontested, to American sensibilities to the extent that they are construed as merely broadening participation, rather than forcing any reconsideration of the basic cosmology of the Blessed State of American Democracy.

In political arenas "reason" is, again, a cloak, quickly drawn over practices of exclusion. For example, campaign events such as debates and "town meetings" can be seen as enactments of short dramas that identify a candidate with a social order in which everything that is, is known and under control. The means to this end can be excluding an awful lot and calling remainder whole. The often preselected questions that citizens pose can be seen as a series of little morality plays in which every concern or potential problem is shown to be subject to reasonable control. In other words, debates function as opportunities to show that the political order is complete. Issues and questions are the raw material for demonstrating that there is no problem (out there) that cannot be reasonably dealt with (in here). The game in the debates, in both the more traditional question-and-answer format and in the town meeting format, is to outreason the opponent. This links the candidate to the promise to make the whole world blessed or, in terms of American democratic ideology, to exercise leadership by proposing reasonable criteria for fulfilling the promise of membership. Every concern, injury, or desire outside the realm of reasonable control is outside the Realm. The spatial arrangement of the television studio "meeting halls" reinforces this notion. The candidates are at the center, as the hub of a wheel around which the citizen-audience moves in place.

The failure of the so-called insurgent candidates in the 2000 presidential campaigns is illustrative. The George W. Bush/John McCain contest was at its best for McCain when it pitted him as a man of principle and principled ideals against Bush, the callow candidate and good ole boy. The fortunes of these two were reversed in the aftermath of McCain's attack on Bush's visit to Bob Jones University. McCain was seen as a one-man inquisition and Bush as a beacon of reason and tolerance in a democratically diverse society. The man of principle was reconfigured as a shrill figure outside the arena of reasonable politics. Bill Bradley's positioning himself against "entrenched power" (read Al Gore) functioned similarly, although not nearly as dramatically.[42] These events disregard both outsider candidates' political biographies as U.S. senators, a very insider place to be, no matter what your politics. The *New Yorker* was only concurring with general critical opinion when it called the two winners "hologram" candidates.[43]

Themes of social inequality and political participation are central to critical social and political consciousness in this country, and they have served to inspire analyses of exclusions by researchers in sociology, political science, and branches of cultural studies such as colonial and postcolonial theory, ethnic studies, and feminisms.[44] A great deal has been let in because Foucault provided the means to articulate this single-minded concern about how things get left out. In this country, Foucault's thinking has been put to work across the humanities and social sciences, not only in philosophy and literary criticism. It has, in fact, added a social science cast to these disciplines. It is seen in the anti-Enlightenment, pro-postmodern maelstrom in cultural studies, in realigned thinking about the relations between knowledge and power in sociology and policy studies, and as an alternative to slavish devotion to empirical research methods across the social sciences. In these, however, perhaps a substratum of positivism has affected the application of Foucault's work. To the extent to which Foucault is understood as exploring a social system as a "thing" to be analyzed, movement between modes, the play of the articulable and visible, and the gaps that movement produces are less likely to be noticed.[45] Uneasiness and laughter have been transformed into new research agendas where excitement is mixed with righteous anger.

Every identified exclusion from full participation is defined against the memory/dream of equality that is this country's political and moral epic. So, to return to the radio example, to say "he was sold" becomes the kind of "event" that Foucault uses to begin inquiry into taken-for-granted regularities and how they structure the syntax of everyday life.[46] This is the cultural context in which Foucault's work has had such resonance. In the main, the notion of the event and the potential of the concept for thinking about possibilities for existence in a porous world have not been so obviously interesting as the potential of Foucault's approach for analyzing exclusions.

There is a way in which reading Foucault has been important for getting on with the work at hand, attending to the political exclusions and the implications of those exclusions for full membership in the American system. In general, the American profile of Foucault tends to deemphasize parts of his work that range too far from discussion of discursive practices and that are less obviously methodological and more difficult from a pragmatic point of view. Although some feminists have worked insightfully with *Herculine Barbin*, other texts, such as *Death and Labyrinth: The World of Raymond Roussel* and *I, Pierre Rivière, having slaughtered my mother, my sister, and my brother . . .* , are not as well known. This is true also of many of Foucault's interviews. Similarly, the details of the histories (for example, visual images that are complicated pictures of how various medical treatments worked and even persisted while what they were supposed to be doing changed) are not often cited. The extent to which Foucault's thinking is spatial, for example, in *The Order of Things*, has also drawn little attention. The concern in the context of American social science has been more about what Foucault offers in the way of tools for thinking about social relations in institutionalized practices and less about what he offers in the way of understanding existence in the spaces we make as we move through them.

Single-minded attention to exclusions can essentialize a liberal ethic. If unsited and not articulated, the ground for arguing against them can become idealized and universalized. This invents and valorizes a Habermasian bias and belief in "Rationality" rather than foregrounding the systems of visibilities in which various rationalities play a role. The perpetual reform notion in the social sciences has the advantage of optimism, of promoting and working for political justice,[47] but it may also have had the unhappy latent effect of leading away from some other major aspects of Foucault's work, including his spatial analysis and interest in heterotopic space, as well his concern with the potential for living life in various registers.

Foucault's spatial analysis and particularly his notion of heterotopic space should sensitize us to expect both productive and limiting aspects of spatial practices. At one point in the *Second Treatise*, as he is describing the state of nature, John Locke remarks that "all the world was America." He chooses America because of how his audience imagined America: as a land of abundance, peopled by "noble savages" who were unencumbered by corrupting forms of civilization and hence had no need for government. In our own time, economic and cultural globalization has been characterized as a different kind of American Moment. Critics argue that in the present situation the "consent" that was central to the move away from the mythical state of nature to legitimate forms of sovereignty is missing from contemporary international economic relations. Thus, reasoned debate and the public good are less important than getting the best deal without the encumbrance of too much public debate. Ongoing events are often presented to the public as presupposed and/or as the result of inevitable forces. Supporters argue that global corporations are vehicles for raising the standard of living in areas of the world bypassed by the advances brought by industrial capitalism.

Whether they are for it or against it, many see a universal urban culture developing. Foucault's work can sensitize us to expect both productive and limiting aspects of this new space. Construction of self and space will be intertwined in somewhat unpredictable ways. For example, the protests that accompanied the meetings of the

World Trade Organization in October 1999 occurred in the middle of one of America's most prosperous cities. At the same time most of the delegates to the World Trade Organization were tastefully dressed in suits and ties of decidedly Western hues.

Perhaps the World Trade Organization can be viewed as the site of a new kind of world government with the consent of those who matter. In this view Locke's noblemen have been transformed into today's corporate elite. Perhaps this has occurred because of the ability to create new sites for the deployment of power—yielding certain areas of state activity to "the people" is part and parcel of making safe space for the exercise of the relations of dominance. The city, then, is not the seat of civilization and governance; it becomes "the street"—heterotopic spaces of expression, sites to protest what the New Governors would like to make invisible. New kinds of urban spaces and urban identities are being formulated and deployed both on and off the streets.

Rajchman's essay on contemporary architecture illustrates how little of Foucault's spatial thought was used by theorists writing as late as the late 1990s. His discussion of Deleuze's interpretation of Foucault presents Foucault's interests as lying beyond the exposure of the limitations of conventional discursive practices. "Visibilities" in Rajchman's treatments are identified with "how things were made visible."[48] He reminds readers that Foucault often presents before-and-after images. One learns how to think differently from comparing the two images. Rajchman emphasizes the language-based components of systems of visibilities in his discussion. "A 'visualization,' a scheme through which things are given to be seen, belongs to the 'positivity' of knowledge and power of a time and place."[49]

Architecture is a particularly difficult example. Although it seems an obvious site for physical spatial practices, haute architecture has had some very textual moments recently. Rajchman's analysis of architecture doesn't discuss new types of physical space, but rather the emergence of a certain kind of self-consciousness about how to inhabit times and places.[50] This is heavily weighted towards the cognitive. In this regard, Ernest Pascucci's review of *Chora L Works*, by Jacques Derrida and Peter Eisenman, in the *Bookforum*, is telling.[51] It said in part:

> The built project never came about, but it did generate a ton of paperwork—Derrida's "Why Peter Eisenman Writes Such Good Books" in both French and English, various seminars in which the word "chora" is endlessly deconstructed, faxes, drawings, etc.—all of which is bound together, complete with holes punched out on every page (replicating the point-grid scheme at LaVillette, which refers to Eisenman's unbuilt point-grid in Canareggio, Venice, which refers . . .)[52]

Rajchman says Foucault's histories "share an *aim* with fiction; the aim not of explanation, or of showing how our ways of seeing and doing are historically necessities, but, on the contrary, of showing how things might be otherwise, beyond our self-evidences."[53]

Foucault's spatial thinking is a component of this move beyond single-minded concerns with exclusions and membership. We can return to thinking in terms of an aesthetics of existence by looking at how space is occupied. To use Lefebvre's terms introduced in the next section, "City," we can look at the gestures that constitute both self and space.

Rajchman's powerful phrases "the *incitement* to see"[54] and "showing how things might be otherwise" begin to specify the location of aesthetics of existence in Foucault's work. On the implications of "the *incitement* to see" for experiencing life, Rajchman is eloquent: "For us the danger is not that we might fail to become what we are meant to be, but that we might only be what we can see ourselves to be."[55] Rajchman only partly ventures into this territory because of how he preprograms the quest: "Foucault's art of seeing is an art of looking out, which would 'give new impetus, as far and wide as possible, to the undefined work of freedom.'"[56] More broadly, the challenge is to use the art of seeing as a different mode: to look in, around, and back and forth at where we find ourselves. Further, the notion of freedom is too limited if it implies only the opposite of being "not free" and only the goal of being untethered, neither one of which should be accepted unproblematically. We don't imagine pirates keeping logs or recognizing border maintenance functions. But their boats go everywhere.

Spatial Presentation from *Las Meninas* to the Afterimage of Modernity

American literary culture includes a tradition of "southern writers." The question of what constitutes a southern writer came up on National Public Radio recently in an interview with the editor of a new collection of southern short stories. At the end of the friendly interrogations, the editor in question volunteered the information that there had been a party honoring the authors of the collection. Since most of them lived in the region, they were able to attend. "You know," she conjectured, "I think that the Yankee writers were jealous. . . . They weren't used to being so friendly with one another." Her speculation was jarring in a mint julep and magnolia sort of way, precisely because in simply saying "Yankee writers" the southern editor had used a hegemonic culture's own terms to escape its space at the very moment *it* was constructing *her* as an exotic object of its own (higher) appreciation.

My reaction to this reversal was to recognize it as a beautiful moment. Southern writers we analyze without pause, but "Yankee writers"? Not since I heard my grandmother's soft voice using *Damnyankees* as one word had I glimpsed this imagined world. It was instantly clear that the radio interview had "merely" been perpetuating an ingrained regional hierarchy. It was publicly exposed to itself with that one sweet phrase.

Regionalism is not an idle thought in the American context.[57] This country's geography cannot be explained only by using a compass. To be familiar with the idea of southern writers requires a reference to cartologies of the United States, both past and present, cultural and geographic. It is the way that "Yankee writers" reverses where we usually stand when reading those maps that made it such an eye-opening comment. The regional anecdote about southern plantation life that opened the previous section was structured in a way to obscure certain aspects of how the physical spaces of the antebellum South worked. The discussion emphasized slavery as a legal arrangement and the discursive mechanisms in contemporary life that hide the shame of those memories—all habits that deemphasize the spaces of the plantation and its regional identity.

There is much to be said and seen about plantation life that involves but also exceeds the informational aspects of language codes. Connection with some of this can occur by recognizing modes of articulation that either flow across the usual boundaries, allowing multiple views, or are heterotopic in the sense that they operate on and off the table. These modes would include, among other things: spatial hierarchies within and beyond the plantation; arenas of clothing and unclothing subjects; spaces that legitimated using, violating, and even photographing bodies by right and in practice; the arrangement of the land itself into adjacent feudal estates; the movement of bodies, by custom, across spaces that have greater reality than kinship ties; and finally, as telling as all these, presentations that escape while being present in these spaces.

Foucault's *The Order of Things* is, among many other things, a methodological guidebook to thinking about space as this kind of "arena of activity."[58] The kind of thought Foucault introduces with the way he writes this book is a mode of seeing space as "practiced place."[59] The conceptual traveling Foucault does is spatial: he develops the tools that make it possible for him to critique the limitations of how he is produced as a cognitive being and that also enable him to site alternative modes.

Foucault's famous interpretation of *Las Meninas,* by Velázquez, appears at the beginning of *The Order of Things.*[60] The spatial approach introduced with the analysis of this painting is the mode in which the whole book is constructed. That is, Foucault does not use only the painting to illustrate his thinking. Similarly, he does not construct only descriptions that use graphics (chapter 4, part 7, "The Quadrilateral of Language") or employ only spatial metaphors to show what he means by cultural contexts (chapter 10, "The Human Sciences"). In the three cases just mentioned the figure *is* the analysis. Foucault deploys forms of thought that emphasize the spatial aspects of order as ongoing processes involving mutually constitutive connections between self and society.

The space Foucault makes with *Las Meninas* is difficult to follow without a reproduction of the painting. A recent paperback edition of *Les Mots et les choses* by the French publisher Gallimard does not reproduce the entire painting but shows only the central figures, highlighting the Infanta Margarita.[61] This is revealing, similarly to how hearing the phrase "Yankee writers" was for me in the story told above.

Concentrating on the Infanta Margarita enacts the biases theorists of modernity such as Foucault, Lefebvre, and Benjamin find in Western thought. Presenting a single image inadvertently privileges the myth of the rational individual by focusing on an important historical subject, ignoring surrounding practices. Carving out the center of the painting and emphasizing a single individual in it leaves behind the constitutive relations that make her who she is. It is as if an entity is displayed but not the activities that constitute her. This Margarita cites the painting; only the painting Foucault has in mind isn't there.

The Infanta Margarita by herself helps to construct a singular, sequential way of looking at the world. One thing leads to another: she is preceded and followed by other royals, each underwriting the next, with none of the fun that can entail being shown. Foucault doesn't reject this mode of thought; he just displays its limitations. Before beginning his consideration of the painting, he provides readers with the names of people depicted on the canvas and then points out that this tends to close off speculation. Names belong to language and hence are the product of the rules that govern language use. "The space where they achieve their splendour is not that deployed by our eyes but that defined by the sequential elements of syntax."[62]

Instead of presenting a succession of elements, Foucault constructs a field of play: a multidimensional, spatial description of the relationships that constitute the painting. He shows readers how to see a number of two- and three-dimensional figures that move across the face of the painting and extend beyond it. Foucault writes spatially; that is, he uses space actively as a form of analysis, beginning with the formulation of an initial scheme based on *Las Meninas* and ending with his consideration of the human sciences at the end of *The Order of Things*.

One of the first figures Foucault constructs from *Las Meninas* is one in which vertical and horizontal lines cross each other. The source for the horizontal dimension is the light that illuminates the painting by flowing across it from a window opening on the right. This is opposite the large canvas on the left, the back of which faces the viewer of the painting. An art historian might point out that this light reverses the convention in paintings of the Annunciation. In this tradition the light comes in from the left, with the Angel Gabriel, and flows across to the Virgin on the right. *Las Meninas* is highly secular, but the light operates similarly to enable the painting. It is active, making it possible to see the figures and calling selective attention to their importance. Dreyfus and Rabinow identify the light with the Enlightenment saying, "Clearly, this is the light of the Enlightenment, which sets up a space in which objects and representations correspond."[63] Foucault does not note either the art history tradition or the Enlightenment, but discusses the operation of the light—the work it does in moving across the painting and constructing a meaningful space.

The differences between the various approaches to the light are the differences between solidifying tradition and activating space. So, for example, rather than to reaffirm the Christian tradition or the history of modernity, the light is used in

Foucault's approach to create a visible space inside the painting. What he does evoke of the Annunciation tradition is the notion of an active element operating in the space of the image.[64]

A horizontal line (the light, the placement of the figures in the foreground) marks the borders of membership inside the painting; a vertical line leading outside marks the occasion of the gathering and the material cause of the painting itself: the way in and also the escape from it. The vertical line makes a dimension that complicates the simple notion of membership. The vertical line connecting the deep background and the outside of the painting upsets the whole question of what belongs where by implicating what may be the "real" subject of the painting. That is, the king and queen who are reflected in the mirror deep inside the painting have to be standing outside the painting.

A second figure Foucault constructs from the space of *Las Meninas* is an X:

The top left-hand point of this X would be the painter's eyes; the top right-hand one, the male courtier's eyes; at the bottom left-hand corner there is the corner of the canvas represented with its back towards us (or more exactly) the foot of the easel; at the bottom right-hand corner, the dwarf (his foot on the dog's back). Where these two lines intersect, at the centre of the X, are the eyes of the Infanta.[65]

The curving spaces of this St. Andrew's cross construct and contain the figures in the painting while also emphasizing the princess and, finally, implicating the viewers outside the painting. Foucault notes the plane made by the lines that lead out of the painting. "It comes from the child's eyes and crosses only the foreground."[66] It does not interrogate the deep inside, but leads out off the surface where the viewers stand, making them an element of the whole.

An issue that drives speculation forward within an art history point of view is the disconcerting relation between the Infanta and the dwarf. Because she is dressed as an adult and he is small with dwarfish proportions, these two figures question and/or throw off and/or draw attention to the perfect exercise of perspective within the painting.[67] The perspective is perfect, except where it is not: the artist is a genius. But Foucault looks at the porousness and instability of the painting rather than engaging this debate.

> The picture accepts as many models as there are spectators: in this precise but neutral place, *the observer and the observed take part in ceaseless exchange.* No gaze is stable. . . . The great canvas with its back to us . . . The opaque fixity that it establishes on one side renders forever unstable the play of metamorphoses established in the centre between spectator and model. . . . We do not know who we are, or what we are doing.[68]

The space does not come to or seek to rest. It exists as long as meanings continue to circulate.

Foucault's use of *Las Meninas* goes beyond being the "classical representation of classical representation" that W. J. T. Mitchell notes in his commentary.[69] Foucault's discussion is a methodological overview of *The Order of Things*. It introduces his approach to thinking about systems of visibilities and his use of spatial presentations to move from an abstract history to active discursive space.

The dilemmas that the painting presents tie relationships and movements that connect what is deeply inside to what appears to be outside. The mystery Foucault produces spatially is how such a bounded space is not contained. Using the language that he introduced earlier, we would say that there is something at the core of *Las Meninas* that is off the table, off with the very fine camel hair brush and the suckling pigs.

This mystery reappears in Foucault's presentation of classical systems of knowledge in section 7, "The Quadrilateral of Language," which concludes chapter 4 of *The Order of Things*. Here Foucault constructs a figure that maps the movements that construct representation in the classical age. Again he includes forms that breach that space as a necessary component of presentation.

For Foucault, language in the classical age is used as a vehicle without itself being an issue. Within this framework, questions about deep meaning that concerned preclassical thinkers fall off the table. The verb *to be* is central: "The function of the verb is found to be identified with the mode of existence of language."[70] Four functions circulate around the verb: proposition, articulation, designation, and derivation. He arranges them as points at the corner of a quadrilateral and puts them in motion in relation to each other. The resulting figure has two diagonal relations. The diagonals cross over each other, and at the center of the figure, playing the same role as the eyes of the Infanta Margarita, is the Name. Of the name Foucault says:

> The entire classical theory of language is organized around this central and privileged entity. All the various functions of language intersect within it, since it is by nomination that representations are enabled to enter as figures into a proposition.[71]

Naming things allows them to be.

> One might say that it is the Name that organizes all Classical discourse; to speak or to write is not to say things or to express oneself, it is not a matter of playing with language, it is to make one's way towards the sovereign act of nomination, to move through language, towards the place where things and words are conjoined in their common essence, and which makes it possible to give them a name.[72]

During the classical age, knowledge was often presented as grids or taxonomies in which all the entities of a certain category were organized. This makes representation as naming seem static. But at the constitutive level this form is active. Naming requires movement of a particular sort within and beyond a space. Just as the light in *Las Meninas* constructs membership, language use that constructs propositions, that articulates, that designates, and that derives belongs to that space, or is on the table, where these movements are possible.[73]

There 'are also movements that break the boundaries of representational space. That is, there are moves in the classical forms of representation that are analogous to the perpendicular lines and triangular and spiral figures that go beyond *Las Meninas*. In the representational space of the classical age this has to do with what cannot be represented. All of creation named and cataloged is the totalizing promise of the classical age. Foucault points out that in order for this conceit to work there must be the ability to differentiate. So although it is unacknowledged in classical thought, "resemblance," the form Foucault identifies with knowledge before the sixteenth century, hovers outside the space of classical language as "the ring surrounding the domain of that which can be analyzed, reduced to order and known."[74] Resemblance makes it possible to compare things to one another, to have identities that are required for naming.

To return to the American context for an example, we can consider spirituality. Here is a space of presentation outside of but against which we activate the reasonable spaces of everyday life. Historically, one of the spaces off the table where the construction and the performance of racial identities superseded imposed identities was the practice of the spiritual. To say that "crossing the river Jordan" is a metaphor for escape from slavery is reductive in the same way as merely identifying subjects of a painting is reductive. One learns nothing about what they mean or how they can be used beyond the power gained by naming them. Tracking the spaces where the river Jordan flows as arenas of social activity provides insight into how African Americans constructed their identity when conventional practices had no room for any such thing.

The river Jordan can be about movement within and towards possibilities, whether "crossing the river Jordan" be about the unknown, and/or spaces outside the known world, and/or going up north over the Ohio River, and/or dealing with death and the blindly promising kingdom that could be the Kingdom of God and complete happiness denied us in this world.

W. E. B. Du Bois called spirituals "the sorrow songs": "They are the music of an unhappy people, of the children of disappointment; they tell of death and suffering and unvoiced longing toward a truer world, of misty wanderings and hidden ways."[75] The spaces that the "ten master songs" he discusses flow across are the spaces of suffering and also of identity. They "tell in word and music of trouble and exile, of strife and hiding; they grope toward some unseen power and sigh for the rest in the End."[76]

There is a narrowness accompanying life in a literate culture that leads to an overemphasis on interpretations based on institutional and sequential language habits. Honoring these approaches exclusively operates as a mode of policing that moves far away beyond the potential Foucault attaches to heterotopic space. One would tend not to ask or evoke the spirituals, for example, "simply" because, having a religious function, they are outside or beyond "rational" discourse.[77] The sorrow songs are interesting to Du Bois not just because they express his people's suffering but also because they are articulations of his people. He traces the distinct memory of Africa in these songs, and then he shows how the American experience is woven into the substance of the songs. He doesn't do that just to show the injustices of race. He does it to show the raw material used by African Americans to forge identities. He does it ultimately to show how black experience has helped construct this country's identity as a whole.

> Here we have brought our three gifts and mingled them with yours: a gift of story and song—soft, stirring melody in an ill-harmonized and unmelodious land; the gift of sweat and brawn to beat back the wilderness, conquer the soil, and lay the foundations of this vast economic empire two hundred years earlier than your weak hand could have done it; the third, a gift of the Spirit.[78]

The gifts are not passive traits of a reduced human nature totally oppressed by inhuman conditions. They are vivid performances of life that have enhanced (by enlarging) the arenas of human experience in this country.

Du Bois asks readers to recognize this heterotopic history:

> Nor has our gift of the Spirit been merely passive. Actively we have woven ourselves with the very warp and woof of this nation. . . . Would America have been America without her Negro people?[79]

Spatial approaches can be used as an instrument to open the door of admission in a way that is prepared to learn something new about what's out there. This is a different goal from arriving at any final destination, such as a well-made analysis requires. For example, to interpret race as a cultural code can produce insight but also the pretense to know all about it. To treat race as the result of constant labor within particular spatial arenas admits, in both senses of the word (lets in and acknowledges), more complexities of race.

To take another example of using space as an instrument of thought, one can consider the photograph as an arena of social activity. How some images operate within and beyond conventional understandings by force of the presentations they make is explored more fully in the next two sections of the book. Here I just want to offer the brief example of the image made famous during the civil rights era of African American children walking into Little Rock, Arkansas, schools through gauntlets of angry white citizens. It is almost self-evident to say that the distance between the two groups was palpable. The image of the distorted white faces of the crowd in juxtaposition to the amazing dignity of the black children entering the school opened up a wide canyon and wound in American culture to public view. But the space is more complicated than a reading that employs oppositional logic would suggest. It was not just rage against dignity. It was the presentation of the spaces of expression that construct the symbolic economy of distinctions. Rage is the low end of a dimension we might call "the troubled right to exercise power over." Dignity is the high end of a dimension we might call "other places in which to stand." "The troubled right to exercise power over" was anchored at the high end by noblesse oblige. "Other places in which to stand" was anchored at the low end by obsequiousness.

If we think of a rectangular space, such as the picture frame with these dimensions cutting through it, we have an "X." At the center of that "X," the St. Andrew's cross as Foucault puts it, is the citizen, the fully responsible, recognizable member. American citizens before the civil rights era resided in a volatile balance, held in place by lines of racial construction that were beyond public discussion. That famous image of children walking into school is the image of that place being reconstituted—their eyes become the center of a new universe.

The space being traversed was not just the linear corridor from street to classroom; it was, for starters, the space of the American educational system that allocates educational capital by the ability to be positioned advantageously. Instead of a national system of educational tracking based on the measurement of intellectual achievement, we have a national system of educational tracking based on the kind of neighborhood your parents can afford and/or are permitted to buy into. Hence, one reason for taking plantation space seriously, in addition to noting the concomitant avenues of escape in religious practice, is not that slavery represents an unusual era when space was used as a mode of governance in our history, but that American political culture has always been and remains profoundly spatial. Regionalism is neither an amusing historical artifact nor an up and coming idea; it is part of the hardware. So to continue with this example, developing the means to track the spaces of regionalism as arenas of social activity means mixing some categories in and out of academic frames while demanding attention to the dynamics of presentation.

Developing spatial thinking is more complicated than bringing in the excluded. That assumes an unproblematic division between inside and outside and ignores the extent to which the vested identities demand border maintenance work by those they "other." This could mean trading in certitude and comfort of our cognitive homes for projects that raise the possibility of a number of destinations. "Space appears once more as practiced place," to repeat de Certeau's terms.[80]

Foucault characterizes space beyond the frames as expressing desires that have no home in language. He cites literature, particularly the writing of Sade, as off-site—operating outside conventional fields of play. Sade is difficult from an ethical and feminist perspective because of his celebrations of power and violence against women. At the very least, the violence in Sade does not appear very unconventional from a feminist perspective.

The problem of the relationship between critiquing violence literally at the expense of examining the relationship of violence to a coherent social order comes up again in another work of Foucault's in which violence is central: *I, Pierre Rivière, having slaughtered my mother, my sister, and my brother . . . : A Case of Parricide in the 19th Century*.[81] Foucault points out that in documents having to do with the case, it was reported that after having committed the murders listed in the title of the book, Rivière "called to the neighbors, not 'I have killed,' but 'I am dying . . . for my father.'"[82]

Foucault puts this in the context of a number of cases of violence among a peasant class shut out and abused by the newly consolidated central government. In this context certain violent acts are acts of discourse.[83] They make sense as political statements, to use Foucault's terminology. In other words they are statements that are instants of engagement by subjects who had to make space for themselves in circumstances that did not provide any.

This interpretation puts violence outside the established order in a simple binary logic. But it also fashions a container for violence. The reach of Foucault's work goes further than he suggests here.

To discuss this, I would like to return to one aspect of Pierre Rivière's case that arrested me when I first read it many years ago: the neighbors reported that as a small boy Rivière had tortured animals. Foucault discusses the recording of this information as part of the attempt to put the case within the preview of emerging professional practices. At the time it struck me that as an arresting concrete detail, it escapes both Foucault's commentary about the murders as discourse and the creation of professional turf, or at least was not totally contained by these interpretations.

It's not the kind of thing you think about a lot, but I remembered it when in the spring of 1998 a boy in Springfield, Oregon, killed his parents and then opened fire in his school cafeteria, killing and injuring many of his schoolmates. The neighbors later said that he had always been troubled, that he had tortured animals. At a dinner I attended shortly after this school shooting, the woman on my right, who was a psychiatric social worker, offered the opinion, while she was digging into chocolate brownies à la mode, that torturing animals is a classic indicator and that somebody out there in Oregon should have noticed. This puts Pierre Rivière and today's parricide on the same table: sociopaths, broken pots from the get-go.

In both cases—the nineteenth century with the insistence on recording and naming, and contemporary life with certitude based on instant sociopathic renderings—the events appear to be totally contained. Violence is brought home again or domesticated. And because the cases of contemporary children murderers and suicides in American schools have continued, there is immense pressure for cultural placement of these events. Analyses of the why-is-this-the-temper-of-our-times type abound. In Oregon, there were many reports of various spokespersons (the governor, school officials, and so on) expressing sympathy and regret for the boy. That shows understanding of a counseling sort, which these days tends to be combined with the rational-legal approach that dictated how Pierre Rivière was treated. Both modes are acts of containment, as leaders are supposed to provide. They are the reassertion of reason and belief in a coherent system, which, if allowed to work, makes the world blessed and gives everyone his or her proper place.

As an alternative, one could choose not to engage the ready-made. If you let yourself feel the effects, hold off for a moment, you will have to encounter this violence close to home in a much more unprotected way. If the acts are close to the people you love, you may feel the urge to resist accepting a discursive space that would domesticate the event right away. We would be better served if the way such events open up conventional forms were kept open.[84] Imagine those yellow stripes they put up around construction sites. They say "Caution" on them.

This is to return to the question of the reasons for recognizing the porousness of space. Perhaps in the classical age it was important to write differently as literature became conscious of itself as a form. In our age, porousness and heterotopic spaces have to do with the willingness just to look rather than always be saying. This is violence to the convention that demands a coherent, blessed world. In some circumstances it may be necessary to violate reasonable order for the purpose of honoring an experience without pretending to know all about it.

The struggle here is not about violence per se; it is about being willing to remain achingly incomplete. The human sciences in modernity place knowledge of Man (*sic*) at the center, where the Name once resided. We could say, using the form of analysis that Foucault introduces with his explication of *Las Meninas*, that the human sciences exist inside the light formed by other intellectual practices. Foucault argues that that place, unlike the eyes of the Infanta Margarita, is troubled.

Foucault follows up on that kind of trouble by rethinking the sovereignty of the social science approaches that place a particular kind of Man at the center. Instead of accepting a history that sees a triumphal ascent—as the natural outcome of a grand march of intellectual history—he creates a spatial image that describes the volatile intellectual space in which the social sciences are produced.

The domain of the modern *episteme* should be represented rather as a volume of space open in three dimensions. In one of these we would situate the mathematical and physical science, for which order is always a deductive and linear linking together of evidence or verified propositions; in a second dimension there would be the sciences (such as those of language, life, and the production and distribution of wealth) that proceed by relating discontinuous but analogous elements in such a way that they are then able to establish causal relations and structural constraints between them. These two dimensions together define a common plane.... The third dimension would be that of philosophical reflection, which develops as a thought of the Same.... Lastly, the philosophical dimension and that of the mathematical disciplines combine to define another common plane: that of the formalization of thought.[85]

One can begin to imagine the space Foucault is constructing using these excerpts. It is constructed from planes or ways of thinking that are linked. These make an active space that also contains space. The human sciences operate in this space in a kind of uncomfortable suspension among the planes the other branches of knowledge define. Again, this figure is not merely illustrative; it is the heart of Foucault's presentation. The object of the human sciences, "Man," as he is known to be, is both beholden to other forms of knowledge and enabling of them, because he is defined by the capacity to represent. Man is suspended within but is also a necessary external presence. Foucault says, "The human sciences thus occupy the distance that separates (though not without connecting them) geology, economics and philology from that which gives them possibility in the very being of man."[86] For Foucault, the position of the human sciences is best understood as active and permeable. Constituent concepts and models from the three major planes of knowledge are alternatively adopted and played against each other. This knowledge is based not in the nature of the object of inquiry but in the shifting spaces that are constructed from surrounding modes of thought. "What renders them [the human sciences] possible, in fact, is a certain situation of 'vicinity' with regard to biology, economics, and philology (or linguistics); they exist only insofar as they dwell side by side with those sciences—or rather beneath them, in the space of their projections."[87]

In contemporary human sciences, the functional perspectives of the founders have been replaced more recently by normative perspectives. This pushes out what is not normal. The human sciences are defined by "analysis ... of norms, rules, and signifying totalities which unveil to consciousness the conditions of its form and contents."[88] If, as Foucault suggests, we think of the human sciences as highly self-conscious, continually interrogating the conceits of knowledge, then the irrational, the pathological, and the aesthetic become vertical lines leading outside their domains. This is another way of saying that spirituality, violence, and art surface in modernity as blatant transgressions of a known reasonable order. In his reading of Foucault, de Certeau suggests that recognizing these things leads to the downfall of the illusion that the human sciences are complete.[89]

Psychoanalysis and ethnology play special roles for Foucault as sites where confrontation with the uncomfortable internal limits of contemporary knowledge are unavoidable. Psychoanalysis pushes beyond rationality into regions of the unconscious. The relationship between the rational and the irrational is an object of inquiry.

Ethnology pushes beyond the rationality of the West to mingle in other cultures. For both disciplines, rationality is the enabling operating mode revealed as restricted by their investigations. Movement outside the spatial practices that contrive to make a knowable world leads to intercourse with the claims that Death, Desire, and Law make. While denying the validity of spaces outside themselves, psychoanalysis and ethnology at the same time push towards this space, that is, towards recognizing the circulation of meanings and real spaces in which meaning plays.

Thus, we strain to stay on and get off the table. The status of heterotopic space in modernity is not only a concern of contemporary theory or of Foucault's. Heterotopias are less an abstract idea than a concrete conceptualization. That is to say, their presence forces them on us if we only look. They are an active component of modernity. This world comes with heterotopic spaces, whether or not we theorize them, or enact policy that takes them into account, or see them in our lives.

Foucault is only one theorist to use uncertainty. In the afterimage of modernity's questions about existence, others have also turned to issues of the possibility of spaces of "real" experience. The next section examines Henri Lefebvre's theories of space in the light of his explicit concern with how to look in modernity for spaces where meaning plays. Lefebvre's spatial theory, his history of urban spaces, and his hope for the future are organized around his concern with recognizing experience in the gestures that make space "occupied" places. Like Foucault, Lefebvre conceptualizes space as a productive process, as permeable, and as interwoven with the potential for experience. And unlike most Americans, he never leaves the city behind.

3

City

Forget your perfect offering.
There is a crack in everything.
That's how the light gets in.

—LEONARD COHEN, "ANTHEM"

The Committee for Public Art and other prestigious civic-minded groups, including the Cleveland Foundation and the Downtown Development Coordinators, recently sponsored a lecture series entitled "Enhancing the Public Realm." The series comprised three lectures: "Cleveland: Rebuilt or Reborn?" "The Cityscape: Public Space for Public Life," and "Public Space: Recent Transformations." Reading these titles calls up Habermas's public men, sitting in black flock coats debating the issues of the day, setting the tone for a democratic ideal that we still warm to. According to background notes on the flyer announcing the series, the first lecturer's "insightful observations are developed through years of research, travel and pounding the pavement to observe the city close at hand."

The logo for the series was an artfully photographed mannequin head. This was not an old-fashioned mannequin with real hair and eyelashes. It was a highly stylized, thoroughly modern mannequin—a she from the get-go, delicately made, shown with the front of her uptilted face illuminated. A beam of light flowed from the square containing her picture. The text inside the triangle the light made said, "Visions for Cleveland's Future."

The flyer announced: "This series is part of a continuing collaborative venture to raise the level of discourse and education in Greater Cleveland." To raise them, I would say, right off the city streets and away from any hint of pounding the pavement. The mannequin's contemplative figure reiterated the notion that we could put that idea right out of our heads. I stopped imagining the men in black flock coats and started staring off into the distance, following the light leaving the city.

In this section I look at theories of space and urban processes that don't leave the city streets but return to them. In these theories the materials of urban culture, particularly street life, become instruments of articulation in projects that seek to engage life in the context of modernity. This turn to the city is linked to attempts to answer the question of how to look in modernity for spaces where meaning plays. Rather than marginalizing the city, presentations of city life discussed below take advantage of the spaces that marginalization has brought.

I begin with Lefebvre's spatial theory because of the explicit connection he makes between physical and social space and his deep concern with "restoring" experience to modern life. Like Foucault, Lefebvre conceptualizes space as active, porous, and inseparable from experience. He connects the formation of subjects to space by gestures of occupation that are constitutive of both self and space. He also goes beyond critique to articulate uses of space that could fully engage life within the context of contemporary urban processes.

On the surface Lefebvre's work is more "literally spatial" than Foucault's, particularly because Lefebvre is so explicit about the relations between social and physical aspects of space. But like Foucault, Lefebvre's work is multilayered, being at the same time historical, methodological, and ethical. Both see space as a productive process for which at some level one must take responsibility.[1] Lefebvre develops a topology of "modes of assembly," which he uses to present the history of Western urban space and to assess its moral future. The critique of capitalism that is a central aspect of this project is tied to what he sees as increasing disregard for preserving the remaining traditional spaces in European cities. For Lefebvre, skewed spatial development is the primary legacy of industrial capitalism.[2]

To introduce Lefebvre's terms, contemporary urban space is dominated by "representations of space," or abstract reason. As a result "representational spaces," spaces that involve noninstrumental and noncognitive dimensions of life, are underdeveloped. Because the city is layered space, former space remaining, and because it can be the locus for unpredictable human encounters, Lefebvre uses *city* as a way to talk about sites where memory and experience can come together. "Urban encounters" reach beyond the programmed demands for labor and consumption made by industrial and corporate capital. "The right to the city" is Lefebvre's phrase for urban experiences that could redeem the abstract spaces of modernity.

Lefebvre is interested in exposing what Walter Benjamin also saw as the modern myths of progress and rationality. His approach uses urban space to reach through the barriers to existence constructed in contemporary urban discourse. For him, the possibilities for an aesthetics of existence are tied to the gestures that would produce spaces and selves that develop our capacities to engage life fully.

Next I look at Walter Benjamin's work. The city was his milieu, both literally and figuratively. His descriptions of actual cities are the staging ground for a mode of analysis that uses the concrete material of modernity to find life within it. Benjamin's method is the result of his labors to escape the limitations of philosophical conceptualizations of experience and to come to terms with his own time. His approach was to develop thought as a mode of participatory reading that collapses the distinction between interpretation and experience.

The work of Walter Benjamin predates that of Foucault and Lefebvre by a generation. Yet his insights into the fragmented way of life that characterizes modernity and his attempts to develop a method grounded in the material of the city are compatible with Foucault's interest in heterotopic space and Lefebvre's focus on how space is occupied. Foucault uses the notion of heterotopic space to make an argument about the sites of experience. Lefebvre critiques the abstract representations of space that characterize life after the rise of industrialization in Europe and theorizes alternative spatial practices. Benjamin moves directly into the streets to find saving grace.

What is relevant to both Benjamin's time and ours is the extent to which conventional expectations and the need to escape them are tied to the politics of presentation. Benjamin uses participatory thought as a grounding in the material world (as it exists) and as a mode of enlarging the capacity of the reader. Whether or not we think of ourselves as visually literate, we operate all the time in environments dominated by images. We are members of the first generations to have been raised by the screen. If representations are the material of our world, Benjamin was one of the first to explore this world seriously as the material for thought. Benjamin critiques the fragmented existence of modernity and then uses montage (the juxtaposition of fragments to attract new meaning) to demonstrate the constructive powers of presentation and to give testimony to the presence of life in the cities he wrote about. Because, as Benjamin argues, we are infinitely far away from our dreams, it becomes all the more crucial to develop ways of moving towards them.

Occupied Space and the Occasion for Urban Encounters

Although Lefebvre's work was not well known in this country until the last decade, it has been foundational to renewed interest in theorizing space in such diverse disciplines as geography, sociology, political science, and urban studies. Spatial theory shows these disciplines to be not as diverse as they first appear. The interest in space that brings them together includes the advantages reaped from acknowledging the materiality of space, from having concepts that interweave the processes of making space with the processes that construct subjectivity, from developing tools for analyzing spatial processes, and from coming to terms with the limitations and possibilities of contemporary spatial practices. As with Foucault's work, certain aspects of Lefebvre's work find a more comfortable habitat in the Anglo-American context than others do.[3] His notion of space as both physical and social is more accessible than his insistence that space be understood as ongoing processes of assembly. The former calls for an expanded program of inquiry; the latter confronts conventional intellectual habits grounded in the logic of discovery. I am concerned here with the implications of seeing space as an activity and will suggest that Lefebvre's notion of representational spaces is another example of the search in modernity for space where experience can play.

What we might call Lefebvre's hope for the city is also not likely to find widespread acceptance in a broadly based suburban society such as America. An exception might be among design professionals with roots in disciplines firmly committed to the city.[4] At the same time, the marginality of city life in this country contributes to the availability of urban space for what Lefebvre calls encounters.

Lefebvre is most accessible as a historian of modernity, one whose inquiry is based on the memory of a lost world. He is at pains to make sense of the disjunctures that accompanied modernity, particularly since the beginning of the twentieth century, which is to say, his lifetime.[5] Two aspects of modernity that concern him are the end of the cosmologies that produced the predictable spaces of traditional life and the ways the traditionally built environment has been destroyed by modernity.[6] One of his most quoted statements expresses these concerns:

> Around 1910 a certain space was shattered. It was the space of common sense, of knowledge, of social practice, of political power, a space hitherto enshrined in everyday discourse, just as in abstract thought, as the environment of and channel for communication; the space, too, of classical perspective and geometry . . . As in the form of the city and the town. . . . This was truly a crucial moment.[7]

The city is not incidental to Lefebvre's work. It is the site with which he must deal. Following in the tradition of other theorists, such as Simmel, who were concerned with the effects of modern city life on the constitution of subjectivity, Lefebvre looks at the relationship between the production of space and the possibilities for human existence. Against the shortcoming of contemporary life Lefebvre asserts the centrality to human life of what he sees as the original conditions of concrete existence. He expresses this as a type of origin myth: "In the beginning was the Topos. Before— long before—the advent of the Logos, in the chiaroscuro realm of primitive life, lived experience already possessed its internal rationality. . . ."[8] His critique of the present centers not just on exploitation of the powerless but also on the fragmentations and lack of coherence that prevail in societies organized by abstract knowledge and technology. Any form of "internal rationality" that humans may have experienced in different time/space is currently displaced by the dominance of abstract space, as is the memory of a previous way of life. This puts it out of reach, that is, difficult to bring into the present. Ideally, physical space and social relations would form a milieu for self-conscious participation in developing spatial practices that promote human experience. But instead the productive forces of modernity have developed in ways that work against imaginative human processes. Lefebvre believes that it has become very difficult to make space in which to be active in our own behalf.

As a methodologist, Lefebvre proposes conceptualizing space as a process. Once space is conceptualized as productive activity, it can be analyzed as a domain or area of activity rather than an empty void or a preexisting area to be filled. In other words, for Lefebvre, space is, first of all, *occupied.* The continuous social and physical activity that Lefebvre calls the assembly of space presupposes occupation. The question is then, What options and opportunities exist for occupying space? A good way to understand the implications of this view is to pretend that one doesn't know what the word *space* means and then to read Lefebvre to find a definition of it. This approach highlights his struggle to reconceptualize space as gestures that make both us and it.

Lefebvre is critical of the structural interpretations of Foucault. But if one imagines space as domain, or area, or region (presented on a table), both Foucault and Lefebvre would have us look at how that space is constructed and maintained in order to understand relations of dominance in society. They both set aside notions of transcendence and look at concrete spatial processes as the source of experience. For both Foucault and Lefebvre, what Michael Shapiro calls "a political economy of intelligibility" sets up the terms of play and constructs the principles of construction, without totally determining what gets to be the case.[9] Where Foucault talks about discursive practices and includes systems of visibility, Lefebvre talks about spatial practices and includes representations of space. Looking at Lefebvre's work after considering Foucault's spatial thought brings physical space and cultural codes even closer together. Processes that produce space as an ongoing practice are what space *is* for Lefebvre.[10] Both physical and social aspects of these spatial processes are constructed according to certain rules of assembly: thus one can analyze how space is productive, building and maintaining a particular social order.

Lefebvre is particularly clear on the necessity of working with the notion that spatial practices combine both physical and social movements. Space brings the two together in ways that undercut the usual ways the material world and abstract thought are separated from each other. If Foucault brings space into language in his spatial thinking, Lefebvre brings language into space with his notion of assembly. All physical space, beginning with the land, is a process linked to a way of life: it is shaped in conjunction with ongoing processes of construction.[11] Lefebvre insists that even, and most especially, our wilderness areas depend on human assembly; that is, they require a syntax to make them what they are. Pretending wilderness is off the table, beyond the reach of civilization, but at the same time demanding that we can still see it in particular ways, is one of the principles of construction that domesticates the heterotopic possibilities of natural sites. We can look, for example, at American wilderness areas. During the construction of the great western highways in the 1920s, Kodak consultants assisted in the designation of scenic lookout points. "The Park Service's Landscape Architecture Division engineered the wilderness to accommodate the new mobility with planned roads and numbered scenic turnoffs."[12] Scenic turnoffs are scenic, that is, culturally defined as photogenic, by design. As conventional photographic views of wilderness space, they offer the opportunity to see and touch the invisible and untouchable all at the same time.

Lefebvre always comes back to *how* space is produced. For him spatial analysis is widely applicable; modes of spatial assembly compose a fundamental conceptual scheme for explaining our times, replacing and expanding Marx's concern with historical forms of constituting value.[13] In addition to conceptualizing space as a process, Lefebvre also presents it as a unitary process; that is, spatial analysis is applicable to different levels of spatial activity. Various examples are easy to imagine: A university classroom, for instance, surely works as a classroom because of the interrelationship of a number of physical and social factors; the university as an educational institution surely includes shifting physical, administrative, and intellectual practices that continually make and remake what it purports to be. On a larger scale, urban processes, both inside and outside the city, that over the last forty years have made us unsure and divided even about what a city is, and the globe, which is characterized by activities that reassert physical boundaries such as those between nations and those that punctuate and reinforce linkages that disregard boundaries, are all processes of assembly. All combine physical and social elements, and at the same time they are porous, requiring boundaries that their fullest articulations demand exceeding.

As a Marxist, Lefebvre is critical of how alienating the processes of constructing space in modern life are. But where Marx examined productive relations using notions of value and focused on the alienating qualities of exchange, Lefebvre makes "the production of space" the source of paradigmatic social relations. He still uses Marxist terms; for example, the reduction of use value and the ascendancy of exchange value, but his analysis is based on conceptualizing how "modes of assembly" operate. The assembly of space is always problematic for Lefebvre. To use the examples introduced above: A classroom is brought together so that the physical spaces and mental activities either cohere or don't; universities are assembling and reassembling themselves within the context of reduced resources and external pressures to demonstrate that they are contributing members of society; for the past two decades American cities have had to deal with the imperative to assemble visible identities in an era where the requirements for physical space of the city have changed, leaving, in effect, an empty shop floor; the notion of a single global existence persists in an era that some days seems above all determined to refuse the very notion of assemblage. Lefebvre calls modes of assembly and the production of space "concrete abstractions," which is the same concept Marx uses for exchange value and the commodity. So although the language of Lefebvre's spatial theory sounds very abstract, he is motivated by the desire to stay connected to the practice of space. Lefebvre is less teleological than Marxist. He doesn't predict any inevitable future, as some interpreters of Marx do; instead he attempts to conceptualize the kinds of space that could overcome the limitations of the abstract spaces of modernity.

Lefebvre's three-part model of spatial processes is useful for showing how the space for life has been reduced in modernity. The model is also a tool for the analysis of space. Finally it gives him a way to articulate alternatives. When Lefebvre writes as a moral philosopher, he contrasts (and employs) the modes of assembly that are characteristic of modernity in developing his conceptualization of encounters in urban space. The opportunity for contemporary subjects to experience themselves as concrete living beings requires the spaces of modernity. For him, as for Foucault and Benjamin, the gestures that constitute space and those that constitute self are inseparable. Again, like Foucault and Benjamin before him, Lefebvre immerses himself in modernity, using it as a tool for experience. His hope for humanity grows out of his critique of modernity.

Lefebvre's three modes of assembly are three concepts that describe how space can be constructed. They are: representations of space, spatial practices, and representational spaces.

"Representations of space" refers to modes of assembly that dominate the construction of space in modernity. They are abstract in the sense that they appear to be self-referential systems. But they are linked to the capitalist political economy and guide practice. Representations of space are similar to Foucault's notion of the articulable in the way that both are concepts that describe the spaces of professional practices. Lefebvre is highly critical of the domination of urban development by representations of space. He points out that planning, including the related design professions, formulates and implements decisions about space without maintaining contact with existing spatial practices. Representations of space operate abstractly in ways that make complicity with relations of production and professional codes more compelling contexts for decision making than is the daily life of the city. As mentioned above, Lefebvre is highly critical of the extent to which contemporary urban space is assembled unproblematically in terms of representations of space, because this mode radically reduces the possibilities for engaged life.

An obvious American example is transportation planning, particularly the highways, corridors, and freeways that carved their way through many American cities in the middle of the twentieth century. Lefebvre would point out that these roads were not the product of highway engineers run amok, but rather the logical application of rational planning. The roots of the rationale for driving corridors in and out of metropolitan areas lie enshrined in the demands of economic forces to reorganize the city for production and the intellectual articulation of these demands in concentric zone theory. As discussed in the section "Urban," an unexamined assumption of scholars of the Chicago School was that urban growth is inevitable. From within this viewpoint, if the city is in decline, the (rational) remedy is to devise institutional arrangements that are believed to foster growth. Transportation planning developed mechanisms that were oriented towards bringing people back to the city by making it convenient for them to get there on their own. The rationale for these policies was rarely at issue. This is the reification into abstract knowledge of the political economy of an internal combustion society and the logic of the industrial city of which Chicago was the primary example. This reification in the form of the ascendancy of representations of space obscures the links between the political economy and "rational planning."

"Spatial practices" are Lefebvre's second mode of assembly. Spatial practices are his way of designating how gestures construct space as life is lived. From some perspectives spatial practices can be thought of as an overarching category of which representations of space are one subset.[14] For the sake of making an analytic distinction, Lefebvre defines spatial practices as patterns of everyday life. These movements construct space in ways that may be congruent with or may challenge representations of space, but they persist nevertheless. An example of spatial practices is neighborhood chiropractors, to whom people go when their backs are giving them trouble. In spite of a systematic program for many years by the American Medical Association to discredit chiropractors, they continue to flourish outside the boundaries of medical science, in part because they make their patients feel better. Community life on a routine daily basis is an example of spatial practices as Lefebvre uses the term.

The city of Cleveland has three commuter corridors leading into it from the near-eastern suburbs. I had never thought of them in any other way than as the roads into work until one of my students presented a project from the viewpoint of residents who live in an area that the corridor I use cuts through. She talked about the difficulty of crossing the street, particularly when walking with children, of getting groceries home, and so forth. From this perspective the corridor is an inconvenient, unsightly, and sometimes dangerous intrusion into the spatial practices that construct community.

In the English translation *The Production of Space*, Lefebvre's third mode of spatial assembly is called "representational space." Elsewhere it is referred to as "spaces of representation." Representational space is a mode of assembly that is tied to participation in the production of meaning. Lefebvre connects "representational space" to "real" or "genuine" life experiences. He introduces representational space as "embodying complex symbolisms, sometimes coded, sometimes not, linked to the clandestine or underground side of social life, as also to art (which may come eventually to be defined less as a code of space than as a code of the representational spaces)."[15]

Representational spaces have the potential for being on and off the table at the same time. Lefebvre values art insofar as it engages this potential in concrete ways.

Because he sees modernity dominated by modes of assembly based on representations of space, space that is not coded in advance carries revolutionary potential for a "real" space of existence outside the spaces of instrumental reason.[16] This is not a matter of the desire to totally escape preexisting representations of space in order to participate in representational space, because the two are interwoven. Spatial processes are a mixture of modes. For example, representational spaces are continually appropriated by advertising and commence in ways that subvert them as a means to produce more compelling forms of human experience. But what looks like simple appropriation is never the complete story. Because the assembly of space is a process, what seems to be appropriation can become the dissemination of sites of opportunity. This provides insight into how Benjamin viewed the tools of modernity, particularly the tools of mechanical reproduction in his own time. To take a contemporary example, hip-hop can be understood as a street form (a spatial practice linked to representational space) that has been appropriated by big business (representations of space). From some points of view, this mixture of culture and commerce is simply appropriation. From another point of view, the commercial success of hip-hop is a victory for black culture, because it is recognized as a creative form identified with African Americans.[17] Furthermore, that form has been made available to the larger culture as part of the language of expression.

The three modes of assembly Lefebvre introduces provide a complex means to analyze space and the relations between space in use and identity in process. As a methodologist he developed conceptual tools with which to investigate how modes of making space are mixed and also to increase our understanding of the relationship between making space and living in a world in which one has a place. Another way to say this is to suggest that representational spaces are active "spaces of presentation." As the example of hip-hop suggests, it is reductive to make space into a static entity or to identify representations of space with Bad Order and representational spaces with Good People. There is some of this in John Allen and Michael Pryke's study of "the production of service space" in London's financial district.[18] They describe the official open daytime space of brokers and financial dealings and oppose this kind of space to the underground space of the cleaners who work at night. They consider closets where personal effects, such as family pictures, are displayed as representational space. There is nothing wrong with this type of analysis, and it does follow from much of Lefebvre's critique of modern life. This approach also has the advantage of showing that the "empty space" beyond official representations of space is very crowded indeed.

But what this form of analysis lacks is emphasis on how space is always in process and, just as important, how the different modes of assembly are connected to identities. Again the question of how space is occupied is useful here. There is nothing politically essential about any of the three modes. In Lefebvre's thinking, it is exactly the condition of contemporary life that social development has lagged behind economic development. Potential representational spaces, such as art, have become accomplices of representations of space. To look again at urban planning: The very phrase "Rational Planning" embodies a highly valued symbol (or representational space) that professional education works hard to inculcate in planning professionals.[19] At one time this notion was the core of planners' identity. This professional space of presentation, which gives special meaning to the "rational," functions to direct attention away from the extent to which the actualization of rational planning on the urban landscape contributed to the destruction of city space as planners conceptualized it and citizens lived it.[20] The notion of "rationality" is heavily loaded symbolically, operating to assemble representational space, in ways that have nothing to do with rationality (representations of space) yet support it. In this case, as in much of the language surrounding planning proposals, a great deal of symbolic space is hard at work to make a convincing case that we are not being ideological. Every zoning meeting mobilizes representations of space that are also being deployed to construct spaces of presentation.

Another example of the complex political valence of the three modes of assembly is the shop-worn critique that American culture is all Disneyland. This critique is the providence of social critics, who may assume they have the intellectual equipment not to be duped. On the other hand, Disneyland, in all its many guises, makes some people very happy. Lefebvre would see theme parks as wanting, because the experiences they encourage and maintain are limited to planned notions of predictable (and expensive) entertainments. The "happiness" they produce is "real," but it does not contribute to participation in constructing the spaces that make us. Themed spaces are about consumption and also have symbolic dimensions, but these are repetitive. When and where the themes come first in contemporary spaces of experience, Lefebvre wants something beyond this—experience that is not completely preprogrammed and is free from the narrow demands on time and space that capitalist production and consumption make.

There are representational spaces in the American landscape that are not destructive or reductive of meaning but instead elicit deep life-affirming experiences among participants. The movements of visitors though the Vietnam Veterans Memorial are some of the best examples of public participation creating spaces of presentation that can expand rather than reduce experience.[21]

Again, the important issue is how space is occupied. For example, when Lefebvre identifies art with representational spaces, he hopes for kinds of involvement that are generative of both physical and social possibilities. In the main, however, he looks to the spatial practices of everyday life rather than to monumental spaces as a potential source. He idealizes spatial arrangements in which abstract space and lived space are integrated. Lefebvre presents this ideal and identifies it with "ancient peasant communities" in his essay "Notes Written One Sunday in the French Countryside."[22] The essay is strongest when it is understood as the presentation of an ideal. Life in actual preindustrial (or nonindustrial) small communities is usually more complicated than Lefebvre's presentation indicates, as he admits.[23]

Lefebvre always addresses space as an activity, looking for the kind of gestures that make occupation meaningful. The three modes of assembly may be present in varying relation to each other. They can reinforce or challenge each other. Each can operate in ways that are system supporting, system challenging, or, most interestingly and as Lefebvre would most hope, in ways that sidestep the system while using it to produce life as a work of art.

Again and again in his work, Lefebvre is highly critical of representations of space that dominate in modernity. In being so, his role as a moral philosopher emerges from his historical and methodological work. He critiques contemporary space in terms similar to Marx's notion of the commodity; that is, it is removed from social relations, and it hides and dominates them. For example, he says: "Symbols have become more and more abstract; in its own way, like money, but on the political level the State is also in a sense a *realized abstraction*, endowed with effective power which is ever more real."[24]

It is central to understanding Lefebvre's thinking to see that he does not suggest merely that representations of space be replaced with other modes. Sometimes Lefebvre expresses his spatial ideal in traditional terms: a return to use value, coherence across modes, and the possibility for human connection. Other times his proposals sound as if they are oriented only to the past or only to the future. But these are not contradictory: he always privileges modes of assembly that would allow social relations to develop in ways that are appropriate to contemporary urban processes but exceed current limitations. The past is for him a Foucauldian kind of history. That is to say, he is concerned with memory, with how and what is brought into the present. So often his articulations are grounded in critique of current conventional modes of assembly. Against this critique he argues for a "*right* . . . to urban life, to renewed centrality, to places of encounter and exchange, to life rhythms and time uses, enabling the full and complete *usage* of their moments and places."[25] This is not a "return" to nature or to preindustrial society; rather it is a development that would bring the social aspects of contemporary life in line with the more developed economic aspects.

David Harvey calls Lefebvre's articulation of an alternative to the dominant abstract spaces of modernity an insistence "that life should be lived as a project."[26] Harvey connects this possibility to Lefebvre's discussion of "moments," which Harvey summarizes as "fleeting but decisive sensations (of delight, surrender, disgust, surprise, horror, or outrage) which were somehow revelatory of the totality of possibilities contained in daily existence . . . Conceived of as points of rupture, of radical recognition of possibilities and intense euphoria."[27]

Lefebvre's evaluation of spatial practices hinges on the extent to which they facilitate the generation of life that engages individuals' powers to the fullest, that is, gestures in which moments are possible. Lefebvre looks for ways to articulate the spatial circumstances that provoke this kind of experience. His hope is "more ambitious, more difficult, more remote than the means, the aim is to change life, lucidly to recreate everyday life. . . . Revealing its positive and negative duality, the critique of everyday life will help to pose and resolve the problem of life itself."[28]

A debate existed between Lefebvre and the situationists about whether moments are chance encounters or whether they can be created with events that are meant to produce them. Lefebvre broke with the situationists in part because of his opposition to manufactured moments. His concerns were broader than the goal of producing individual momentary experiences of heightened awareness or even pleasure. Lefebvre's idea of the moment is closer to Foucault's notion of heterotopic possibilities. As a Marxist, Lefebvre was committed to the promise of the revolution and to the belief that the working class is the true agent of social chance. But his concerns were also broader than a class-based revolution. His working out of an alternative to the dominance of abstract reason is oriented towards creating a potential for personal involvement in making space.

Just as preindustrial peasant life is the raw material for generating an image of ideal spatial practices in Lefebvre's work, the city becomes the raw material for generating an image of a mode of life that would offset the fragmentations, separations, and loss of coherence that have accompanied modernity. His discussion in his essay "The Right to the City" presents moments as spatial circumstances that are generative of engaged life experience. This goes beyond conceptualizations of moments as individual instants of heightened consciousness or even as sparks that could ignite revolution.

"The Right to the City" is written in the French context where working-class housing had removed the working class from the center of the city. Because his (Marxist) hope for the future is based on the working class, it follows that Lefebvre argues for returning the working class to the city. But to take this only literally is to reduce his argument.

The implications of Lefebvre's presentation reach beyond this immediate contingency and the Marxist perspective that leads him to be so hopeful about the working class. It is not just a literal return to the city that Lefebvre desires. In the same way that heterotopias are not real *or* virtual but both, the right to the city is about making space that makes room for modes of existence. If we consider Lefebvre's larger analysis of modernity, he is not saying that only members of the working class live fragmented lives. The spaces in which time and attention are parceled out according to the needs of global capital or of some of its many supporting institutions are much broader. It is not just the working class that is wooed and bought off by the pleasures promised by a consumer society.[29] Marx himself argued within a relational framework. That is, what was so destructive in industrial capitalism was that it established constitutive relations that led to reduced identities for labor *and* for owners, that is, for everyone regardless of his or her material wealth. Lefebvre is critical of the extent to which a similar reduction of humanity exists in contemporary society. Contemporary urban space is organized by the demands of both productive relations and consumer relations. In America, for example, a broad-based middle class (loosely defined in various ways) lives in suburban circumstances and is just as surely party to pacts where time and autonomy are traded for mobility and the means to acquire consumer goods as the French working and middle classes have been. Lefebvre's critique and his return to the city as the site for reconnection speak to circumstances beyond Marxist theory and the situation in France to the circumstances in modernity in general. Lefebvre the moral philosopher is concerned with how to live.

In the first section, "Urban," Bier's recommendations for regional policy suggest that the city and the suburbs are no longer useful as separate categories. In the context in which Lefebvre writes, the city and the country are no longer useful categories. In each case the spatial practices that gave each spatial entity its distinct identity have been gutted. But there are aspects of both city and rural life that Lefebvre values. These he would revitalize for the sake of producing an urban society.

In "The Right to the City" Lefebvre presents cities as sites of layered history. To return to the city is not an act of historical preservation. That would be to pretend to be able to restore traditional ways of life. Lefebvre means acts of memory. Encounters are possible in the city because urban space has the potential for bringing memory and experience together. As the public gatherings on the site of monuments reproduced in Néstor García Canclini's article on hybrid culture (discussed in the "Urban" section) showed, memory can become a ground for political activism. This is only one available mode of participation in urban life. Lefebvre tries to articulate various kinds of spatial activity that would involve moderns more fully in their own lives. He describes these broadly as "encounters" in urban space—spaces of presentation that occur on the street.

In claiming a right to the city, Lefebvre argues that "urban encounters" can overcome the separations and spatial distances that characterize our age. They can be the means for wrestling back autonomy—the taking of time for one's own use. This is in contrast with the more familiar exchange of time and control of time for compensation. Encounters in the city between memory and experience are profoundly noninstrumental. They are examples of life as an engaged art.[30]

One way to reduce Lefebvre's thought is to imagine the right to the city literally, as the right to return and walk down those historical streets. Another reductive approach appropriates Lefebvre's and the situationists' ideas and argues that we need to make permanent areas in the city for festival and entertainment events—returning to the city by staging moments of touristic joy. This caricature of the latest in economic development fads is too literal and misses the point—at the same time it accurately describes the current "vision" of planning professionals in some American cities.[31] Festive market places are basically tourist places. Lefebvre's critique of modernity is that we have become tourists in our own neighborhoods. As Jonathan Culler suggests, "The tourist is interested in everything as a sign of itself. . . ."[32] The joy of visiting festive market places such as South Street Seaport, discussed above, is contained within a set of signs; in the case of South Street Seaport, it is New York's seagoing past. This kind of experience is organized by abstract representations of space that give pride of place to the economic potential of urban space. Urban encounters as Lefebvre conceptualizes them are not predictable and hence their promise. They are themselves: mutually constitutive encounters between memory and experience, whose outcomes are not thought out in advance.

In "The Right to the City" Lefebvre is very clear that a literal interpretation of the phrase stops well short of his meaning. He points out that it is not even clear what the city is anymore. There are two misleading aspects to current representations of urban space. First, analyses of the city are always strategic. We saw this above in Beauregard's study of the rhetoric of urban decline. A cultural agenda organized the description of cities in decline in the so-called objective media reports. Second, there is no city. As Lefebvre puts it: ". . . the object, the city, as consummate reality is falling apart. Knowledge holds in front of itself the historic city already modified, to cut it up and put it together again in fragments." Further (as Boyer's analyses of New York illustrates), Lefebvre goes on to say, "The city historically constructed is no longer lived and is no longer understood practically. It is only an object of cultural consumption for tourists. . . ." What remains is a virtual object, leading Lefebvre to raise a question Foucault would recognize: "If man is dead, for whom will we build?"[33]

What Lefebvre would build is a new urban society, a project inseparable from building a new humanity. He promotes active participation in unplanned urban encounters. These spaces of presentation don't merely challenge the pious spaces of abstract reason. They stand in opposition to the themed existences in contemporary urban processes of which Lefebvre is so critical. Because the focus in Lefebvre's thinking is on space as occupied, this implicates not just city space but the selves that inhabit the city.

For street photographers, awareness of the connections between self and space is illuminated in those instants when the body, the camera, and street life are joined in momentary arrest of their separate existences. These instants become "urban encounters," the representational space that Lefebvre calls for in modern life. One of the ways these moments bear close family resemblance to the experience that Foucault seeks as heterotopic possibilities is that they are often overlooked, being somewhat "off the table." There are two levels to the lack of such moments in daily life: a lack of awareness and a lack of opportunity. Lefebvre is critical of both yet still sees modernity as the site where such instants must be found. Urban life *is* modernity; that is, the spaces we necessarily occupy are always suspended between glimpses into forgotten worlds and views of unattainable futures. Lefebvre seeks experience in connections between the two.

In the chapter entitled "Spatial Architectonics" in *The Production of Space*, Lefebvre opens with a discussion of the body. This is, among other things, a way of emphasizing the extent to which space and selves are interwoven. He sets aside the homey conviction that the body is a secure, bounded thing, existing in space. He points out instead that a great deal of social energy must be expended to naturalize separations and boundaries that are presumed to mark the edges of bodily entities. This notion links the self and the city in fundamental ways. But if bodies are usually busily involved in the politics of securing their own inviolability, it is difficult to bring instants when the relationship between space and self is unstable to the fore.

One of the great urban novels of modernity, Dostoevsky's *Crime and Punishment*, links self and the city at the level that Lefebvre discusses.[34] *Crime and Punishment* opens with the central character, Raskolnikov, walking into the city, and from that instant on it is impossible to imagine him without the city of St. Petersburg. It is just as impossible to imagine St. Petersburg without Raskolnikov and the other characters that Dostoevsky presents. Even the crime and its interlinked punishment (which coexists with it, even before the crime is committed) require the city in order to be what they are.

It might seem logical to identify city life with "traces" (of events) or with marks (made in the world). But because the occupation of space is an ongoing activity implicating spaces and selves at the same time, we must consider the city a composite of "gestures." "Gesture," says Lefebvre, denying the reader the comfort of a definition, "should be taken here in a broad sense, so that turning around may be considered a gesture, one which modifies a person's orientation and points of reference."[35] The gesture is fundamental to the occupation and assembly of space and self. Even wholly predictable space is not possible without it. Further, because gestures must be repeated as part of continued occupation, there is always the opportunity for an enactment in which who we are and the type of space in which we move change. Urban encounters recapture the gesture for consciousness, as an instrument constructing who we are.

Lefebvre is not recommending a theory of gesture. Participation in the gestures that assemble space is more an orientation: "I speak of an *orientation* advisedly. We are concerned with what might be called a 'sense': an organ that perceives, a direction that may be conceived, and a directly lived movement progressing towards the horizon. And we are concerned with nothing that even remotely resembles a system."[36]

The city is the place of potential encounter with new experience and a depository of memory. It provides the context for chance and the bringing together of differences. The countryside was the place of coherence and also festivals that celebrated engaged spaces of representation. Bringing the potential of city spaces and rural spaces together is not an abstract proposal for Lefebvre. He is not suggesting a program for planning theory. The possibility for urban encounters lies in the uncelebrated spatial practices of daily life. Lefebvre felt that the need to gather our own time around us, to encounter chance and live life inside our culture is a societal need, beyond the revolutionary potential of any one class. The right to the city is both an awareness of and a call to participate in heterotopic moments. In the same way that Foucault's notion of heterotopic space applies to possibilities both inside and outside and running between the articulable and the visible, the right to the city is profoundly sited but also untethered. It is escape based in immersion and chance. Lefebvre is talking about the potential of urban encounters when he says:

> The *right to the city* cannot be conceived of as a simple visiting right or as a return to traditional cities. It can only be formulated as a transformed and renewed *right to urban life*. It does not matter whether the urban fabric encloses the countryside and what survives of peasant life, as long as the "urban," place of encounter, priority of use value, inscription in space of a time promoted to the rank of a supreme resource among all resources, finds its morphological base and its practico-material realization. . . .
>
> Urban life has yet to begin.[37]

Coming to Terms with "The Responsibility of an Heir"

The Sunday *New York Times* recently presented a chatty piece about photography at the Getty Museum. The curator being interviewed explained that the museum uses two categories to organize its photographs: Art and Anthropology. He discussed art photography as being about "Time," while anthropological photographs are seen as providing interesting information about other peoples and places. To divide photographic images into the abstract categories of art ("time") and social science ("information") is to reaffirm a history that is also a hierarchy. Our formal categories beat your informative details every time.

Material manifestations are needed to outfit this scheme, hence, full speed ahead on Getty's acquisitions program. It is fun in this regard to remember that Atget insisted that his images of Paris were not art but "documents," that they were made long before the Getty Museum existed, and the Getty will be lucky to get as many Atgets as it can, and they won't go into the Anthropology section.

For Christine Boyer the museum is a "deliberate" instrument of "collective memory."[38] Museums have played an important role in verifying a history whose trajectory begins long ago in other places and ends now in Western civilization. This history is prior to the artifacts that verify it (although the material collections always threaten to exceed the carefully crafted stories that bring them together in the first place). This approach has its roots in the aesthetics, philosophy, and ethics of distinction in which the abstract is ranked above the material. These notions predate modernity, of course, but have continued to have power within it as a powerful cultural convention in which "the material" is secondary to the power to organize it. But the role these biases play in thought is complex. At the same time as these codes are used as foils against which cultural producers and theorists have sought to reclaim the world, they also provide the raw material for reclamation.

In his "Critique of the Hegelian Dialectic and Philosophy as a Whole," Marx indicts Hegel for giving abstract thought priority over nature. "Mind has *nature* for its *premise*," Marx argues,[39] but in Hegel's thought mind is put before nature because nature is *"superseded"* by consciousness. To put this in terms of the Getty example above: This is the same as saying photographic images have status only as examples—at the highest levels of the timelessness of art, or at the middling levels of the variation of human experience. In Marx's dialogue with Hegel, he begins a critique that figures the relations between the world and systems of mediation somewhat differently. One has to return to this argument about what philosophy and thought and human experience are in order to understand how Walter Benjamin and later theorists such as Lefebvre and Foucault pick up their Western cognitive baggage. Each theorist is involved in a struggle with and against conceptualizations of humanity that give consciousness and language systems pride of place. For them the concerns listed above, "about what philosophy and thought and human experience are," become reversed in order of importance to be: "about what human experience and thought and philosophy are." All three also look to space and the visual to find more open fields of play. Understanding the components of these struggles will provide a context for the discussion in the next section, "Streets," which ties visual experience, the materiality of image making, and the potential of photography together as instruments for producing urban encounters.

Marx shows how Hegel links the definition of humanity to the ability to act. The kind of action Hegel tracks moves away from the material world, but without erasing the generative functions of action. In Hegel's system the categories of existence evolve, becoming more abstract as "man" develops in moving through them. Marx finds fault with Hegel for leaving the "real" world behind in the course of climbing this ladder of abstraction. He is critical of the notion that the spatial practices that "remain in existence" are visible only as markers of higher levels of abstractions. Marx explains Hegel's approach as follows:

In Hegel's *Philosophy of Right*, *Private Right* superseded equals *Morality*, Morality superseded equals the *Family*, the Family superseded equals *Civil Society*, Civil Society superseded equals the *State*, the State superseded equals *World History*. In the *actual world*, private right, morality, the family, civil society, the state, etc., remain in existence, only they have become *moments* of man—state of his existence and being—which have no validity in isolation, but dissolve and engender one another, etc.[40]

What Marx does draw attention to as a positive contribution is the way Hegel posits that "positively self-deriving humanism, *positive humanism*," comes into being through relational activity. This is possible only if the annulling effects of abstraction can be overcome. Marx points this out by saying:

This is the insight. . . . Concerning the *appropriation* of the objective essence through the annulment of its estrangement; . . . Only through the annulment of this mediation—which is itself, however, a necessary premise—does positively self-deriving humanism, *positive humanism*, come into being.[41]

The distance between us and the world is overcome if the movement through it is active, making connections between us and our world. Connection to the world is the result of labor, activity that returns to it, not denies it. More directly, Marx says:

> Hegel conceives labour as man's act of *self-genesis*—conceives man's relation to himself as an alien being and the manifesting of himself as an alien being to be the coming-to-be of *species-consciousness* and *species-life*.[42]

Marx's use of labor is similar to Hegel's in that both see labor as generative of humanity while also being alienating. For Marx the alienating aspects of labor are not essential but are tied to the dominate modes of production, in particular, to industrial political economies. That is, he identifies estrangement in industrial societies with the material conditions of existence in modernity. Marx's discussion of alienation is a systemwide critique. The constitutive relations of industrial capitalism were alienating, for both capital and labor. To put this in a more positive way: The importance of making space for activity in one's own behalf cuts across classes. It is harder, given the working conditions of the time, for the bourgeois to see themselves reduced by the system that appeared to reward them so grandly. One of the reasons for looking at Walter Benjamin's work is that he studies how the material and imagistic spaces of bourgeois consumption are central to an alienating system that keeps moderns from themselves. The famous surrealist notion that "life is elsewhere" would not mean outside his class and time but mean outside the ways in which his class looked and acted.

If philosophy itself is a betrayal, there is a kind of anti-intellectualism that accompanies critical thought. Against this background, Benjamin's use of the moment, or "flash of recognition," is understandable as an instant when the possibility of breaking through the alienating systems of thought and presentations of history that are modernity's origin myths occurs. The modern world that is the source of alienation is also a source of tools that can be used to resist the estrangement of modern life. Through Marx, Benjamin is predicted by the previous work of Hegel. He and Marx are its heirs—especially in the way that they take responsibility for exceeding their own positions.

In *Specters of Marx*, Derrida theorizes the relationship of intellectuals to their (Marxist) past in terms that activate this relationship at a constitutive level. His challenge is that "there is no inheritance without a call to responsibility."[43] If an issue for artists and intellectuals is what should they do, Derrida's notion that they are "bearing witness" is a response that changes the nature of the question.[44] It is not what artists and intellectuals should be doing (that they are not); it is that bearing witness is what they do. As Derrida puts it, "The responsibility, once again, would here be that of an heir."[45] The situation in which we find ourselves (first) is one in which we are witnesses and cannot not respond. That position, to be a witness and to bear witness, is a form of deeply responsible action in the face of modernity. For some theorists and cultural producers in modernity, this became a life work.

As a young man Benjamin wrote an essay, unpublished in his lifetime, entitled "On the Program of the Coming Philosophy."[46] In it he outlines a program for thought in which the responsibility of the heirs to the Western philosophical tradition would be to address the shortcoming of Kantian philosophy. Benjamin conceptualizes this first as the need for philosophy to be able to justify itself, second, as the importance of addressing the reduced notion of experience in current thought, and third, as a reach for connection with the metaphysical. He begins with the importance of justifying knowledge and moves through a critique of current thinking to develop suggestions for future work. His hope is that philosophy will develop in a way that will honor the richness of experience. He is concerned that philosophy become the source for reaching higher existence while proceeding within a Kantian framework. It is important to him that modes of presentation be the focus of investigation and that the connection between experience and language be understood. Benjamin was born in 1892.

"Theses on the Philosophy of History" was completed by Benjamin in spring of 1940—over twenty years after "On the Program of the Coming Philosophy" was written. Instead of the carefully formulated logical argument that characterizes the first piece, the "Theses" is presented as fragments. There are numbered paragraphs, each complete in itself. At the same time, they relate to each other and present an overall position. This is different from the "argument" form that is conventional in the humanities and that Benjamin used twenty years earlier. In the "Theses" Benjamin redefines the responsibility of thought and the spaces in which thinking develops— together, as the same project. Further, experience is redefined in conversation with historical materialism, not in conversation with an abstract philosophical tradition. In the earlier work, Benjamin builds an argument that moves towards and finally addresses the metaphysical. In contrast, in the Theses, he *begins* very early with the notion of redemption and our situatedness, not in a philosophical tradition, but in a set of circumstances between past and the future. He says: "There is a secret agreement between past generations and the present one. Our coming was expected on earth."[47]

In paragraph 5 of the "Theses" the difference between a logical argument and a more vivid form of awareness is articulated. "The past can be seized only as an image which flashes up at the instant when it can be recognized and is never seen again."[48] Rather than being memorable because of the points they make as the argument unfolds, the theses are memorable because of statements and groups of statements that are unforgettable and have taken on a life of their own. For example, there is the famous, "There is no document of civilization which is not at the same time a document of barbarism."[49]

To read "On the Program . . ." is to seek to understand the logic of the argument. After one has done that, rereading can yield a more in-depth understanding of Benjamin's critique and an acceptance or rejection of his proposals. The reading and rereading of "Theses" are not so clearly related to each other, because the various paragraphs can be interpreted and reinterpreted a number of ways. So much depends on what the reader brings to them: so much depends on where the reader can take them. The "Theses" is, among many other things, the flowering of an alternative form. As Benjamin suggests, it is not the sequence of events but "constellations," or connections between time and space, that are important. It is, to use the language I introduced earlier, the relationship to memory, how things are brought into the present, that thought should attend to, (1) because that is how thinking works, whether we acknowledge it or not, and (2) because awareness of "the time of now" is "shot through with chips of Messianic time."[50] The responsibility of the heir has been reconfigured to be the responsibility to tell the truth, and the nature of truth has been reconceptualized in terms of our capacities: as situated, as connected to that we cannot reach, and as volatile.

Benjamin and Marx both recognized uncertainty. The redeeming confrontation with materiality is a relationship of possibility, but also one that may not be fulfilled. Redemption can never be a matter of a simple reversal of roles between the oppressed and the oppressors. For example, Marx argues in his short discussion in "The Power of Money in Bourgeois Society" that money is such a powerful system of mediation that it is exceedingly difficult to formulate alternative modes of valuing—whoever is in charge. "Since money, and the existing and active concept of value, confounds and exchanges all things, it is the general *confounding* and *compounding* of all things—the world upside-down—the confounding and compounding of all natural and human qualities."[51] Money is still the root of all evil—the form this evil took in industrial capitalism was to separate humanity from the power to engage. To apply this insight to the present is to ask what activities are possible in particular settings. Looking at past-industrial cities such as Cleveland, one can ask why in times of economic prosperity such high poverty levels persist. Why, goes this line of questioning, after minority mayors have been elected haven't they improved the conditions of their people? In response one can look to the difference in this country between the electoral process and the governing process. To get elected one promises to work for what the voters feel is best. To govern on a daily basis one negotiates with forces that can make or break the city. Since American cities are not supported by the federal government but must raise much of their own revenue, mayors must deal . . . One of the reasons it has been so difficult for mayors of any ethnicity to pursue redistributive policies in urban areas in this country is that they must operate within political economic space oriented towards accumulation.[52] Because American cities raise their own revenues, it is difficult to win support for policies based in redistribution or nonaccumulative cultural values, such as communal life and the beauty of urban encounters. With the homogeneous forms of valuation that money imposes, there is little discursive space to articulate alternatives. Political discourse becomes a dialect of political economy.

What cultural critics hope for, of course, is the kind of activity where the confounding presence of exchange value is overcome and "*man* and his relationship to the world can be a human one."[53] But that doesn't happen in isolation; it must be done in relationship, by changing the nature of the space in which we are constituted. Marx expresses this in startlingly lyrical way: "If you love without evoking love in return—that is, if your loving as loving does not produce reciprocal love; if through a *living expression* of yourself as a living person you do not make yourself a *loved person*, then your love is impotent—a misfortune."[54]

The potential for love is the opportunity to bear witness. The method is making connections. Perhaps to break through the barriers to human existence beyond the modernist myths of the rational individual is to claim an inheritance we have been neglecting. At least this is a project upon which some cultural producers have embarked—devising methods to encounter the city.

Benjamin's own success in this regard is announced by his dedication to his short book *One Way Street.*

> This street is named
> Asja Lacis Street
> after she who
> like an engineer
> cut through the author.

"Cut[ting] through the author," in Benjamin's dedication, implicates him as party in a relation. Victor Burgin points out how the erotic image is reversed from normal expectations: her voice penetrates his writing.[55] Within the highly gendered society in which Benjamin lived, the announcement can be interpreted as an admission of being dominated. But this simple topology diminishes the implications of Benjamin's dedication. Benjamin's statement is tied to a mode of being based on making connections. If we take this interpretative strategy, Benjamin's dedication is also about method. He himself is not complete, not a closed mind going off on an investigation. He and the world around him are receptive, more open than what Buck-Morss calls "the myth of rationality" would have us think possible or appropriate. We can think similarly about the city in modernity. The particular city in which and about which Benjamin wrote a series of magazine features with Asja Lacis was Naples.

The very rock of Naples is volcanic, and hence porous—we could call it a space with uncertain boundaries.[56] Drawing on the work of Benjamin and Lefebvre, Ian Chambers has reflected on contemporary Naples as a place where representations of city space as organized and planned are happily, hopelessly punctured by the activities of living. The spatial practices of everyday life of this city upset the pretensions of rational systems, such as urban plans. It is not clear what *urban* is coming to mean in the jumbled organization of real and virtual productions that are the daily life of any city, but Benjamin searched for means of articulation in the streets of specific cities.

Together, Benjamin and Lacis found Naples open and wonderfully varied. They participated in the porousness of this city's life in three ways:

1. They used it as a vehicle for critical analysis:

With the pawn shop and lotto, the state holds this proletariat in a vice: what it advances to them in one hand it takes back again with the other.[57]

2. They saw it as a place of festival where they were welcome to participate:

Even the most wretched person is sovereign in the double consciousness of playing a part in every corruption, every never-to return-image of Neapolitan street life, enjoying the leisure of their poverty, and following the grand panorama.[58]

3. Finally, they used it as the site for methodological experimentation. In describing the essay "Naples," which Benjamin wrote for a German newspaper in 1926, Buck-Morss says:

There is no explicit political message [in the essay]. Rather, hardly noticeable to the reader, an experiment is underway, how images, gathered by a person walking the streets of a city, can be interpreted against the grain of the literary style. *The images are not subjective impressions, but objective expressions.* The phenomena—buildings, human gestures, spatial arrangement—are "read" as a language in which a historically transient truth (and the truth of historical transiency) is *expressed concretely.*[59]

Benjamin sees active engagement with the material of the world as generative. His relationship with the city is not subjective, of the lone witness to events, nor is it objective in the positivist sense, of the discoverer. The relationship is performative and mutually generative. A space that attracts meanings is made as he moves through the city. In other words, Benjamin and Lacis's relation with city space functions as cultural dreamwork. They are not reporting as a correspondent would or assuming a correspondence with the truth. They are generating, using themselves as the instrument, "Naples." Naples is also the material at hand, the raw material from which they fashion a "Naples" that can be conveyed to readers. The life of the city and the life of its artists are intertwined as the fragments of modernity are reconfigured into a montage based on encounters with the city.

Naples was not just a city of exotic possibilities whose material sights and sounds could make interesting human interest reading for rational northern Europeans. It was an opportunity being constructed before readers' eyes, first by making available the raw material Benjamin and Lacis provide, but then by adding the capacity for making sense of these fragments that readers bring. Their memory and the experience of the city make spaces of presentation at the same time as they are faithful witnesses testifying in behalf of the city. It is the combination of being a faithful witness, the opportunity to testify, and the participatory reading of the audience that together enlarge the experience of the city.

Whereas both Hegel and Marx could talk about a system and even hypothesize historical trajectories, both Lefebvre and Benjamin recognize themselves in the fragmented world of modernity. Using fragments that are physical "gestures" to occupy space and using fragments that are images to construct new meanings are both ways to display our situation while also making some repairs. If modern identities must contend with the master myths of instrumental reason, Lefebvre and Benjamin use the material of the world to supersede those myths. The "responsibility of an heir" becomes for them the mandate to testify on behalf of life in the world using the material of that world.

Participatory Reading and the Means to Testify

In his essay on early cinema, Charney notes that initially the technology of film did not allow for narrative. As a result, the first films presented viewers "with brief images that would shock, thrill, or incite curiosity." This was called "cinema of attractions": "for instance," he says, "the 1895 Lumière short of a train arriving at a station; or the 1903 Edison short in which an elephant is electrocuted, falls over, and dies."[60]

Testifying as a faithful witness in encounters with the city is more at the moving-train end of things than at the killing-elephants end of things. The latter is to send in the shock troops of the cultural imaginary first, rather than to play with chance in the city. The inherently compelling material the city "naturally" provides is, of course, anything but natural. It is what Taussig calls the second nature created by culture.[61] In contemporary urban culture, the city does not come with attendant dangers and seductions; it *is* those dangers. The dangers of some streets are all too easily conflated with a taken-for-granted notion of the city as a dangerous place.

I have shown the Lumière piece Charney cites in classes many times, and it is still thrilling. Much of the early Lumière work is. One begins to appreciate trains in the way he shows them, as a deep diagonal approaching and cutting into space as their arrival takes it all up. How to glimpse the world as it is and testify to existence within it are difficult issues: it is cheating to approach the city with an elephant gun. That approach dissolves the question of how to testify to life in the city by answering it ahead of time—and not very originally either.

Benjamin addressed the question of how to testify by linking the montage principle to physical engagement with urban space. He uses the material of everyday life as "construction material" both in his walks through Naples and in his lengthy encounters with Paris. He arranged concrete images of life in beautifully imperfect juxtaposition. Demonstrating this method, "the dialectics of seeing" was one of the major projects of *One Way Street*, but it also appears in his memories of his childhood in Berlin and in his essays on other cities, including Moscow. The last is a particularly beautiful example of this art, because it is so unpretentious. He moves though Moscow, linking a number of fragments, seemingly guided by chance events of the days rather than any narrative goal. Reading this piece does not leave one with the impression of just being with a very engaging guide, as travel pieces often do. It is more profound. Benjamin relates daily occurrences, but this Moscow involves the reader as it seems to unfold its being. In the end you feel as if you have experienced something important about this city at a particular time in its history and also about the experience of urban life and the moments that make up life in general. Forget what we thought we already knew about revolutionary-era Moscow; forget the chronological events of the day leading to some kind of climax. The effect is like really noticing a train coming in for the first time.

A contemporary artist who approaches contemporary urban culture in a similar fashion is Victor Burgin. In *Some Cities* he presents a combination of photographs and textual images from his travels to cities in different parts of the world.[62] The two kinds of images are interwoven and function the same way. They are fragments that make connections for readers that exceed their individual insights. The effect is cumulative and also requires active reading—one is always aware of being shown a world and being allowed to savor its possibilities. That the montage is constructed from images and text makes no difference to the reader-viewer. In other words, the images go beyond illustration; they are part of the presentation. Both images and text are interwoven spaces of presentation. There is work to do of the deeply satisfying kind in reading this book. The rewards are great, including a new self-awareness of what it means to be visually literate. Benjamin and Burgin are both present in their city works in a limited autobiographical sense until they meet the right reader-viewers. The irony of the potential of montage as a mode of testifying is that it requires what is outside one's self to make any testimony valid.

Benjamin's method was never to leave the ground through which he was traveling but at the same time to juxtapose fragments of urban life. The "content," to use his term, leads. The reader moves through the text in the usual way, but the chance impressions of urban space that he presents "accumulate," attracting meanings. Benjamin's use of montage brings memory and experience together in the urban encounters he finds and in those he facilitates. He says:

> The currently effective messianic elements of the work of art manifest themselves as its content; the retarding elements, as its form. Content makes its way toward us. Form holds back, permits us to approach. The retarding (formal) elements of music probably dwell in the memory, where listening forms an accumulation. In any case, art of every kind and every work of art contains something that causes perception to accumulate, and this is the essence of the artwork's form.[63]

Benjamin's use of montage creates the environment for the accumulation of meaning. It is a form that duplicates the porousness of the city in Lefebvre's work. The montage principle can be used, as Benjamin used it, to engage the city in the same way the city engages its witness. There is nothing determinate or totalizing about this approach. Individual encounters are open to chance, and the resulting images could always go together differently. Again one is reminded of cultural dreamwork. The combination of images is a generative process, attracting meanings that use and expand the significance of any single part of the montage. This was influenced by, but also differs from, a surrealist notion where the items of modernity are used as gateways to the unconscious. Benjamin did not bind himself to psychoanalytic discourse. He also uses multiple images rather than composing a single image from improbable juxtapositions. Nor do his combinations of textual images aim towards any final Truth. Even for readers sixtysome years later, it is the activity of participatory reading that makes the pieces work.

When Benjamin wrote about the camera, he considered it a paradigmatic tool of modernity. Photographic images remain strongly connected to the material of the world, and they are tailor-made for the presentation of fragmented experience. The fact that they do not present an explicit narrative leaves more room for the multiplication of meaning. In advertising, this possibility is reconnected to narrative fragments with verbal and visual images that activate the desires and anxieties of potential customers. In contemporary urban life, consumption has expanded into a required recreational activity, the mall being the field of play. As opposed to this, making an engaged art means using images to return to existing material space to find that life is still there. For Lefebvre this kind of engagement presupposes the porousness of spatial practices. For Benjamin the openness of boundaries is combined with constitutive participation by the writer/viewer/reader. In the face of the dangers of orienting oneself towards the ready-made, Lefebvre and Benjamin offer the alternative of using the fragments of modern life to participate in the life of the city. Their methods require bodily engagement in the material of the city.

Because modern bodies are visible in public only when clothed, and these clothes must be bought, our bodies are usually considered in the way of things, unless and until they can be mobilized (or more often immobilized) in the service of capital. The properly clothed mannequin is more a citizen in some fluorescent-lighted venues than an improperly clothed human being.[64] Walter Benjamin used mannequins and fashion to illuminate the deadening aspects of modern subjectivity. Fashion requires the ever new in order to continue to exist. Yet mannequins are dead, and the cycles of fashion deny the life cycle. They celebrate a frozen time of life and individual style over relationship. Mannequins are frozen forever in youth, unable to move or reproduce.[65] They are nevertheless often beautifully arresting.[66] They may have been constructed only to hold clothes for sale in a beguiling way, but in doing this they do much more. Mannequins repeat the position of the subject under modernity and at the same time train her to it. Simmel suggests that the stimulation and impersonality of the city threaten to overwhelm individuals' "most personal core": "He [the city dweller] has to exaggerate this personal element in order to remain audible even to himself."[67] Mannequins are aids to audibility, but the cost they exact is participation in existence. As Pogo would have said: "Mannequins are us."

Currently, we have had doubts not only about our personal cores but also about the status of the gesturing body itself. A. R. Stone explores the body both unsure of its own boundaries and also gesturing wildly into virtuality. She considers cyberspace an arena of social activity, including even, and especially from a marketing viewpoint and in the activities of certain enterprising spirits, an arena for sexual activity. Stone's work gives some insight into Lefebvre's critique of the narrowness of contemporary gestural practice and Benjamin's analysis of mannequins. We are, as Marx might have dryly pointed out, loving "without evoking love in return—a misfortune."

Walter Benjamin was determined to search through what he saw as the material wrappings of modernity for the raw material with which to piece together a fruitful involvement with the world at hand. His "constellations," as he called his use of the montage principle, were physical gestures that continue to attract meanings the way good images do. "Construction Site," from *One Way Street*, reintroduces readers to productive practices they may have forgotten:

Children are particularly fond of haunting any site where things are being visibly worked on. They are irresistibly drawn by the detritus generated by building, gardening, housework, tailoring, or carpentry. In waste products they recognize the face that the world of things turns directly and solely to them. In using these things, they do not so much imitate the works of adults as bring together, in the artifact produced in play, materials of widely differing kinds in a new, intuitive relationship.[68]

Juxtaposition is a mode of construction based on making connections, being in a generative relationship with the material world. This is a much more complex involvement than ones based on good design or displaying found objects so they can be seen to the best advantage. Not that that is easy either. But the point of the literary montage as Benjamin developed it is to attract new meanings using the material at hand. Montage moves the writer/reader/viewer by making the writer/reader/viewer the prime mover. Movement though the material works as connections to the point or to many points. The material becomes an agent of thought.

Benjamin's early experiments with montage were literary, for example, his essays on Naples, Moscow, and other European cities. The essay, and later the book, would remain for him the natural venue for putting the fragments of modernity in juxtaposition.[69] His method in *One Way Street* was to organize "literary snapshots" in a similar way to American artists and at the same time as they were developing photographic sequences.[70] Verbal (or visual) themes are introduced and reintroduced. Instead of moving linearly from the beginning to the end, the book becomes an interwoven set of themes moving the reader though encounters with modernity.

Choosing the book as a space of presentation means confronting the issue of how to construct it as a site of engagement. It is not just a matter of setting fragments next to each other. It is to use the physical book, and by extension the page, as a resource. The montage principle is an active collaboration by the author with deliberate chance and the minds of readers, who become creators in their turn. In order to write/read/view one has to be active in relating to the meaning systems that precede one. This is another way in which philosophy is a betrayal from Benjamin's viewpoint: it doesn't leave any space for the kind of connective gestures needed to attach experience to memory.

The montage principle reintroduces physicality and thus performance to the book. It becomes a space under construction. Layout, the relationship among pages, and between images and text all become provocateur to an engaged readership. One kind of book that is constructed as a physical object is the artist's book. This is a kind of exceptionalism—a special type of art that has its own problems if it becomes too "precious" or too formal. But the artist's book does treat the book as a performance venue.

The montage principle works only if and because of how readers feel connected to the material through their own experience. That is, readers must be given a reason to move through the material. The movement the montage principle requires includes a constitutive relation to the reader. Setting up paths of suggested, suspected, and possible connection is integral to achieving this kind of successful relationship. As Gilles Deleuze suggests with his use of the term *negotiate*, there is no final ending, just the beauty of participation.[71]

It's less about securing identity and more about accepting responsibility for statements that mean. These continue to proliferate in what Deleuze refers to as the ascendancy of AND over the verb *to be.*[72] Identity and the book based on the montage principle continue to be works in process as long as the creative gestures of writing/reading/viewing continue. It is possible to make the argument that this is how reading works in general, but in the kind of work represented by the montage principle, self-conscious reading is pushed to the foreground, to be hoped for, actively acknowledged, and expected.

In a book that is foundational to postcolonial theory, *Orientalism*, Edward Said argues that the nineteenth-century "Orient" excluded oriental subjects except as needed to fulfill their role in Western (mostly English and French) requirements for the Orient. In this influential example of discourse analysis, Said begins by writing, "I have found it useful here to employ Michel Foucault's notion of discourse, as described by him in *The Archaeology of Knowledge* and in *Discipline and Punish.*"[73] Said is writing social critique, a "history of the present" oriented towards revealing exclusions.

Said notes how Arabs were excluded from participation in shaping human affairs, what Said calls "history" or "narrative." He notes how the West is made to move forward while the East is static: "The complex dynamics of human life . . . become either irrelevant or trivial in comparison with the circular vision by which the details of Oriental life serve merely to reassert the Orientalness of the subjects and the westernness of the observer."[74]

Even when Arabs were drawn into Western wars, thereby threatening to become part of history by putting themselves on the map, they were excluded in a process Said calls "the defeat of narrative by vision": "There is no recourse beyond 'the Semites' or 'the Oriental mind'; these are final terminals holding every variety of Oriental behavior within a general view of the whole field."[75]

The Oriental was produced as a missing subject—one without wit or agency, although heavily endowed with emotional and erotic possibilities—at exactly the same time as Europeans were constructing identities for themselves organized around rationality. Hence, in a nontrivial sense, the need for the Grand Tour to the Orient. Said is insightful on Gustave Flaubert's trip, on what Flaubert articulates about the Orient and the intersection between what he sees and how he takes his pleasures.

Orientalism is well over three hundred pages long. Readers with a hermeneutic bent might struggle on in vain waiting for Said to say, finally, what the Orient and Orientals "really" are. Said doesn't even begin to deliver on this score, saying his "project has been to describe a particular system of ideas, not by any means to displace the system with a new one."[76] It is, in fact, the genius of *Orientalism* that it enacts what Said is analyzing. There are no definitive or even speculative statements about the nature of the absent Orientals. As excluded, they simply do not appear, while obviously underwriting the whole enterprise.

Even though Said uses the word *visibility*, using Deleuze's terms we would say that he is interested in how the articulable constructs a coherent system. He analyzes "the discursive apparatus in the learned professions, the universities, the professional societies, the explorational and geographical organizations, the publishing industry" as means of "delivering Orientalism."[77]

In that context there is much to say, but not about the links between seeing and saying inside and outside the discursive apparatus Said investigates.[78] For this reason I have always been interested in the painting used as the cover of *Orientalism*. It is one of a genre of richly presented paintings of the Orient by Western artists from the period. On the one hand it seems to be a perfect representation of the exotic, erotic East, site of mysterious pleasures. On the other hand the background of this painting is writing (on the walls)—the very measure of civilization to Westerners.

Said's choice to focus on the discursive follows, as he himself says, from the methodological discussion in Foucault's *Archaeology of Knowledge*.[79] It is also simply the choice he made about what to study. His choices are much different in a later work, *After the Last Sky*,[80] where he moves from critique to testimony. One can understand the method of *After the Last Sky* by imagining the static world identified with "the Oriental" in Said's earlier work being pushed to the fore and found to be not static at all. Said and Mohr's investigation illuminates some of the many layers of previous and present occupations of the central site of "Orientalism"—the place where a Palestine might be. Said's orientation in *After the Last Sky* shifts from applying a method of analysis to working out the problems of presentation. He enters into a porous relationship between the articulable and the visible, using himself as an instrument. The basis of his presentation is a montage of many elements, including himself as an active writer and reader of his own situation. At the same time he is negotiating the identity of a modern Palestinian.

After the Last Sky is a collaboration between Said and the photographer Jean Mohr. Mohr took photographs of Palestinians in various Middle Eastern venues where they reside and Said wrote the text. Said begins with a recounting of a predictable history told from a respectable distance. But because he interweaves his narrative from the beginning with commentary connected to Jean Mohr's images, any hopes of continuing to tell the story without material involvement are undercut immediately. In the beginning it seems as if the ghost that haunts this book is the ghost of history.[81] This is also what the reader comes to this book expecting.

The project has the initial appearance of the famous professor becoming accessible. He describes photographs; he intermixes personal recollections with the presentation of a political history. One assumes this will be easy to summarize as a predictable ideological position. But Said has been accessible in public forums many times before, on the radio, in public lectures, and through his political activities, so he really isn't opening up new territory in that way. As the book continues, one realizes that if a ghost does haunt this book, its name is "representation"—and the reader learns not to know what to expect.

As I tried to understand what was going on in the book beyond what I originally expected, I was reminded of how I use the zoom lens on my camera. When it is pulled back, everything is in view. When I see the space I want to use to make an image, I close in on it, composing through the viewfinder. If the image works, the composition may be tight, but it opens up a world. Said closes in on himself in this way. The author of *Orientalism* does not concoct a more accessible self, as if he were leaving out theory for the benefit of his reading public. Instead he turns around his lenses, that is, his ability to conceptualize and his concern with the politics of representation, to look at himself in relation to the Palestinian space that helped make him. And then he closes it down. The reader realizes that the book is an arena for negotiation, and Said is presenting himself as a subject in process.

I'm not saying that he talks only about himself. This would not be very useful. Instead, the space of Palestine and the identity of the Palestinians are shown to be joined and also not separate from who Said is. These identities are negotiated on the pages of the book as they are on the ground. This is a great contrast to the method Said used in *Orientalism*. There, the careful presentation of evidence was produced without the benefit of Edward Said's personal presence. The book didn't need him. As I said above, this absence is a reenactment of the method by which the systems of visibilities that constructed the Orientals did not require their active presence. "Of course," as a veteran of the colonies might be imagined to say, "you could never know what 'they' are thinking." But this was because "they" weren't constructed as thinking beings in the sense of being articulate or even understandable.

As a reader continues to move in the space of *After the Last Sky*, Mohr's images of Palestinian space and Said's concrete memories are made into encounters with the politics of history and geography. These are placed in juxtaposition with Said's attempts to write about them. The battle with presentation—continuing to make space for encounters in which he and his readers must deal with interpretation/experience—is what gives the book its force. As this happens, Palestine becomes a more vivid site, and the issue of how to reach the Palestinian experience through dominant systems of mediation becomes more pressing. The reader is implicated at both the level of political space and the level of self.

For example, the fluid course of Said's commentary on Mohr's images is interrupted when Said admits to recognizing a woman in one of the images as an old friend of his family's. This unsettles any workmanlike approach that he and we may have had in mind. In speculating about what he can really know about her from the image, Said writes, "Something has been lost. But the representation is all we have."[82] Those representations are the material with which he and we must negotiate whatever connections are possible.

In many places, Said articulates how presenting the spaces of Palestinian lives is a process in which the Palestinian situation and the limitations of his own situation as one who has taken on the responsibility of bearing witness have no final meaning. How to testify is not as simple as a universal humanistic model based on intercultural goodwill and common sense might suggest. The task of making space for existence calls for the production of space that doesn't yet exist. Said is brave enough to provide readers an example of the shortcomings of straightforward universal goodwill in his own writing when he comments on images of Palestinian women of different ages and positions. He understands the Palestinian male "warrior" identity that is disregarding of women. He admits that women have suffered greatly and have great resources, and he is surprised at their capacity for joy. At the same time as he can talk about how the image of (warrior) men and (their) women function in the dynamics of Palestinian cultural space, he cannot address the questions these women's images raise for him. Their strength, their joy remain somewhat mysterious. In relating a story that involves his mother as a newly married woman having her passport voided, he says she became "a mediated person."[83] And when he admits to being unable to articulate the experience of Palestinian women, he is also saying that he is a mediated person, that by extension so are his readers. The subtext then becomes about the inescapability of systems of presentation that are beyond us and also are our raw material. It becomes a way of admitting the limitations of the productive forces that make us what we are. Because of the space we have, there are places we cannot easily go.

The main work of this book is to fulfill the authors' promise to testify. They do this on many levels. Said says of the Palestinian's situation, "Homecoming is out of the question."[84] He says this of his own situation—again, not just because his parents were born in places he can't go back to, but because those places don't exist anymore. He uses his own identity as a case in point.

In *Orientalism*, Said expanded the discursive spaces in which the general reader can understand the Middle East. In *After the Last Sky* there is a tremendous leap off the table of the oriental into the space of a living people. But the presentations he makes are not just encounters with *their* lives; they are encounters with his. Said describes himself and the people with whom he identifies as "immigrants and hybrids. We are in, but not of, any situation in which we find ourselves."[85] The lives covered by this statement are Palestinian, like Said; academics, like Said; immigrants, like Said; and all who develop hybrid identities because there is no home to return to, like every one of his readers.

The ghost of the politics of representation haunts us all, and Said's gift to readers is to use the paradigmatic case of our times to show how this operates on the ground. He connects the situation of having no one place to the situation of having to make a place for yourself in the world.

W. J. T. Mitchell has called the photographic essay, including Said and Mohr's work, "labors of love in which we are enjoined to collaborate."[86] The reach for existence is enacted in the desire to testify, in the commitment to bear witness. This kind of love cannot be a misfortune.

In the end (or in the beginning) the desire to participate in attracting meanings is not as simple as a desire to (finally) tell the truth. This orientation moves forward from the intellectual activities that take critique or exposure as their final purpose. Said's work is an example of what Lefebvre reaches for and what Benjamin was also seeking in the city streets of Europe and especially in the arcades of Paris: the means to testify. The authors of *After the Last Sky* gesture in the direction of using themselves as instruments in the enterprise of exploring the particular occupied space in which they found themselves.

Both Lefebvre and Benjamin provide theoretical underpinnings for the development of this kind of testimony because of how they took up their own responsibilities as heirs to philosophical and Marxist traditions that preceded them. Lefebvre argues that we think of space as always occupied and that occupation constructs not only environments but also identities. The dynamic that links space and self is the gesture. The gesture leads, and space and self follow. The gesture is the site of experience that Foucault seeks in heterotopic space. The gesture is the move Benjamin makes with participatory reading. The reasons for venturing into city spaces are expanded far beyond the city's familiar roles as suburbs' other and as the site of economic aspirations. Instead, it is possible to rewrite the terms of engagement, to be oriented towards testifying on behalf of the ongoing occupation of city streets. We can evaluate, know, and exist in spaces according to how we participate in their occupation. Gestures of occupation are what one looks for when photographing the city.

4

Streets

Photography, if practiced with high seriousness, is a contest between a photographer and the presumptions of approximate and habitual seeing. The contest can be held anywhere—on a city sidewalk or in a scientific laboratory, or among the markers of ancient dead gods.

—JOHN SZARKOWSKI, *Looking at Photographs*

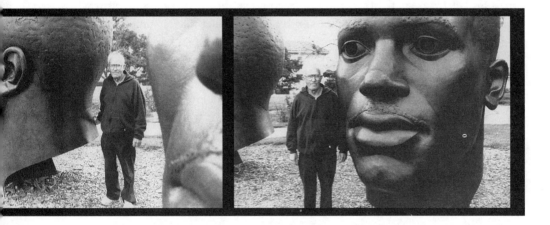

I n this country, public radio must attract sponsors in order to survive, which leads to commercials of a restrained sort. This morning there was a tasteful advertisement for business suites where traveling executives have access to teleports, scanners, printers, and a feeding station. *A feeding station*: If this is for people, wouldn't you call it a dining area, as you would in any self-respecting estate ad for an apartment in the city or a home in the suburbs? A feeding station can exist only in the context of a certain kind of executive identity, where professionalism is all about being on the move and being oriented towards the task at hand as defined by one's corporate or government sponsor. This "working environment" also involves a way of life that doesn't recognize boundaries of time or space.[1]

Of course, executives on the move are not at home. But there is an even bigger difference between the feeding station and café society than there is between work and home. One of the spatial innovations of modernity for the middle classes has been the separation of productive and reproductive functions. The feeding station way of life brings them together again in the interests of production. It is difficult to imagine Lefebvre's right to the city in the spaces this way of life requires. Similarly, the potential for heterotopic moments at the feeding station seems rather remote. Executive suites are paradigmatic "non-places."[2] They feed the troops while providing urban experiences that don't need any particular city. To return to the cultural confusion between "urban" and "the city": Feeding stations illustrate how it is possible to be both immersed in urban space and separated from the city. This can trigger some interesting questions, not just about the dining experience available at feeding stations, but also about the connections between these supremely utilitarian but statusy sites and the subjects moving through them.

Contemporary urban processes include a wide range of activities that don't involve particular cities. Many, in fact, avoid them. In this section I take the camera into the streets in the sense that I explore photography as an instrument that engages the city directly. I argue that by so doing we can return our culture to ourselves.

If, as Lefebvre's spatial theory suggests, to move through space is a constructive gesture, this section is an urban renewal project. But rather than assume city space is in decline, I look at how photography, a technology identified with modernity, can be used to connect to spaces of life in city streets. If the city is the raw material for production, for economic development, and for academic research, it has also been available to artists. Dorothea Lange called the camera a tool for teaching people to see without the camera. Alternatively, one can learn to see *with* the camera. Photographs can function as sites of participatory reading that provoke urban encounters, first, in the relationship between the photographer and the city and, second, in the relationships between viewers and the city images.

De Certeau describes how Foucault "saw" things that surprised, startled, and/or pleased him, leading him to investigate the source of his reaction. De Certeau says of these "bouts of surprise": "Something that exceeds the thinkable and opens the possibility of 'thinking otherwise' bursts in through comical, incongruous, or paradoxical half-openings of discourse."[3] His characterization of Foucault's bouts of surprise bears a family resemblance to Lefebvre's hope for urban encounters and the way Benjamin engaged the city. Participatory reading was key to Benjamin's presentation of the city, and it is also a key to understanding how the art of street photography works. Jean-Pierre Montier describes Henri Cartier-Bresson, the acknowledged and rarely surpassed founder of the genre, as "recognizing (rather than capturing) the life present in all phenomena at the moment in which their potency and vitality are at their height." The photographer "does not embalm time, he questions it, recreating its delights and sensual pleasures."[4] Cartier-Bresson himself says: "As far as I am concerned, taking photographs is a means of understanding which cannot be separated from other means of visual expression. It is a way of shouting, of freeing oneself, not of proving or asserting one's own originality. It is a way of life."[5]

It is important to note here that Cartier-Bresson is explaining himself and his photography at the same time and that both are described in terms of how to occupy space. When asked what he would photograph, he replied, "You never know. . . . I cannot predict what will happen. One can also be indiscreet sometimes with regard to love. . . ."[6] As singular as Cartier-Bresson's work is, his use of this notion of love is not idiosyncratic. It appears again and again in writing by photographers on photography. What "love" means in this context is one of the issues of this section. One can begin by noting that this love is a notable move away from critique that seeks to "supersede" the world and a move towards participation in world making. It is love that is not, as Marx would say, "a misfortune."

There are as many approaches to the camera as there are to the city. So it is less the inherent qualities of the camera as a tool than how that tool is deployed that is of interest here. Photography is a medium of great accessibility. Cameras are easy to get and convenient to use. Photographic images are widely available and put to a broad range of uses. I'm interested here in showing how, as a tool of modernity, photography can be deployed to make connections to aspects of city life that are visible, fleeting, and not ordinarily noted. It is hard to imagine Foucault of *The Order of Things* or Lefebvre of *The Production of Space* bouncing around always on the move, as Cartier-Bresson was described as working. But this is because of how we usually imagine them.

The transparent use of the camera is understood in terms of explicit claims to represent the world, but at the same time this use implicitly reinforces preexisting cultural codes. In contrast with this, my interest here is in conceptualizing more active relations between photography and urban space. When used to make connections to the city, the camera is not an instrument of representation; it is a way of making space and attracting meanings. The camera becomes an active tool, not of representation, but of presentation.

If photography is seen as the art of making (not taking) pictures, the possibility emerges for using it as a productive part of city life. From this perspective photographic images bring memory and experience together, attracting meanings in the process of stopping time and presenting a space. Photography's unique gift to modernity is its power to arrest: to stop time, to demand attention. In addition, in a way counter to more traditional visual arts, such as painting, the camera requires a referent. This means it maintains a connection to the material world. Take the camera out into the street, and the potential for unpredictable encounters with the city is built in. The camera also has an active relationship to time. Photography holds up (stops) the world to hold up (to future scrutiny) the ambiguities of that world. The "arrest" that the camera makes allows the luxury of time outside instrumental time to be productive in the making of meaning. These are traits Lefebvre found crucial to "the right to the city."

The performative force of the camera is open. Once images leave the site where they are made, they are incorporated into the abstract and material practices that we call our culture, being regularly deployed for and against the dominant forces in that culture. This freedom that is part of the camera's operation makes it eligible for a number of cultural chores—both public and private.

So at the very same time photography is a taken-for-granted component of themed existences, photographic images regularly transgress the ready-made. The space of the photographic image is never closed and must be continually made intelligible by the labors of viewers. The nature of the relationship among the world, the photographer, and the viewer is unstable, even when the photographer and the viewer are the same person.

Garry Winogrand is reported to have responded to the question, "How long did it take you to make that picture, Mr. Winogrand?" by pretending to consider and then replying, "I think it was a hundred and twenty-fifth of a second." He was right, of course, but only in the most immediate sense. All of what Lefebvre calls the gestures, traces, and marks that make the space of American political culture precede *and* follow him. Garry Winogrand is a paradigmatic street photographer in the way he was stalked by American urban culture. He responded with magnificent vengeance by shooting back. This is the context in which to understand one of his most quoted (and misinterpreted) statements: that he photographed in order to see what the things that interested him looked like as photographs. John Szarkowski interprets Winogrand (and Edward Weston) as expressing "a shared fascination . . . in the difference between photographs and the world they describe, and in the possibility that the former may nevertheless, if good enough, tell us something important about the latter."[7] Similarly, Hill and Mora see Walker Evans's photography coming of age at the point when his work embraces a realistic approach. But this is not a matter of simple correspondence. They suggest, "From now on every one of his subjects had to be shown as a photographed, not a photographic, subject."[8]

Acknowledging the radical openness of photography requires a willingness to relinquish the ideology of control. The potential of image making as performative space is tied to admitting (and admitting to) viewers as active participants. Earlier I suggested thinking of the Vietnam Veterans Memorial as representational space (as Lefebvre uses the term). In many of the public statements that Maya Lin, the designer, has made about this work, she reiterates that the memorial is not her work alone, but that it becomes what it is because of what visitors bring to it. This is, in fact, one of the most compelling aspects of her monument work.[9]

For example, in discussing the garden that Lin and her brother designed for the Cleveland Public Library, she said that there are many things about the garden that cannot be known until it has been in place for a while. How the space is used is central to her notion of it as a space. The space can be analyzed in terms of its formal design. She adds to this such questions as whether it is a good place in which to eat lunch and how the foot traffic will pattern. Direct experiences that cannot exactly be predicted are aspects of both heterotopic space and "the right to the city." Making meaning in this sense, in the city with a garden or using photographic images, is based in making connections. In the garden this is a matter of attracting visitors. With the photographic image it is a matter of attracting participatory readings. In the city we can entertain the idea that it is a matter of reaching for the real.

Because photography is connected to the world—it is handmaiden to light—the space it makes has the potential to operate heterotopically, both inside and outside its original context, both for and against order.[10] Walter Benjamin saw the possibilities in the camera's facility for decontextualization and recontextualization. He expressed great insight into the potential of photography to witness, and at the same time he was fully aware of the dangers lodged in the ways it decontextualizes images. Photography is the tool par excellence of advertising and political propaganda as well as for defining normalcy in the family snapshot.[11] It can also be used as a "faithful witness" in coming to terms with the city. The notion of faithful witness was originally based in a realistic approach to the photographic image, but the idea of witnessing also describes an ethics in which the arrest the camera makes and its connection to the world are used as a site for experience.

Photography is a creation of modernity; it is a means to testify to, for, and against modern experience. In the process of using photography to help negotiate our way in modernity, the connections between approaching the city as raw material for production, making space, and making images become clearer. All these activities engage, require, and become the material of the world. In ways parallel to Foucault's hope for heterotopic space and Lefebvre's plans for urban encounters, street photography is a demonstration project for "the right to city." Making images is a mode of bearing witness, not just to the city, but also to the existence of ourselves as producers.

The discussion below brings photography into the previous discussion of presentations of urban space, spatial theory, and the potential for experience. It begins with consideration of the use, operation, and potential of the camera as witness; moves to explore challenges to reason in modernity that admit the loquaciousness of the image; and finally looks at connections between photographic testimony and the search in modernity for life worth living. As the camera moves into the streets, the limitations of seeing cities as dystopic space become clear.

Photography as Faithful Witness

It is practically a prerequisite in writing about the photographic image to link the ethics of photography to a definition of the camera based on its capacity to present evidence about the material world. Tracing shifts in how this relationship is understood is central to understanding photography as a spatial process. This is a different and much more fruitful exercise than discussing photography from within a paradigm based on truth or falsity. Just as various approaches to the city were shown above to be interconnected, various approaches to the camera are layered within each other.

What John Szarkowski calls the "faithful witness" approach to photography is the conventional wisdom or taken-for-granted way of thinking about the relationship between photography and the world. As he describes it, in this approach the most usual assumption is

> that for the purposes of visual knowledge a mountain and a photograph of a mountain are fundamentally the same thing. Presumably no one has really believed this, but it has been a convenient and useful fiction. It has not generally been in the photographer's interest to make an issue of the fact that the photograph of the mountain was only one man's opinion, for his customers did not want opinions. . . . The popular formulation of this convention was expressed in the claim that the camera does not lie.[12]

Not only is it taken for granted that the camera does not lie, as Szarkowski's commentary notes, but also the use of photography to construct an approved world is usually not questioned. To use images in this way is to participate in a set of related practices that have been major visible gestures in the direction of putting a there there in the space of American culture. To participate in that deployment in a reflective way is to lay claim to the capacity to produce meaning. A strong tradition of this kind of witnessing is foundational to street photography. The photographer W. Eugene Smith wrote about his Pittsburgh project in a way that sounds as if it were constructed within a true/false framework, but on close reading gives a sense of how complicated the notions of truth and falsity become in conjunction with photography. Smith wrote: "To portray a city is beyond ending: to begin such an effort is in itself a grave conceit. For though the portrayal may achieve its own measure of truth, it still will be no more than a rumor of the city—no more meaningful, and no more permanent."[13]

Smith is taking a position here in which the use of the camera is an activity. It is more like an encounter than a historical record. In his hands, the presentation of (no more than) a rumor of Pittsburgh was a great achievement—"its own measure of truth."[14] The photographer's mountain is still present, but it is a different thing from the photograph of the mountain. We understand the making of an image of that mountain in a different way. The photograph works as testimony, not just as an instrument of visual correspondence.

Lincoln Kirstein's comments on Eugene Smith's work give us some language for understanding how the power to witness goes beyond the pretense of faithful representation. He calls Smith's images memorable: "I see Gene Smith's best photographs as icons, like those thank-you pictures painted by grateful craftsmen, set up as tokens before altars of their favorite name-saint intercessors, who saved their lives from tuberculosis, mad dogs, or an automobile accident. Without self-pity or vanity. Possibly hysterical. Possibly insane. Memorable."[15]

Szarkowski's comments on Helen Levitt's work also move away from an appreciation of her art based in correspondence theory. He expands the notion of faithful witness, showing just how complicated it becomes when the photographer encounters the city:

> Some might look at these photographs today, and recognizing the high art in them wonder what has happened to the quality of common life. The question suggests that Levitt's pictures are an objective record of how things were in New York's neighborhoods in the 1940's. This is one possible explanation. Perhaps the children have forgotten how to pretend with style, and the women how to gossip and console, and the old how to oversee. Alternatively, perhaps the world that these pictures document never existed at all, except in the private vision of Helen Levitt, whose sense of the truth discovered those thin slices of fact that, laid together, create fantasy.[16]

Levitt's images are presentations based in the material life of the neighborhoods she photographed. The "fantasy" she creates is not fantasy in the sense of being an individual psychological invention. It is encounters with the urban—complicated spaces that don't just picture the city but also participate in urban processes. They are a part of the cultural space they portray. Undeniably urban, rarely singular portrayals of individual subjects (as portraits aspire to be), their meaning is generated in the relationships they capture and the connections between those relationships and the street. Edward Agee saw a wildness in these everyday compositions: coming from the middle of the city, they also stood at the borders of what we call civilization: "The overall preoccupation in the photographs, is, it seems to me, with innocence—not as the word has come to be misunderstood and debased, but in its full, original wildness, fierceness, and instinct for grace and form. . . ."[17]

Agee is not describing a *private* vision. A private visual language could not connect viewers to the city in the same way Levitt's images do. The space these photographs make is in between what they show and what we see. This complex relationship among the photographer, the photograph, and the viewer constructs a form of public space. Levitt worked from the material she saw in plain sight, never leaving the street. The silent partner enabling the connection between her images and Agee's reaction was a time/space in American cultural life when cities, communal life, and the street as a public area were suspect, becoming even more déclassé, actually being planned out of existence in many eastern cities. Opposed to this, the country was collectively envisioning clear, crisp, clean green suburbs for new suburban identities. Levitt's images are not images that were made to sell in the interior decoration sense. Her images create spaces somewhat tangential to realms that require pleasant images, choosing instead to say a great deal about what was being subtracted as a people fitted themselves for the homogeneous comfort of material democracy constructed for them in the wake of the Second World War.

From this viewpoint, the faithful witness notion stretches far beyond "simple" representation. The subject-camera-object relation is better thought of as a web of the many gestures that constitute the activities of image making.

Two theorists of modernity who paid serious attention to photography are Walter Benjamin and Roland Barthes. For both, the power of photographs to become sites of experience is connected to how the process of making sense of photographic images necessarily involves the viewer. The status of photography as art or the nervous question of whether photography is a substitute for painting was less important to them than how photography could reveal modernity to itself. Visual theorists of Benjamin's era, such as André Bazin, were interested in understanding how the photographic image (both still and moving) was integral to late-breaking modernity. Bazin tied the creative force of the camera to the production of material space in the world: "The photograph as such and the object in itself share a common being, after the fashion of a fingerprint. Wherefore, photography actually contributes something to the order of natural creation instead of providing a substitute for it."[18]

Benjamin's discussion of photography introduces two themes that continue to appear in his and others' work: the connection between photography and the world, and the function of the viewers' participation in making photographic space. For example, in speaking of a single image, he says:

> If one concentrated long enough on this picture one would recognize how sharply the opposites touch here. This most exact technique can give the presentation a magical value that a painted picture can never again possess for us. All the artistic preparations of the photographer and all the design in the positioning of his model to the contrary, the viewer feels an irresistible compulsion to seek the tiny spark of accident, the here and now.[19]

The spark, as Benjamin calls it, links the referent, the time/space of the camera in use, and the capacity of viewers to experience. This experience exceeds the individual image and the individual viewer but at the same time is derived from both. Both making and viewing images make new space. How this works is most clearly articulated in Roland Barthes's short book *Camera Lucida*.

Barthes does not speak as one who takes photographs or as one who is interested in being a subject of photographs. He writes from the perspective of the viewer. His project in *Camera Lucida* is most usefully understood as a guided tour of the camera's capacity to attract meaning in which the tour guide uses himself as the primary instrument. Barthes finds the photograph to be a space of articulation that engages him in the world in a mutually constitutive fashion. His discussion of this perspective is a detailed analysis of photography as faithful witness. Instead of the "useful fiction ... of unchallengeable and objective truth" (as Szarkowski had it), he uses photographs to bear witness to the conditions of our existence. In this small book he enacts the ability to experience ourselves deeply in the space made by a single image. In the beginning this seems a very complicated and wonderful thing that he makes the camera do for *him*. But this is not only an individual experience: he uses his experience to show how the cultural capacity to stand inside meaning can be reclaimed. Viewing the photographic image becomes a mode with which to encounter the urban, not as a static environment, but as a boarding house with certain vacancies where temporal experience need only apply.

Barthes constructs a typology of two types of witness. The first, the *studium*, is the most familiar. It is a culturally coded, nonsubversive mode of operation. The field of *studium* is not without emotion. It can shock, gladden, or enlighten the viewer, but it always works within frameworks that are already familiar. Thus *studium* is the practice of cultural codes. This kind of witness relies heavily on a realistic approach to the camera in which (to requote Szarkowski) "the mountain and the photograph of the mountain are fundamentally the same thing." Looking at a powerful image in this way may change one's thinking but without challenging the perspectives within which one knows how to think. This has nothing to do with the issues of whether an image is good or the value of a photographic project.[20]

To the *studium* experience Barthes gives "polite interest." He then turns his attention to ways in which photography has greater potential. "Photography is subversive not when it frightens, repels, or even stigmatizes, but when it is *pensive*, when it thinks." He means pensive in an active way. In talking about a photograph that has this potential, Barthes says, "It is fantasmatic, deriving from a kind of second sight which seems to bear me forward to a utopian time, or to carry me back somewhere inside myself."[21] This language of return (to the self) recalls Foucault's heterotopic space and also Lefebvre's encounters insofar as they are connected to the desire for unthemed existences.

The aspect of photographic action that moves Barthes he calls the *punctum*, or wound. It is something that "happened to be there."[22] For Barthes the *punctum* has "the power of expansion." Like Lefebvre's "moment" and Benjamin's "spark," this "wound" is an "extra" element that, in the end, is all. Barthes repeatedly comes back to the fact that the camera requires a referent, a connection to the world. When combined with the viewer's experience of the *punctum*, the image expands into an encounter and, hence, participates in making a world.

Barthes writes beautifully about a photograph of his mother, ending by saying, "I had understood henceforth I must interrogate the evidence of photography, not from the viewpoint of pleasure, but in relation to what we romantically call love and death."[23] This position is initially understandable in the context of what an important figure Barthes's mother was in his life and how deeply he felt her loss. But as he goes back over his reflections on photography in connection with viewing this image of his mother that touched him so deeply, we see him presenting the gift of his experience to the reader as a way of illuminating the potential of a certain kind of photographic experience in general. Barthes also describes this process in terms of an "arrest." He uses *arrest* in two ways. *Arrest* means "stop" (as in time), which is how the camera works. *Arrest* also means "to take into custody"; this is the wound Barthes mentions. The photographic image "works" with a combination of referent, time, and what Barthes in another context has called "buttonholing" the viewer.

John Berger calls this "reacquiring a living context." In his words: "Photographs are relics of the past. They are traces of what has happened. If the living take that past upon themselves, if the past becomes an integral part of the process of people making their own history, then all photographs would reacquire a living context, they would continue to exist in time, instead of being arrested moments."[24]

In other words, the potential of photography is not guaranteed. Arrest can become arrested development. Angela Davis writes about this third kind of arrest in an essay about the proliferation of photographs based on her 1960s "radical" hairstyle. Many years after the fact of her choosing to use her personal style to make a political statement about African Americans' constructing a positive identity of their own, what has also occurred is a recognizable hairstyle that in the case she discusses was used to sell clothes.[25] Davis's essay on this personal history illustrates how difficult it is to achieve Berger's ideal of a living context. At the same time both Berger and Davis recognize that no arrest is final. Images are always on the run from attempts to reterritorialize them. The image space is continually being constructed by a number of forces. Without any special efforts they are always available for encounters with new viewers. The photograph maintains the connection to the past that Berger comments on above and continues to be constructed in the present and into the future.

Photographs combine "the voice of banality" (everybody knows that) with "the voice of singularity" (allowing the viewers to experience meaning).[26] "Reacquiring a living context" is based on an encounter. As Barthes explains: "The photograph's essence is to ratify what it represents. . . . The important thing is that the photograph possesses an evidential force, and that its testimony bears not on the object, but on time. . . . *The power of authentication exceeds the power of representation.*"[27]

The arrest that the photograph of Barthes's mother makes of him has everything to do with the way that it engages him and very little to do with what she "really" looked like. "The power of authentication" is the ability to witness, not the ability to catalog.

The power of authentication can have a broad reach; it is not just at home in the mind of the photographer/viewer, although that is the beginning of the process. Janet Malcolm discusses one of Diane Arbus's images in terms of how it allows the viewer to witness:

> The picture shows a plump woman, wearing a striped cotton dress and sneakers and no socks, lying stretched out on the grass on what must be a warm summer day. She lies with her arms extended luxuriously behind her head, and with one leg also stretched, while the other is bent at the knee to allow a sneakered toe to push against the grass. . . . Arbus has put us in the presence of one of those moments of existential rapture in which the phenomenon of human happiness seems *proved*, as if in math.[28]

This is a fantastic way to encounter Arbus's images, which are almost always discussed in terms of the marginality of her subjects. This image, as Malcolm astutely observes, opens the door to a certain kind of experience. The fact that this image is part of Arbus's asylum series is neither determinate nor incidental to the opening to heterotopic space it makes. We might also want to make such a place for ourselves.

This is another way in which the arrest Barthes has in mind is not "merely" a representation. He points out how photographs don't reproduce a past; they block it. Or more accurately, they can fill up the space of memory, becoming the official record. He says, "The photograph is violent: not because it shows violent things, but because on each occasion *it fills the sight by force*, and because in it nothing can be refused or transformed. . . ."[29] For example, looking at images of important family events is complicated by the way in which those images may initially differ from the experience as remembered. As time goes by, the images may become that experience, raising all kinds of interesting questions about truth and timing. Which wedding comes first: the one we planned or the one we attended or the one kept in the album? Photography not only records events but also constructs those events. You can look at old photographs of the domestic scene to see how you did and/or to present the argument that you are familial. Or like Ralph Lauren (see the summer ads), you can begin with clothes and put the patrician family inside in hopes that people will confuse the two and purchase the latter.

The camera uses light and time to create a grounded space in which meaning plays. What direction that meaning will take—if it will provoke an encounter as a faithful witness or if it will construct a world already totally known and made—depends in part on the relation between the subject and the photographer and in part on the relationship between the image and the viewers. The photographic gesture seems straightforward: the camera uses time and light to capture space. What that space will become is not so simple. It depends on what kinds of connections are possible among referent, camera, photographer, and viewers. At the very least, to photograph an urban scene that exists only for the time it takes to make the picture or to make a picture of a building that no longer exists pulls the rug out from under a strictly empirical approach to being a "faithful witness." But this seeming weakness is also the source of the "power of authentication." Faithful witnessing is a productive activity: making the image and the viewer. So in the end the "violence" of the arrest that Barthes notes does not always lead to "arrested development." It can be enabling— pushing the space of the image forward in the quest to attract meanings.

Barthes returns to the image of his mother to explain this: "It (the image) accomplishes the unheard-of identification of reality (*'that has been'*) with truth (*'there she is'*); it becomes at once evidential and exclamative; it bears the effigy to that crazy point where affect (love, compassion, grief, enthusiasm, desire) is a guarantee of Being."[30]

The photographic image does not always function this way. As *studium*, part of the image repertoire of everyday life, photography is usually used as a kind of insulation from stepping outside a common cultural code, from falling off the table, from this guarantee of Being—what Barthes also calls "the wakening of intractable reality."[31]

Barthes uses language similar to Foucault's notion of "exceeding syntax" to articulate how the photograph can provoke experience: "I then realized that there was a sort of link (or not) between Photography, madness, and something whose name I did not know. I began by calling it: the pangs of love. . . . In the love stirred by Photography (by certain photographs), another music is heard, its name is oddly old-fashioned: pity."[32]

This is an issue Barthes grappled with for some time: how to say what the image shows. He resolves the issue by saying what it does. In an earlier essay, "The Third Meaning," there is a preliminary statement of the power an image can have. Here he examined movie stills and noted how limiting conventional ways of understanding them are. Describing the power of images in terms of connotative and denotative meaning does not explain everything about how images work. There is a further meaning having a particular effect: it "seeks me out." He calls this obtuse meaning: "I believe that the obtuse meaning carries a certain *emotion*. Caught up in the disguise, such emotion is never sticky, it is an emotion which simply *designates* what one loves, what one wants to defend: an emotion-value, an evaluation."[33]

The power to "authenticate" and "designate" describes connections of the sort that the theorists of modernity wanted to provoke. It is the use of the material of modernity to find life within its limitations. This "guarantee of being" breathes life into the faithful witness notion by showing the special power of photographic presentation. Witnessing is a generative relationship.

In Barthes's now classic treatments, the camera can be an instrument of deep meaning, connecting the scene to the viewer and the viewer to existence. The height of attainment, or using the language of theorist Eduardo Cadava, "the height of responsibility,"[34] obtains when images exceed the pious verities of the world they also reproduce to become tools of our irretrievable connections to life and death. If Barthes calls this love at one point and then pity, he is in both instances talking about moments when life is fully engaged.

Returning to Szarkowski's comments on the camera as faithful witness is to recognize this potential in a broader sense than it was originally meant. The arrest the camera makes is the space for witnessing in the sense of being joined to the material world in ways the image makes possible. Photography, particularly street photography, can exercise this power of authentication. To be a faithful witness is to join the spaces in which we are immersed; it is to acknowledge the joy of mutually constitutive relations.

The notion of a life-giving relationship was key to Barthes's reflections on photography in *Camera Lucida*: my implication that his reflections on his mother's photograph do not involve just what the photograph does for *him* was not very well put. It is better to say that in presenting the function of the photographic image in the way that he does, Barthes both expresses and enacts a solution to a central problem in modernity. This problem is the need to be directly involved in making a place for oneself in the world. The weight of convention is a heavy load that pits the demands of social order against the formation of an active subject. Barthes is making the argument as a kind of gift to the interested public that (1) the project of making a place for oneself in the world is the project of modernity, and (2) as a part of modernity, photography can be employed in service of that project. The activity of witnessing that the camera facilitates also gives life to the witness.

My Country 'Tis of Thee

Merce Cunningham, the great modern dancer, was interviewed recently on *NewsHour with Jim Lehrer* as part of an ongoing celebration of his eightieth birthday. When asked about his recent work, which incorporates computer-generated images, he said, among other things, that dance is a visual experience. I wanted to respond, "But isn't dance a performance art?" But then I thought, we experience dance visually. Being able to see it that way allowed Cunningham to mix genres, to cross categories, to make new kinds of dance, and to help digital artists learn what their art can do.

Sixty-nine years ago, when Cunningham was a young man, Walter Benjamin wrote in his essay "Little History of Photography," "'The illiteracy of the future,' someone has said, 'will be ignorance not of reading or writing, but of photography.'"[35] In the time since then, we haven't done much about visual literacy, even though we live in an increasingly visual culture. So we now have children raised by the screen who may be trained in life styles and skills through advertisements and visual media such as television, but who are still educated to recognize the word as the only instrument of thought.

Benjamin is usually recognized as a founder of cultural studies. Cultural studies can be confused, both inside and outside the field, with the study of isolated idiosyncratic activities and marginal groups. Benjamin's conceptualizations of visual and material aspects of modernity are still outstanding because of how he understood the technology of modernity as both integral to structures of dominance and also the raw material with which to search for existence. Benjamin saw the material of modernity, even such peripheral beings as mannequins, as organizing components of the myths of rationality. Mannequins, for example, wove fantasies that were so immediate they helped make the assumptions of historical progress and instrumental reason unassailable.

Modes of presentation, especially the tools of mechanical reproduction, such as the camera, were central to Benjamin's explorations. He was struck first of all by their power to attract attention. In comparing the visual culture of modernity to traditional social thought, he points out that it is "not what the moving red neon sign says—but the fiery pool reflecting it in the asphalt" that commands our attention.[36] The image, particularly when used in advertisement, works in a mode that Benjamin describes in noncognitive terms, saying, "Sentimentality is restored to health and liberated in the American style"[37]—by which he means, roughly, in your face. More politely we might say the immediacy of visual culture makes it almost impossible to ignore.

Like Foucault and Lefebvre, Benjamin was sensitive to both the dangers and the promise of modernity. While visual experience frames the world we live in in unavoidable ways, its functions are not predetermined. Benjamin's interest in illuminating the myth of historical progress that so captures the cognitive capacities of modern being is linked to the potential of the image, particularly the image of the street. The image is not less important than the word, nor is it inherently trivial while language is serious.

From this viewpoint, images have more profound uses than to illustrate thought. They are capable of thought. Or to say this in another way, the image is an instrument of human experience with special potential because of how language has been corrupted by its own pretensions. In this way of thinking, the image is close to poetry. It is capable of a flash of insight beyond the pious conventions that seem normal but are also incomplete.[38] To take this further, one can reverse the order of importance and argue that the guarantee of being an image can provide a guide to how good writing works. This changes the usual order of valuing images and text. It also leads to questions about the claims we usually make for logic as the instrument of reflection. Furthermore, flashes of insight may be the best we can hope to experience, and explaining our insight in discursive frames is a secondary (in the sense of logically later) activity.

Photographic images can engage the world in compelling ways, because they operate as the sites where the relationships among systems of meanings are both displayed and exceeded. This is not a simple distinction between a law-abiding text and the wayward image. Nor is it exactly the distinction between cognition and emotion, although as Barthes's analysis suggests, a cognition/feeling distinction is useful for establishing initial grounds for consideration. One of the disadvantages of our usual habit of characterizing cognition and feeling as separate areas of experience is that when words such as *feeling* or *sensation* are used in the literature to explain how certain types of total engagement reach beyond the world of "simple" cognition, these experiences are elevated and/or separated from our way of life, rather than being situated within it. Or they are devalued and separated from serious thinking[39]—again, rather than being situated within life. In addition, thinking along the lines that separate a sensible linear order from a specially charged aesthetic realm can begin the slide down the infamous slippery formalist slope leading directly to the individual artist as a heroic, complete, and woefully ahistoric figure.

Ian Chambers aptly castigates words for "their custody of reason,"[40] echoing Lefebvre's critique of abstract representations of space. Leo Charney's essay on "the category of the moment" also situates the "moment" beyond the word. He places it as an alternative to (but also of) the social order of modernity, that is to say, the city and urban culture. The moment is a brief experience of a heterotopic world. Both Chambers and Charney have a tendency to essentialize the categories they use, but they do acknowledge and explore the spaces of concrete experience in modernity. For both, the city is a privileged site of this exploration.

The "category of the moment," as Charney uses it, means, first of all, an instant of intense feeling or awareness. Short duration and deep feeling are combined with an ability to articulate the moment only after it is past. So one would recognize the moment while it was happening but would be able to say what occurred only after it was gone. This is very much how Lefebvre defines moments. Charney is most interested in the moment as an aspect of the motion pictures, but his treatment applies to still photography as well. He does not make an argument that modern mimetic technologies such as the camera make it possible to arrest time in order to experience a true representation of reality. Nor is he pitting the validity of the moment against the limitations of thought. Instead, he argues that the way to explore the moment is to examine how it appears in various spaces of modernity as a component of modern existence. He sees the moment in modernity as life reasserting itself against instrumental reason. The hegemony of systems of visibility and abstract representations of space "requires" a shock, to get our attention, to get there. In this context, one is reminded of the "blasé" attitudes Simmel saw urban subjects developing as their only defense against the overstimulation of city life. One is forced to consider the ethics of deployment: how instruments of the moment can and should be used as a faithful witness in the context of contemporary urban processes. This question was pursued during the past decade by critics of the National Endowment for the Arts, without the advantage of too much reflection.

Walter Benjamin connected "momentary sensation" to vision through what he called in his Arcades Project the "now of recognizability."[41] Benjamin's conceptualization of the moment connects it to an ethics, to political responsibility. Recognition is tied to movement in and out of the space made by interaction with the material world. Lefebvre refers in a similar way to gestures that can construct spaces of representation. As Michael Taussig puts it so forcefully, the experience of recognition is "not in the head, but where we see it."[42] Charney's treatment also emphasizes the visceral aspects of experience of the moment in ways related to Taussig's notions of "seeing" as "feeling"—recognition is a tactile relationship entailing a moment of contact.

Recognizing the capacity of photography to become an instrument for moving though modernity and contributing to the creation of heterotopic space is not the usual history of mechanical reproduction. The well-worn story of photography moves in a linear trajectory from the early days of experimentation and portraiture, to the pictorial tradition, to the realistic aspirations of straight photography, to a hypersensitivity about the camera as an instrument of unfair advantage (a "taking"), and on to digital possibilities. This history is the field on which Szarkowski's playful dig at realism, as "a convenient fiction," plays. Some theorists look at photography in modernity and ask what convenient fictions have been entertained and why. Charney ties the experience of the moment to defamiliarization or shock that can take the viewer outside (while making sense only within) the confines of the rational order that constructs the spaces of modernity. This analysis is simpatico with the search of other philosophers of life, such as Foucault, Benjamin, and Lefebvre. They are united in the search for spaces of return and redemption missing from modern life. This search is sited here, not confined to redemption in the sense of an afterlife or limited to a new life brought about by political revolution. It centers on situations, gestures that construct habitable space, space in which one has a place.

There is a theoretical tradition that emphasizes the ways in which image-making instruments such as the cinema, the screen, and the camera function as distancing devices by presenting the world as spectacle. This leaves out the capacity of images to present moments. In between frames, there is a pause that is not a pause: in between the world the photograph presents and the world the viewer sees in the image, there is a distance that is not a distance. Contact with the "strangely familiar" can reach life beyond themed habits that usually organize us.[43] In other words, barriers to participation in constructing experience are porous.

Benjamin's notion of a flash of insight refers to a mode of seeing through and into existence. It is not a literal metaphor for photography. That would deemphasize photography's active relation with the world. Producing moments, as if they were only products, is not the goal. That would be to imply that photographing the city is important if you produce a certain number of moments with your images. The moment is an instance of connection to urban life that is constructed anew, even if somewhat differently, in each viewing.

It is too easy to assume that photography resides in the camera. In a consumer society this is a handy reason to keep improving the technology, and this is useful for the commodity and collector subcultures of photography. It also makes the camera into both commodity and Deity of Vision. But the difference between the very latest in camera technology and a pinhole camera is nothing. My pinhole camera was originally a Quaker Oats box. Fully outfitted it cost roughly three dollars, and it came with all those extra oats. The first time I used this camera, as part of my nephew's science project, I realized, with a great deal of anxiety, that I didn't actually believe in the pinhole camera. Seeing the image coming up in the developing solution, I had that feeling of wonder that newcomers to photography often report. It made me rethink photography. Photography is not in the camera. It is in the world, more specifically, in the way light works. Everything after that is a matter of elaboration. And given who we are, that elaboration is often in the direction of gaining more control. But the world remains ahead of this game. The optics of the newest lenses are impotent (to use Marx's term) unless the world is already willing. The ability to make space in its own image, which we can think of as a miracle, is the way light works. A photograph is not of an object; it captures the light coming off that object. Understanding photography as the connecting light between the subject and the image the viewer experiences is one way to see how photography engages the materiality of the world in the process of witnessing.

For Michael Taussig, the materiality of this process is crucial to how the image is redemptive. In what he happily admits is an idiosyncratic reading of Benjamin, he suggests that the dialectical image is not only a visual image. He asserts, "A first step here is to insist on breaking away from the tyranny of the visual notion of the image."[44] This situates photography in the world by drawing attention to its physical components. Taussig connects Benjamin's nostalgia for the storyteller to his hope for the revolutionary aspects of instruments of mechanical reproduction such as the camera. Traditional storytellers are connective instruments. They link audiences and the world in ways that give life to both. The modern storyteller, photography, "preserves—indeed invigorates—the gesticulating hand in the form of the tactile eye."[45] Taussig's principal concern is to make the argument that the mimetic faculty is "the nature that culture used to create second nature."[46] Instruments of mechanical reproduction make contact by entering into relation with the world. But this relationship goes beyond a static representation. Instead, the relationship is a process of presentation. That is, as part of what makes it possible for them to work at all, the tools of modernity slip the cultural harness of "second nature" to open nature. Photographic images are not in the subject, or in the camera, or confined to cultural codes: they only require these things to connect light to experience.

This is not to say that photography has to be employed in ways that appear to be revolutionary on the surface. It is to say more: that photography can be used in ways that are radically open. As Barthes clearly knew, advertisements use the same tools to shape desire to the ends of consumer capitalism as the processes that produced the important image of his mother. The issue this raises is the politics involved in the ongoing deployment of the image. Images are so much a part of us, but what that part is, is always being addressed anew by photographers.

Writing during the same era as Benjamin, Lincoln Kirstein was just as conscious of the relations among the image modernity and the modern subject as Benjamin was. In his 1938 essay on Walker Evans's *American Photographs*, he said, by way of making space in which to interpret Evans's work, "It is a good deal easier to look at a picture than to read a paragraph. The American reading public is fast becoming not even a looking public, but a glancing or glimpsing public."[47]

Charney and Schwartz take the position that to see film as an invention of modernity is only the beginning of asking how it is a part of modernity. They explore how "society was cinematic before the fact."[48] Put in this context, Kirstein's remark implies that photography is one tool in use by the preexisting, modern glimpsing public. Perhaps the glimpsing public "needed" a means for gaining some perspective on the complexities of modernity; perhaps it needed a mechanism that also kept that complexity at bay. Both have to do with using the material of the world to come to terms with it. Instead of a protective wall shoring up or punching through the boundaries of the world, Walker Evans used photographic images to assemble active space with which viewers could find themselves. These are the aspirations with which Kirstein surrounds Evans's work. He is suggesting that we see Evans as articulating the daily minimum requirements of his age.

Walker Evans created a culturally active form of presentation, the photographic sequence. As Alan Trachtenberg has pointed out, these sequences were presentations to be read.[49] The glimpsing public was invited to move though the images, making connections, witnessing America and themselves as part of American spaces.

Walker Evans and, after him, Robert Frank are usually identified with this particularly American approach to photography. There are two aspects of their approach that are particularly illuminating here: montage and the everyday. In each case there are parallel developments in European photography. But montage and engagement with the everyday took different forms in America from those they took in Europe. These differences are understandable in exactly the ways in which modern American sensibility differs from European sensibilities.

Walker Evans's *American Photographs* was first presented as a photographic sequence on the walls of the Museum of Modern Art in New York City. It was later published in book form, presented as two linear sequences. Robert Frank's book *The Americans* is also organized as a long photographic sequence broken into segments.[50] In fact, it was originally composed physically on walls, as if the exhibit also came first. In both cases, the photographs are not meant to be understood only as individual images, but take their meaning from each other and from the connections viewers make by moving back and forth among them.

Photomontage was developed in Europe at approximately the same time Walker Evans was working. In the hands of its best-known practitioners, the Berlin dadaists

Hannah Hoch and Raoul Hausman, it usually took the form of a single composite image. Similarly in the antifascist work of George Grosz and John Heartfield, parts of various images were juxtaposed with text to make one image. In both American and European versions of montage, the montage principle is the same: the artist places images in juxtaposition to attract meanings beyond what is readily available from viewing the single components in isolation. Both recall exactly Benjamin's notions of using fragments to construct constellations of meanings.

In the American context, connections have been made by movement through images. A kind of cultural language is created and deployed with the photographic sequence.[51] For example, in both Evans's and Frank's work, themes that construct an American experience become more and more obvious with repeated readings. The reading of montage is not only linear. It circulates through while making a space. The reader goes back and forth among related images: the car and people moving across America in Evans; the flag and the raw diversity of life as it appears spread out across the American landscape in Frank.

This leads to discussion of the second way in which Evans and Frank present American sensibilities with their work. They never leave the cultural ground they are moving within. This differs from the psychological and explicit political aspects of European montage work. In the European style, movements between the elements of an image connect to the psyche (or what was thought of as unconscious reality) or to important political issues. This way of thinking does not draw on the great abstract themes and eternal verities of traditional philosophical thought, but it is very different from the American mode of boring into the details of everyday life. Although Frank is Swiss, not American, and although he was trained in Europe, his work since *The Americans* has been marked by an intense exploration of the everyday.[52] In both Evans and Frank, the mundane material realities of the life are the life. If we are to construct meaning, it will be here on earth, and these are the materials with which we must work.

Movement is an aspect of both men's work. Movement through the images is like the movement of the car in the landscape. Frank's images are literally the result of a road trip across America. Evans before him concentrated on the American Northeast and South, but still there is the feeling of movement—through the images as well as through the space they make. So in tempo, subject, and mode, photographic montage as it has been developed in the American context is wholly congruent with the national sensibilities attuned to open spaces, movement, and regional ground. The intricacies of European thought did not fall on fertile ground in this country. The impulse to use photography to make a place in which to stand resonated in both arenas, but res-onated differently.

The desire to make photography an active tool engages the time/space of the material at hand in a fight for life in this world. This orientation contrasts vividly, for example, with medieval murals that also require active participation by readers but that cite time and space outside viewers' own. The meanings medieval murals attract make life on earth richer through the retelling of beloved narratives, such as the life of a saint or of Christ. The goal is to make life here richer by making connection to the divine. Modern American street photography seeks connection to life by presenting existence here.

This is most clearly illustrated in the anguished life and work of W. Eugene Smith.[53] Smith could be understood as having large ambitions and obsessions within a framework in which the important image is understood as the same thing as an important career. His famously difficult and troubled personality is seen as unfortunate or as an example of the romantic loser, depending on your point of view. If the romantic loser narrative is followed, Smith's earlier personal career ambitions are seen as being transformed by his experience of combat during the Second World War. He became engaged in a deeply quixotic attempt to use photography as an instrument of Truth. This handy narrative sidesteps the issues that arise from focusing on his actual photographs. It becomes possible to chuck about bad habits and the impossibility of Truth while deeply admiring his skill. His photographs are allowed to be beautiful, overwrought, and dismissable because that is what peace in a contemporary urban culture calls for, and Marx and Freud saw it coming, providing the analytic tools with which to name names. This masks and radically diminishes Eugene Smith's attempt to employ the camera as witness.

Smith's postcombat work was created in the overtly homogeneous time/space of the United States following the Second World War. This is the era in which the suburban promise of American identity by subtraction spread out across all classes (except the very poor) and all ethnic groups (except by reason of race). In other words the material promise of democracy was extended and detached from the city and the immigrant identities that characterized city life. If we look at Eugene Smith's work—both his notes and images—we see him trying to get to places where the placid demands that the buttoned-down world makes don't reach. This explains why his strongest photographs are from the edges of society. His "Country Doctor" and "Nurse Midwife" essays may have appeared in the mainstream magazine *Life*, but these images are kin to his unfinished Pittsburgh work and his private images of jazz musicians.[54] He moved away from the success his early ambitions promised—if his images are understood only as objects to be appreciated on aesthetic or ideological grounds. He moved towards something more profound and more difficult to define. He says of this movement: "I can't stand these damn shows on the museum walls with neat little frames, where you look at the images as if they were pieces of art. I want them to be pieces of living."[55]

In other words, photographic images are modes, not things. In other words, the camera works with the material at hand. It is heir to the conditions in which we find ourselves. To say the camera is an instrument for reporting on what you see is to say it carries a certain responsibility. When Eugene Smith held the camera, the modern hand-held camera to his eye, he was testifying to life in his time.

A contemporary ethics of photography takes responsibility for the relationship among the world, the camera, and the viewer. Opening urban space to the public is a central issue in a world where the spread of privatization in so many realms once considered public signals withdrawal from dealing with the unpredictable. This is the space in which Eugene Smith's best city work moves. Walter Benjamin noted that disconnection from the outside world is both a marker of modernity and a distinction of position within it. Ethics that promote a strategy of engagement and encounter put aside the tendency to gain distance and distinction by leading with your formal categories. Instead, one agrees to make art from the material at hand.

Sweet Land of Liberty

There is a famous story that might be true in which a student asks Minor White if he thinks that he (the student) can ever make good photographs. Minor White responds by asking, "Have you ever been in love?" "Yes," the student replies. "Then," White says, "you can make good photographs."

The space of the photographic image is itself a field in which culture plays. That so many photographers talk about image making in terms of love raises the issue of what this means in the time/space of contemporary life. The profound notion of love that Barthes talks about in conjunction with his experience as a viewer gives some insight into what photographers mean when they invoke it. It is also informative about the work art does in contemporary life.

Instances of connectiveness with existence make street photography part of the art of existence. This always occurs in the context of particular situations and often fleeting spatial arrangements. This is not a matter of "getting" a particular subject on film. Nor is it a matter of adopting a particular style of photography. As Colin Westerbeck puts it, "It is the capacity to make your work both a reflection and an expression of your own culture, rather than an extension of someone else's modernism, that makes a street photographer great."[56] Both making and viewing images can become "events" that are not merely sociological but go further to articulate the beauty of being connected. In Foucault's reflections on his work, he credits events with provoking further investigation of the rules of formation of sites from which we develop identities and also from which we get the urge to move "off-site." "Reflection" and "expression" of the known are in a sense only the beginning. Currently the notion of the event and the category of the moment are both in retreat from the appropriative arm of official Art understood as the power to shock. But the connectiveness that photographers can find has nothing to do with shock in this sense.[57] Instead the potential to connect, to love, becomes a radical act in a hyperindividualistic society such as our own. Urban photographers who face the city without the prior commitment that literal shock is necessary or desirable are claiming a right to participate in constructing the life of the city. They are not engaged in illuminating our preexisting prejudices about urban space.

In an interview about the boxing images that make up his "Times Square Gym" series, John Goodman explained what he saw there:

> The Times Square Gym was a "home" for many young boxers. There is almost a genetic connection between the older trainers and younger boxers. It's beautiful to watch all the wisdom and love, which is probably surprising. That is what I was interested in, not necessarily the combat.[58]

When asked why he is a photographer, Goodman responded by saying:

> I think it's the process of connecting. Making a picture reconfirms your existence. . . . There is a certain feeling I get when I'm taking a picture. I know that I'm there . . . it's not ego. It's "This is right." It's like breathing air.[59]

The themes of love and connectedness appear again and again in photographers' written accounts of their work. I could just as easily have quoted Harry Callahan or a number of other photographers working in the street tradition.

This is often combined with a genuine surprise at what happens when one photographs. If Goodman describes it as breathing and Cartier-Bresson as life, this is not to say it is predictable or given. Martine Franck describes her commitment to photography as follows: "What I like about photography is precisely the moment that cannot be anticipated, one must be constantly on the alert, ready to acclaim the unexpected."[60] Acclaiming the unexpected is also a shout of joy at being alive.

It is humbling and also useful in terms of understanding the importance of the connections that these photographers make to note that theorizing about the potential of heterotopic space, the urban encounter, and participatory reading is logically after, not before, these artists chose to engage the streets. Deleuze insists on a "relay between theory and practice."[61] Philosophers of the moment and street photographers both use the material of modernity to address the issue of what Foucault calls "having an experience." This suggests that the reach towards caring in the sense of being committed to the space of our existence is a great issue of our age.

As discussed above, John Rajchman characterizes Foucault's work as "the incitement to see" and expresses the moral implications of this by saying, "For us the danger is not that we might fail to become what we are meant to be, but that we might only be what we can see ourselves to be."[62] Rajchman characterizes the potential for exceeding ourselves in terms of freedom. But "freedom from" does not connect to the spaces that make us; it does not locate life in the concrete flow of events. Working with fragments of modern urbanism, American street photographers testify to life by using the material at hand. Thus they address their country not as a *sweet land of liberty* but as spaces of indebtedness.

The physical and cultural spaces of the American landscape are the raw materials with which contemporary photographers work. In conjunction with the use of this material, their images reach beyond conventional views to present gifts of recognition—"*of thee I sing.*" Their images are spaces in which viewers can also "have an experience," reiterating the photographers' initial finds. The combination of a localized origin and the attraction of meanings that constitute experience is also a description of Lefebvre's right to the city.

American street photography is a presentation of the gaps in the connective tissue in the culture. The classic street images of Helen Levitt, Eugene Smith, and Garry Winogrand discussed above each stand in the middle of conflicting dimensions making up the American urban scene—becoming, in effect, what I called earlier "the troubled eyes of the Infanta Margarita." Specific struggles to claim a right to the city are present in their images at a constitutive level. Pairing each of these photographers with another working at the same time highlights the dimensions of these American spaces under construction. Examining this work doesn't completely explain the spaces of indebtedness it bears witness to or why the work remains compelling. But it can bring some of the trials of love to light.

Of Thee I Sing

By Oneself or in the Company of Friends

The work of Helen Levitt was used above as an example of street photography that acknowledges life in the city at a time when Americans had aspirations to leave it behind.[63] The photographic images Levitt made are rarely representations of single subjects. They are complex compositions that link subjects to each other and to the urban space that surround them. These undeniably urban subjects and the streets they inhabit are interwoven. The images show people in relations. They are group shots, not in the sense that a gaggle of people is gathered at attention in the middle of the image space, but in the sense that the construction of the image requires these relations in order to be what it is. These are less images of individual subjects and more orchestrations of human presence in city space.

James Agee is quoted above describing the wildness in the innocence of Levitt's street images, particularly those of children. This wildness is shown in the city at the same time the city was being marginalized in the general culture. There is something about "ordinary life," if it refers to ordinary life in city spaces, that implies transgression. Levitt presents these ambiguities in her images simply by being there and seeing the way she did.

Levitt is an heir to the tradition of Cartier-Bresson and Walker Evans. She is credited with intuitively understanding Cartier-Bresson's project of participating in the life of the city. He spent time with her when he was in New York and showed her many images not publicly known. She also worked directly with Walker Evans on some of his city projects. All three occupy a tradition in which the photographer understands the world as space that offers revealingly beautiful instants of perfection. In Levitt's work these instances are often what we would describe today as edgy. They differ from the graceful site that Cartier-Bresson makes of Paris. Levitt's genius is in the way she presents the raw energy of New York neighborhoods in the 1930s and the 1940s.

Her spaces are urban, always suspect, always outside the rural, now suburban, ideal. This urban society is unpredictable, often vaguely foreign; yet it remains necessary to the city, organizing the core of what has been called civilization. Her images come from a time when America was moving to institutionalize the rejection of the city. Levitt used that rejection and ambivalence to lay claim to life in the city. She made images that show how life arranges itself in unpredictable ways, is dependent on connections, and continually makes and remakes itself. The spaces she created are alive, because the spaces she saw were animated by the gestures of communal life.

Dorothea Lange was Levitt's contemporary, and she was as attuned to the times as Levitt, but with a different sensibility.[64] The origin myth of Lange's concerned photography has her leaving her studio, where she ran a profitable portrait business, and walking in the streets where she made an image of a man in the White Angel bread line. What is immediately noticeable about this now-famous image is that it is of one man. Even though the picture frame is crowded with other people, he is what we see. He becomes the Great Depression in the City.

If Helen Levitt's images depend on conjunctions in city space, Dorothea Lange's images depend on recognizing the singular individual. The images of each of these photographers work very differently. The coincidences, the wildness, the compression and display of city space as a locus of humanity are the spaces of Levitt's images. The singularity, the dignity, and the worthiness of the individual are the spaces of Lange's images. Lange's best-known images are her photographs of farmers fleeing the dust bowl. The usual critiques about the implicit ethnic biases and the manipulation of images have all been made of Lange's work. They are boring and inadequate to her work, especially when seen in the context of her images of the American South. What might be true of her collaborative work with Paul Taylor is true of all lobbying efforts. They were active in making a case for congressional support of migrant farm workers. To do this they used the rhetoric of American political ideology. At the time this included a certain nativism recognizable in ethnic terms and articulated as respect for the virtues of hard work, long suffering, and fair play.

Beyond specific policy agendas—remember it was Lange who said that the camera is an instrument for teaching people to see without the camera—making her subjects into subjects worthy of attention was in a larger sense Lange's project from beginning to end. She never stopped being a portrait photographer. To be able to have a portrait made of oneself in this society is to be able to lay claim to a certain status as a notable individual. As much as Levitt's images are human experience in action, Lange's images are formal compositions that elevate the human subjects they present. The space of her photographs is a space in which the form of the individual dominates the space. This is true even in her group images such as the well-known migrant mother. Mother and children are presented as a unit. This space makes the kind of sense it does in the context of a culture that celebrates the singular life.

Lange looked at outsiders in America and made claims for them on the basis of the individual dignity she presents them as having. She acknowledged the American landscape as a backdrop. She presents her subjects for the viewers' recognition rather than displaying spaces of sociality, as Levitt does. American culture focuses on the individual, making the measure of a person the position he or she attains. This tends to exclude the human connections that are necessary, not just for success, but also for survival. In shooting her subjects in the rural landscape, on the road, and so forth, Lange mobilizes the conditions most likely to devalue them as the material for making space for them. Her images of farm workers or women and children in the fields or on the road are images of individuals of substance. She makes them that way by making the most desolate rural landscapes into a studio where her subjects reside with grace.

Sociability is usually not an explicit referent in claims to American identity because of this culture's commitment to the singular hero. Following Foucault's model for spatial analysis, the play between identity and sociality can be conceptualized as dimensions making the figure X across the space of American political consciousness. The high end of the social dimension recognizes the ties that bind as a life-giving support system, and the low end focuses on the restrictions of communal life. The high end of individualism is the rational self-governing citizen, and the low end is rampant disregard for others. Levitt and Lange stand at the center and focus upward, drawing viewers in to recognize the spaces of existence outside the insecure middle, in which they are likely to reside.

In Search of Peace

Roy DeCarava and W. Eugene Smith both produced images so beautiful that it is difficult to study them at first.[65] The art of printing for each centered on the uncommon use of darks. Their work stands in great contrast to the tradition in printing, which is centered in midtones and reaches towards the highlights and shadows. One result is that both DeCarava's and Smith's images call attention to themselves as images. As strong as Levitt's and Lange's images, their works seems to have a decontextualized force. But this is misleading, because, also like Levitt and Lange, both men were deeply involved in presenting existence in sites most problematic for American culture, not as a matter of an overt political agenda, but as part of what they did and who they were. Both men were deeply involved in siting/sighting peace and violence. For both, the search for peace included complicated relations with the city and with the conventions of urban culture. Both worked on the margins, but from different loci of enunciation.

Smith became known as a photographer for *Life* magazine and then became famous as a combat photographer in the Pacific theater during the Second World War. His notebooks clearly state his commitment to "show it like it is." Hence he photographed war as death and destruction that entangled all who were involved. Although many of his images of the Second World War are now part of the general cultural memory, others were not printed at the time and are less well known. This is in part because his editors at *Life* thought some of his images did not show enough patriotic devotion to the war effort. They operated outside the required syntax of wartime America and presented more of what Smith saw.

Smith himself was badly wounded during the war. When he began photographing again, he recommitted himself to presenting truth with his images. If we take him at his word, which everything about him suggests we should, we have to ask why he headed for the margins in this quest. His postwar photo essays show him searching beyond the domains of mainstream middle-class American life. The "pieces of living" he presented are outside the newly emerging suburban spaces. He went both inside and far outside the circle of green where the new materialist suburban culture was realizing itself. In other words, he turned his back on the consumer society that was America's homecoming to returning veterans and presented peace elsewhere. For example, his photo essays "Country Doctor" and "Nurse Midwife" contain images of rural and black America. They have nothing to do with the well-padded life; they have everything to do with lives dedicated to social good using very few goods.

The country doctor story is made up of images of a man working long hours, caring for his patients, and fighting off the death of a child. The midwife story is a portrait of a southern midwife, making the rounds among her clients, witnessing the beginning and end of life. In his notebooks, Smith refers to his remarks about Maude Callen, the midwife, as a "love letter."

Smith stepped "off the table" to find his subjects. His flight from violence is calculated, directed towards lives, and then towards moments where life is worth living. At the same time the violence of industrial and segregated American spaces made the sites he found what they were. The marriage of the opposition between peace and violence is highlighted in his Pittsburgh work and in his jazz series. These were images, made over the course of several years, of after-hours jam sessions in the New York loft where Smith lived. This was also one of the most difficult times in Smith's life. He was unraveling and heavily invested in substance abuse but still photographing and taping these sessions. It seems to me that Smith was also seeking peace, and this series highlights the cost he paid for his quests.

Although his photo essays contain many images that appear to be intimate and he committed a great deal of energy to learning the territory before he shot, he always made images from outside. Even his famous image of a Spanish village wake, inside the small room, was taken as an outsider. He looked into a situation in order to present it, but he was not in a position to negotiate a presence for himself. This is more central to understanding why his images are American icons than the vigorous controversy about his manipulation of images. The central issue is not whether he "really" did straight photography; it is what kind of testimony he fought hard to produce. The "violence" to the cultural code of the straight image is analogous to going off to strange places to attract meanings that reach towards truth and the peace truth promises.

For example, one of Smith's combat images shows three soldiers in a foxhole. This image was exhibited recently at the Cleveland Museum of Art. The image is riveting in its presentation of fear. As I was realizing this while looking at the image, I also realized that the eyes of at least one of the men look bleached. My initial thought was, he didn't have to do that. The image is powerful enough, they are scared enough, the situation is terrifying as it is. But it obviously wasn't. There was a need to produce a heterotopic space that broke through while being within the moralizing syntax of the wartime mentality. The folks back home could not be counted on to assume terror automatically. Smith felt required to point out to viewers what they should be seeing. This decision is part of a process of authentication that Smith was dedicated too. He was not a court recorder, but the manipulations are also tokens of his outsider status. The violence he did to his images is part of seeking to reach human experience beyond the conventions of seeing in which he worked. This is the same way in which, like the readers of *Life*, he remained outside the peace he sought. His work was in the service of making it possible for them to see what he saw from where he stood.

Roy DeCarava photographed at the same time as Smith.[66] His images are also beautifully composed, using the whole image space. But where Smith shot as an outsider to the violent legacy of racial separation in America's culture, DeCarava photographed from inside. As an African American he was a direct heir to cultural violence, and he also lived in that space. The racism of everyday life was the ground he walked on and lived in in his photographs of Harlem. So in navigating the spaces of peace and violence, both men used the tensions of their era, but they navigated differently.

In city spaces often closely identified with violence and outsider status, DeCarava made beautiful images that express both the violence and the possibilities of making peace. For example, his Harlem Project photographs don't present the kind of longing Smith's do. DeCarava's eyes see troubling things, but his position with respect to them is untroubled. The Harlem Project was supported by a grant from the Guggenheim Foundation that he received in 1952 but was eventually published as *The Sweet Fly-paper of Life* with a prose poem written by Langston Hughes. Both Hughes and DeCarava were directly acquainted with life in the mostly invisible spaces that Harlem Americans made for themselves. DeCarava's eyes are untroubled as they look out. He is in the same room with his subjects when he makes images of their intimate daily routines.

DeCarava is also known for his photographs of jazz musicians, *The Sound I Saw.* Again, whereas Smith's images of jazz are mostly private images of jam sessions outside the public venues where people go to hear jazz, DeCarava recorded the fabric of an ongoing way of life. His images acknowledge jazz as a collective, public component of city life, and they were shot from within the culture that supports it.

DeCarava's early training was in printing and painting, and, as in Helen Levitt's work, the whole image plane is his canvas. But like Dorothea Lange, he often used human subjects to make beautiful formal compositions. Whether in homes or on the streets of the city, he was at home, producing images that are both intimate and a complete visual experience.

DeCarava stood in the center of where he was when he made his images. In this way he and Sister Mary Bradley, the character Langston Hughes created to accompany his images, would have understood each other. She says, "Me, I always been tangled up in life."[67] This is the mode in which DeCarava used the material of his world to show viewers the moments he experienced. He stepped beyond the spaces of violence that racism makes by being in them. He made peace at the center.

Smith was better known by the general public than DeCarava, but part of the burden of this was that it supported his stiutation of being off to one side of what he photographed. Smith was finding his truth away from the spaces to which his fame, his ethnic and class background, sought to assign him. This led him to spaces outside the conventional boundaries of the culture, spaces to which he himself was marginal. These are complexities DeCarava did not have to deal with in the same way. He shot where he was; these were the spaces he occupied. The city of Harlem may have been created by systematic spatial exclusion that we have to call violent, and being black in the 1950s was often dangerous, but DeCarava used this material to produce images of loving connection.

Our image of this country in the 1950s is a contradictory mix of political complacency and material well-being spiced with fear of communism and active red-baiting. One aspect of this era was that the new American suburban subjects were not deeply involved in political activism. Not only did they have lawns to mow and mortgages to pay; they are often portrayed as faithful followers, "corporation men" (and mothers and children). This is a generation that lived an increasingly privatized lifestyle—the transition from the Monday night card game to Monday night football. As an alternative, outside the borders of these politically atrophied lives, the beginnings of the civil rights movement were stirring. Off-site, the heterotopic possibilities of making peace were being enacted. Smith and DeCarava occupied this space also, but they occupied it differently. Smith, by birth and experience, was an outsider to the spaces he wished to inhabit. DeCarava, by birth and experience, was an insider to the spaces he presented in his images. Both made images that in very different ways provide glimpses of peace and connectedness that rely on, while also escaping, the conventional violence of their time.

The Deeply Feminine and the Reach for Existence

Garry Winogrand was a fierce street photographer who burned up the city streets with his images.[68] A loose male cannon on the urban landscape, he later became a desperate kind of street walker who shot endless images from his car window. This memory of him has a certain appeal, but we could easily make too much of it as an explanation of his slightly off-center images. And it means ignoring the fact that what he did as a photographer was shoot what he saw. This is clear from his statement quoted earlier: that he photographed in order to see what the things that interested him looked like as photographs. Among other things this statement is an admission of guilt at being seduced by the found. Winogrand's images are not staged. What he photographed was already there. What he chose to photograph takes on the meaning it does in a culture that likes to look at women in ways mistakenly called objective, likes to find any abnormality shocking, and romanticizes the lone wolf. Winogrand's suburban images are just as devastating as his city work, but the city is really his milieu. His images are so right about the painful contradictions in American culture in the 1960s and 1970s that it takes your breath away. The complicated eastern tableaus, the disturbing images of the handicapped and walking wounded negotiating city streets, and the women—always the women, personified by an image of a leggy West Coast woman with her long blond hair at play in the wind—all imply certain amounts of disengagement *and* attraction. The lady lioness on the street is presented from a distance because she was what he was not. That kind of shot makes him into what he was. The man disconnected at the same time and in the same ways as his culture disconnected.

Winogrand's images often show people together, but they are very different from Levitt's images. They ought to be relating, but instead a hyperindividuality is on display or a cultural subtext is working that undercuts connection. In the famous image of Muhammad Ali, the photojournalists gathered around him may or may not be smirking. The equally complicated shot of John F. Kennedy's acceptance speech at the 1960 Democratic National Convention shows Kennedy's (real) back and his face talking on a television screen facing the viewer. Winogrand's subjects are shot from a distance, not quite as we would like them to be, and it is not always easy to articulate why.

Winogrand is the master of the tilt. It is his angle. He takes a distance we call male but also modern. If irony is a survival tool in modernity, Winogrand deploys it again and again and shows communal life dissolved and the sense of common space scattered—suggesting it is unwise to believe.

Sally Mann's work has been as unsettling to many viewers as Garry Winogrand's.[69] At the same time, if his work is identified with a certain distance, critics and Mann herself use the word *intimacy* to describe her work. For example, Mann calls the large format landscapes she made of Georgia and Virginia a "record of intimacy and quietude." Lyle Rexer's review of her latest work is titled "Marriage under Glass: Intimate Exposures."

Mann's earlier images of young girls make people uncomfortable for reasons they can't always articulate. Sometimes this is expressed in general terms: it just doesn't seem right to photograph them "like that." Her photographs of her children evoke similar responses: "Are they really without clothes so often—where did those children get those poses, those faces that stare back?" On the one hand Mann has done little to reduce these worries. One could say that she plays on them. The text that accompanies her images of twelve-year-olds touches on the porousness of taboos in the lives of the (real) girls she photographed. The autobiographical notes published with images of her children chat on about growing up with sexual openness and rural purity. She repeats both in her public presentations. But in the end, naughty is not why her images are upsetting. Her positioning herself against bourgeois convention can be read as posturing. The voyage of the Sally Mann is about positioning herself in relationship to Art and being an Important Photographer.

But all this aside: she *is* an important photographer, one whose images are successful because they have the power of authentication that Barthes talks about, not because she has portrayed her children as free spirits with attitude. Furthermore, Mann's images are not rural images except in the literal sense. The subjects may live in rural settings, but the images depend on sensibilities that are thoroughly modern and thoroughly urban.

In this context the larger challenge her work presents is connected to the intimacy she and others see in it. She stands in a place that Winogrand was intuitively attuned to and mirrored as its other. Mann asserts a claim to the deeply feminine. Her images don't cover this up or veil it. They are built from a way of inhabiting the world that the culture as a whole leaves very little room for. The deeply feminine is so deeply unsettling in contemporary American culture because our way of life depends so much more on calculation than it does on immersion. Moderns have worked long and hard to keep the juices and connective tissues of life off-site. Happy or not, respectable or not, Mann's images testify to the trials of the deeply connected. It is entirely without accident that one of the exhibitions of her southern landscapes was called "Motherland." That is where she has always come from.

In the review mentioned above, Rexer gives us two insights into how Mann situates herself. Her husband of thirty years was diagnosed with muscular dystrophy in 1997, and the couple decided to document the progression of his illness. Also Mann chose not to exhibit or publish the series (images from the whole of her marriage). This is an expression of intimacy that deserves our deep respect. It also shows the contrast and similarities between her and Winogrand. He confronted his destiny by spinning out of control with his images, refusing with his unrestricted shooting to make them mean. She has settled in, joined with her world.

Simmel argues that the demands of the modern metropolis are numbing. Modern subjects must learn to shield themselves against the overestimation of city life and learn to live with instrumental, fleeting relations. At the same time, in order "to remain audible even to themselves," as Simmel puts it, they must find a way to shout.[70] Winogrand and Mann have both worked during the "culture wars," when gender was unraveling in public and the society then reacted by coming up male. The definition of male became enlarged enough to include some of the ladies interested in power dressing. Many of the rest became temporary hippies until the workplace reeled them in. The realignment of where and if and how to place desire is addressed in both Winogrand's and Mann's images. They don't resolve the problem, but they do show more clearly than much of the debate on the subject.

Acknowledging what I am calling the deeply feminine as one place in this world where meaning can play is too isolating and too costly most of the time. Winogrand could see it. The honesty with which he presented the alternatives that we allot ourselves is numbing. The claims of the deeply feminine that Mann makes are actually much stronger in exhibit than in book form. It is not because this is the challenging art of an important photographer—it is this only in a reductive sense. The gesture of real importance that Mann makes is to present the deeply feminine as part of existence.

Spaces of Indebtedness

It is often remarked of the inherent impossibility of rejecting modernity completely that eventually you will have to come to town. All of the photographers discussed above came to town in the sense that their work makes the sense it does in the context of particular unresolved dynamics of modernity. Their contribution has been to keep certain dilemmas unresolved while presenting aspects of American culture in ways that allow viewers to participate in negotiating them. That is the way the site of enunciation of this work is urban. Thus metaphorically we can say that the city is the occasion for engaging life, for shouting, as Cartier-Bresson put it. It is redundant but also right to return to the theme introduced earlier and to characterize this art as acts of love.

Understanding photography as active in this way moves away from the business of producing predictable statements. It is to sign on to the realm of what Foucault called "the event" and Lefebvre "the right to the city." In Foucault's reflections on his own work, he credits events with provoking reflection on the naturalization of sites from which we seek comfort and also from which we get the urge to move "out of site." Events are heterotopic situations as are moments. I suggested above that notions of "the event" and the category of "the moment" receive less attention in official Art circles than the power to shock. In this context it becomes a radical act to face the city without the prior commitment that literal shock is necessary or desirable and to live in the space made by the more fundamental tensions that construct modernity.

It is remarkable to note that more than fifty-five years after Benjamin's death and fifteen years after the English publication of *Camera Lucida*, the same terrain, that is, the distance between making images that present the known world and making images that require some renegotiation, is still the stage on which the photography plays. This issue is not about the power to shock literally but about the power to alter and hold open judgment to reach existence.

The January 1997 issue of *Artforum* contained examples of each approach. Alexander Alberro wrote about Roy Arden's color photographs of the cluttered, run-down, and generally unattractive aspects of Vancouver, British Columbia. His remarks evoke Photography as Art—as an official and formal practice that constructs its own context. He begins:

Arden's approach hovers somewhere between the pictorialism of early Modernists like Alfred Stieglitz and the more positivistic practices of documentary photographers like Walker Evans, who worked under the auspices of the Farm Security Administration. In the spirit of Evans (who appropriated the photojournalistic model to propose it as a new kind of art photography) and of photo Conceptualists such as Edward Ruscha, Dan Graham, and the Bechers, Arden gazes directly at his subjects. In his work optical conventions such as perspective are viewed not as a restrictive "norm" to be subverted with gimmickry and darkroom manipulations, but as the device for the construction of a rationalized vision. . . . At the same time these deadpan images . . . evoke the prephotographic or protophotographic tradition of "realist" painted representation. . . . Arden thus attempts to reclaim painting as a vehicle for serious historical, philosophical, and political expression, while giving it the documentary weight particular to the photographic.[71]

This is nothing if not the presentation of an original *studium*—which is to say, not very original at all. The domesticated spaces of Photography as Art lead. The challenge is that there is no challenge, only the potential that Arden's images are stronger than their press.

Another recent work, a book by the young British photographer Richard Billingham called *Ray's a Laugh*, introduces vastly unsettling spaces but also a different kind of challenge. Jim Lewis, writing again for *Artforum*, gives a sense of what that challenge is:

The book is a collection of photographs of the apartment in a lower-middle-class British housing project where his [the photographer's] parents live. His primary subject is his father, Ray, an everyday alcoholic who rarely leaves the house; instead he stays in and drinks home brew, puttering around while wearing a series of drunkard's expressions: delighted, dazed, about six inches short of dead. Aside from Ray there's a behemoth mother, a brother who comes and goes peripherally, a dog, and a cat.[72]

In other words, this book is a series of snapshots of an very unaesthetic group. Charles A. Hartman, writing in *See*, the journal of the Friends of Photography, essentially gave up after brief praise and concentrated on how wonderful and courageous the layout of the book is. After starting out to confront the material in *Ray's a Laugh*, he retreats into abstract categories: "The harsh color images, unadorned and uninterrupted, connect with viewers in myriad ways, and the book's format and design encourage individual experience. . . . That Billingham's monograph is made up solely of images may further signal a significant cultural movement, both forwards and backwards."[73]

In his review in *Artforum*, Lewis took a direct approach to the problem presented by Billingham's photographs. Like Barthes, many years before him, he works at resolving the issue of why these images move him as a viewer. In the case of *Ray's a Laugh* a literal answer to this question would be the power to shock. But just as Barthes's interpretation of the image that moves him only begins with its literal content, Lewis also goes further. His understanding of the problem brings together material conditions, photography as an instrument of engagement, and the compulsion to witness. After describing one of the more unsavory images in the book, Lewis asks why he finds Billingham's work so beautiful. His remarks deserve reproduction, both as an example of courageous writing and as a powerful expression of the reach of photography within and through modernity.

I've argued before, and will assert again here, that photography, more than other forms of image making, is a form of love: the photographer's love for the sitter, and the variations on attention it inspires. Because the photographer watches the way a lover watches, with a regard at once rapt, alert, fascinated, and ecstatic. I should say that by "lover" I don't mean, or don't necessarily mean, an erotic partner, or even a family member or close friend. My point is that photography is a form of devotion: we take pictures of the things we adore, and adore the things we take pictures of. I know I said that photography was exploitative: I don't think that's incompatible with what I'm saying now. What makes some photographs great is precisely the balance they strike between devouring their subject and adoring it, and the surprise they inspire at the idea that whatever they're picturing can bear the weight of just that contradiction.[74]

Lewis is making the same moves Foucault does in the beginning of *The Order of Things* when he uses Borges's Chinese encyclopedia to contemplate the implications of moving on and off the table at the same time. Both are articulations of spatial processes that use the material at hand to reach the unreachable. Lewis explains photography as a tool of life.

What moves Lewis about photography is similar to the redemptive search for infinity that Benjamin engages in, the way Barthes explores the depth of his feelings about the image that moved him, and the way Lefebvre searches the spatial practices of modernity for meaning. In a world dominated by instrumental reason and rigid moralities, an encounter with love makes as great a claim to the mantel of transgression as Sade's dungeons and Foucault's murderous peasants. In other words, I am suggesting that engagement and encounter are heterotopic situations, off-site in a world preoccupied with the anxieties of maintaining order. Lewis sees photography as one mode of testifying to the alternations that dwell among us.

To photograph the material of everyday life is to become an heir to the storyteller, infinitely productive, a faithful witness, bearing a happy responsibility for the spaces in which you find yourself.

Acknowledgments

This author exists because of ongoing support from many quarters. Dan Melnick, Tayyab Mahmud, and Rachel Carnell are my partners in reading and discussing theory every other Friday. They will recognize some great afternoons past and the extent to which they have contributed to what is developed in this text.

My seduction by photography would not have happened without the initiative and ongoing support of Masumi Hayashi. She is an artist of the possible. My teacher in photography has been Nat Eatman, production manager and chief photographer at Instructional Media Services, at Cleveland State University. One of the best things I learned from him was the joy of looking over contact sheets. I also spent a summer learning the nuts and bolts with Denis Breno. Workshops with Nathan Lyons and with Philip Brookman and Jim Goldberg were foundational to my explorations of the grammar of photographic sequencing.

The institutional support of the Levin College of Urban Affairs and of Larry Lederbur, associate dean of research, gave me the space in which to work. On several occasions Larry mentioned that he couldn't remember when I wasn't working on this project; I am grateful that he never let that bother him. Susan Petrone of the Urban Center was my software coach and local editor without peer.

David Perry of the Great Cities Institute listened with rare attention and offered critique that almost always led to refinement of my conceptualizations of the dynamics of urban life. Joe Fusco has been my collaborator on several projects, generously giving both muscle and insights into creative processes and the potential of public art.

In my role as case 8692029 I would like to acknowledge Paula at Apple Support. She and I were getting to be like family there for a while.

Carrie Mullen at the University of Minnesota Press has been the editor authors would like to invent. Her understanding and support have been major factors in keeping the show on the road during both the ups and the downs of working in two media at once.

This project is dedicated to Bri, Danny, and Joey-John, who in the time I worked on it became Brian, Dan, and Joe and then seriez@ . . . , retsnag@ . . . , and rabid_ jackalope@ . . .

Notes

Introduction

1. David Harvey credits Henri Lefebvre with conceptualizing this shift. See his afterword, in Henri Lefebvre, *The Production of Space* (Oxford: Basil Blackwell, 1991), 430–31. "But consideration of the urban question quickly led him to deny that the city was any kind of meaningful entity in modern life. It had been superseded by a process of urbanization or, more generally, of the production of space, that was binding together the centre and the periphery, in new and quite unfamiliar ways." See also the work of Manuel Castells and Paul Virilio, among others.

2. Walter Benjamin argued that authors/artists should use technological innovation against the forces of production and in the service of what he called "a revolutionary useful value." See Walter Benjamin, "The Author as Producer," in *Reflections: Essays, Aphorisms, Autobiographical Writings*, ed. Peter Demetz (New York: Harcourt Brace Jovanovich, 1978), 220–38, 230.

3. "Either ethics makes no sense at all, or this is what it means and has nothing else to say: not to be unworthy of what happens to us." Gilles Deleuze, *The Deleuze Reader*, ed. C. V. Boundas (New York: Columbia University Press, 1993), 78; quoted in Marcus A. Doel, "A Hundred Thousand Lines of Flight: A Machinic Introduction to the Nomad Thought and Scrumpled Geography of Gilles Deleuze and Félix Guattari," *Environment and Planning D: Society and Space* 14 (1996): 421–39, 432.

4. One morning, after working on this project for over two years, I read: "While taking part in a radio programme dedicated to his exhibition at the Grand Palais in 1970, Cartier-Bresson economically defined photojournalism as 'a means of testifying' and became annoyed when invited to discuss his oeuvre, taking advantage of the transmission to launch an appeal to the public, asking them to campaign in order to save four journalists, including Gilles Caron, whose whereabouts were unknown at the time." Jean-Pierre Montier, photographs by Henri Cartier-Bresson, *Henri Cartier-Bresson and the Artless Art* (Boston: Little, Brown, 1996), 164. I decided not to mind about not being entirely original.

Urban

1. Harry and David's *Best Price Sale Catalog* (January–March 1996), 5.

2. Ibid., 5.

3. This notion of relays is derived from a discussion between Michel Foucault and Gilles Deleuze, reprinted as "Intellectuals and Power" in Michel Foucault, *Language, Counter-Memory, Practice: Selected Essays and Interviews*, ed. Donald F. Bouchard (Ithaca: Cornell University Press, 1977), 205–17.

4. For a discussion of the politics of presentation of public issues see Helen Liggett, "The Play of Approved Method and Authorized Value in the Administration of Public Issues," *International Journal of Public Administration* 20, no. 11 (1997): 1955–78.

5. See, for example, Elvin D. Wyly, Norman J. Glickman, and Michael L. Lahr, "Top 10 List of Things to Know about American Cities" (7–23); and Michael B. Teitz and Karen Chapple, "The Causes of Inner-City Poverty: Eight Hypotheses in Search of Reality" (33–70); both in *Cityscape* 3, no. 3 (1998). *Cityscape*, a journal of policy development and research, was published by the U.S. Department of Housing and Urban Development during the Clinton administration. It contains the work of leading urbanists and is distributed to scholars and policy makers.

6. Witold Rybczynski, *City Life* (New York: Scribner's, 1995), 112.

7. Ibid., 114.

8. See also chapter 3, "Home, Sweet Home: The House and the Yard," in Kenneth Jackson, *Crabgrass Frontier: The Suburbanization of the United States* (Oxford: Oxford University Press 1985), 45–72, especially 68–72; and chapter 1, "Themes and Texts," in Robert Beauregard, *Voices of Decline: The Postwar Fate of U.S. Cities* (Oxford: Basil Blackwell, 1993), 3–33. See pages 13–17 for discussions of some of the early sources of antiurban biases in American cities.

9. Rybczynski, *City Life*, 82.

10. "The true issue is not to make beautiful cities or well-managed cities, it is to make a *work of life*. The rest is by-product." Raymond Ledrut, "Speech and the Silence of the City," in *The City and the Sign: An Introduction of Urban Semiotics*, ed. Mark Gottdiener and Alexandros Ph. Lagopoulos (New York: Columbia University Press, 1986), 114–33, 133.

11. The phrase "making space" is David Perry's. See his "Making Space: Planning as a Mode of Thought," in *Spatial Practices: Critical Explorations in Social/Spatial Theory*, ed. Helen Liggett and David Perry (Thousand Oaks, Calif.: Sage Publications, 1995), 209–42.

12. Thomas Bier, Charlie Post, and Winifred Weizer, *Tax Base Disparity: Development of Greater Cleveland's Sapphire Necklace*, Urban Center, Levin College of Urban Affairs, Cleveland State University, 5 December 1997.

13. Ibid., 1.

14. Cleveland shares this geography and this conventional figuration with Chicago, which is situated on another of the Great Lakes and is the home base of mainstream urban theory.

15. Aid to Dependent Children has been replaced in Ohio by Ohio Works First.

16. For the quoted suggestion, see Bier, Post, and Weizer, *Tax Base Disparity*, 23.

17. See Janet L. Smith, "Interpreting Neighborhood Change" (Ph.D. dissertation in Urban Studies, Cleveland State University, 1998) for a genealogy of traditional theories of neighborhood change, including notions of invasion-succession, filtering, life-cycle models, racial tipping, and gentrification and revitalization. Smith is particularly concerned with linking the Chicago School to American cultural preferences for social and spatial segregation and in showing how this logic has continued to influence subsequent conceptualizations of neighborhood space.

18. Beauregard, *Voices of Decline*, xi. I've added the word *American* because, as will be clear below, European and South American urban theorists do study representation.

19. The main resource for Beauregard's sources was *The Reader's Guide to Periodical Literature*. He "selected any title that suggested a general discussion of urban decline." See chapter 14, "Methodological Note," in *Voices of Decline* for further details (331).

20. Ibid., 5.

21. However, as Beauregard points out, any periodization of cities, including the one used in his research, blurs upon closer examination; thus his presentation is not strictly chronological. Ibid.

22. Ibid., 17.

23. The movie *Avalon* (dir. Barry Levinson, 1990), about a Jewish family being transformed from an inner-city extended immigrant family to a number of suburban nuclear families during the boom period after the Second World War, is one of the best portrayals of what "moving to the suburbs" meant in terms of life as lived.

24. For further discussion of the influence of notions of the urban and antiurbanism on contemporary spatial patterns in America, see Judith DeNeufville and Stephen E. Barton, "Myths and the Definition of Policy Problems," *Policy Sciences* 08-09-87 (1987): 1–25; Kenneth T. Jackson, *Crabgrass Frontier* (New York: Oxford University Press, 1985); and Neil Smith, "The Ideology of Nature," chapter 1 in *Uneven Development: Nature, Capital, and the Production of Space* (Oxford: Basil Blackwell, 1991), 1–31. For two primary sources in architecture and planning, see the various writings of Frank Lloyd Wright and Lewis Mumford.

25. Beauregard, *Voices of Decline*, 290. Further, as in most discussion of poverty, notions of poverty among rural, white, elderly, and the disabled take a back seat to the urban stereotype oriented towards race.

26. Robert A. Beauregard, "If Only the City Could Speak: The Politics of Representation," in *Spatial Practices*, ed. Liggett and Perry, 59–80.

27. P. Stallybrass and A. White, *The Poetics and Politics of Transgression* (London: Methuen, 1986), 5.

28. Beauregard, *Voices of Decline*, 282.

29. Robert Dahl's *Who Governs?* (New Haven: Yale University Press, 1961) was a primary text in the community power debate. It was also the basis for the development of an empirically based democratic theory. Dahl studied the decision-making activities of Mayor Lee during the implementation of urban renewal in New Haven.

30. Urbanists in this country participate in the tendency in American culture to disregard the existence of the whole rest of the world in every topic except food and fashion. *Voices of Decline* reflects the same tendency as in the popular literature, thus identifying northeastern industrial cities with cities in general. The different political, symbolic, and spatial economies of southern and western cities in this country are not considered.

31. M. Christine Boyer, *The City of Collective Memory: Its Historical Imagery and Architectural Entertainments* (Cambridge, Mass.: MIT Press, 1994).

32. Ibid., 411.

33. Steven Marcus, "Reading the Illegible," in *The Victorian City Images and Realities*, vol. 1, ed. H. J. Dyos and M. Wolff (London: Routledge and Kegan Paul, 1973), 257–76.

34. Ibid., 258.

35. Ibid., 268.

36. Ibid., 268–69.

37. Ibid., 269.

38. Ibid., 257.

39. Boyer, *The City of Collective Memory*, 151.

40. Ibid., 173.

41. Ibid., 159.

42. Ibid., 163.

43. Ibid., 169.

44. Mark Wigley discusses the reversal of decoration and structure in his essay "Untitled: The Housing of Gender," in *Sexuality and Space*, ed. Beatriz Colomina (Princeton, N.J.: Princeton Papers in Architecture, 1992), 327–89, 366.

45. Boyer, *The City of Collective Memory*, 138.

46. Ibid., 138.

47. See M. Christine Boyer, "The Great Frame-up: Fantastic Appearances in Contemporary Spatial Politics," in *Spatial Practices*, ed. Liggett and Perry, 81–109.

48. Boyer, *The City of Collective Memory*, 426.

49. Ibid., 436.

50. Ibid., 440.

51. Ibid., 464.

52. Ibid., 411.

53. Ibid., 476.

54. William Menking, "Elected by the Property Owners: Redefining City Government in Mid-Town Manhattan," in *Strangely Familiar: Narratives of Architecture in the City*, ed. Iain Borden, Joe Kerr, Alicia Pivaro, and Jane Rendell (London: Routledge, 1996), 67–71.

55. Boyer, *City of Collective Memory*, 484–85.

56. As discussed in "Space" (the next section of this book), Lefebvre conceptualizes space in terms of its porousness. This makes a parallel point.

57. See Michel Foucault's discussion of rules of formation in *The Archaeology of Knowledge* (reprint; New York: Harper and Row, 1972).

58. Néstor García Canclini, "Hybrid Cultures, Oblique Powers," in his *Hybrid Cultures: Strategies for Entering and Leaving Modernity* (Minneapolis: University of Minnesota Press, 1995), 207–63.

59. Ibid., 231–32.

60. García Canclini interviewed residents and asked them to respond to photographs, telling him which ones best represented Tijuana. He reviewed popular arts such as graffiti and comics and talked with artists and publishers. Ibid.

61. Ibid., 236.

62. Ibid., 261.

63. See Foucault, *Archaeology of Knowledge*.

64. García Canclini, "Hybrid Cultures, Oblique Powers," 237.

65. Michel Foucault, *The Order of Things* (New York: Random House 1973), xv–xxiv. This is discussed in the following section.

66. García Canclini, "Hybrid Cultures, Oblique Powers," 212.

67. García Canclini uses documentation of monuments in Mexico assembled by Paolo Gori and Helen Escobedo. Ibid.

68. Ibid., 214.

69. Ibid., 219.

70. Ibid., 222.

71. For examples of the recoding of public monuments that is explicitly concerned with using monuments to challenge the political economy of neglect, see Rosalyn Deutsche, "Krzysztof Wodiczko's *Homeless Projection* and the Site of Urban 'Revitalization,'" in *Evictions: Art and Spatial Politics* (Cambridge, Mass.: MIT Press, 1996), 3–48. Wodiczko projected symbols and materials used by homeless people onto the statues of well-known (mostly military) heroes in New York City.

72. What Foucault calls "aesthetics of existence" is embedded in his discussion of memory and experience as components of spatial processes and in his working out of possible relations between subjects and the social order. Rajchman suggests that this issue was the driving force in Foucault's work. John Rajchman, "Foucault's Art of Seeing," in *Philosophical Events: Essays of the '80's* (New York: Columbia University Press, 1991), 68–102.

Space

1. See Susan Buck-Morss, "Aesthetics and Anaesthetics: Walter Benjamin's Artwork Essay Reconsider," *October* 62 (fall 1992): 3–41. She suggests Benjamin means "aesthetics" to represent the kind of interface with the world that is tied to all the senses (wherever the body and the world meet). This is opposed to the more familiar notions of aesthetics that remove "art" from the materiality of the world. "Life as a work of art" is the title of an interview with Gilles Deleuze about Foucault's thought and Deleuze's book *Foucault*. Gilles Deleuze, *Negotiations, 1972–1990*, trans. Martin Joughin (New York: Columbia University Press, 1995), 94–101.

2. Michel de Certeau, "Story Time," chapter 6 in *The Practice of Everyday Life*, trans. Steven F. Rendall (reprint; Berkeley: University of California Press, 1988), 77–90, 82. See especially the section titled "The Art of Memory and Circumstances."

3. Michel Foucault, *Remarks on Marx: Conversations with Duccio Trombadori* (New York: Semiotext(e), 1991), 33.

4. On Foucault's writing as rhetorical, see Michel de Certeau, "The Arts of Theory," chapter 5 in *The Practice of Everyday Life*, 61–76. On Foucault's writing as visual, see John Rajchman, "Foucault's Art of Seeing," chapter 4 in *Philosophical Events*, 68–102. Also see Gilles Deleuze, *Foucault* (Minneapolis: University of Minnesota Press, 1986).

5. For a systematic spatial explication of Foucault's work that places it in the context of political theory's concern with freedom, see Tom Dumm's *Michel Foucault and the Politics of Freedom* (Thousand Oaks, Calif.: Sage Publications, 1996).

6. Foucault, *Remarks on Marx*, 33. In a similar vein Roland Barthes remarks that "language is, by nature, fictional," in *Camera Lucida: Reflections on Photography* (New York: Hill and Wang, 1981), 87.

7. Deleuze, *Foucault*.

8. Walter Benjamin, "On Some Motifs in Baudelaire," in *Illuminations*, ed. Hannah Arendt (New York: Schocken Books, 1978), 155–65.

9. Roger J. Steiner, *The New College French and English Dictionary* (New York: Bantam Books, 1980), 226.

10. See the introduction to Michel Foucault, *Herculine Barbin, Being the Recently Discovered Memoirs of a Nineteenth Century French Hermaphrodite* (New York: Pantheon Books, 1980), vii–xvii.

11. Foucault, *The Order of Things*, xv.

12. Ibid., xvii.

13. Ibid.

14. Notable exceptions include Michael J. Shapiro, "Spatiality and Policy Discourse: Reading the Global City," in *Reading the Postmodern Polity* (Minneapolis: University of Minnesota Press, 1992); Dumm, *Michel Foucault and the Politics of Freedom.*

15. Michel Foucault, "Of Other Spaces," *Diacritics* (spring 1986): 22–27, 23.

16. Deleuze, *Foucault*, beginning on page 31 and as a continuing theme.

17. Adapted from the lyrics to the Leonard Cohen song "Anthem," on *The Future* (New York: Columbia Records, 1992): "Forget your perfect offering. There is a crack in everything. That's how the light gets in."

18. Foucault, *The Order of Things*, xviii.

19. Ibid., xvii.

20. Foucault, "Of Other Spaces," 24.

21. Ibid., 25.

22. "Cases of this are rest homes and psychiatric hospitals, and of course prisons, and one should perhaps add retirement homes that are, as it were, on the borderline between the heterotopia of crisis and the heterotopia of deviation since, after all, old age is a crisis, but is also a deviation since, in our society where leisure is the rule, idleness is a sort of deviation." Ibid., 25.

23. These are institutions Foucault also sees as spaces of deviation and, in the case of prisons, a kind of model space for understanding what he calls "the disciplinary society." See Michel Foucault, *Discipline and Punish: The Birth of the Prison* (New York: Pantheon Books, 1977).

24. I do not mean that the world would not be a better place if emotional ties and loving support were valued more highly. Just that in this particular world there often doesn't seem to be time for these things.

25. Foucault, "Of Other Spaces," 27.

26. Deleuze, *Foucault*, 49–50.

27. Foucault, "Of Other Spaces," 27.

28. Mary Douglas, "The Abominations of Leviticus," chapter 3 in *Purity and Danger* (London: Routledge, 1966), 41–57.

29. Quoted in Douglas, *Purity and Danger*, 42–43.

30. Ibid., 44.

31. Ibid., 48.

32. Ibid., 48.

33. Ibid., 47, 48.

34. Ibid., 50.

35. Ibid., 56.

36. "'A polluting person is always in the wrong." Someone who cannot claim to be blessed endangers the world and everyone in it. Ibid., 113.

37. Winner of the National Book Award for nonfiction in 1998, Edward Ball, *Slaves in the Family* (New York: Farrar, Straus and Giroux, 1998).

38. See Elizabeth D. McCausland, "Dirty Little Secrets: Realism and the Real in Victorian Industrial Novels," *American Journal of Semiotics* 9, nos. 2–3 (1992): 149–65, for an analysis of how representations of the urban poor in novels function as a middle-class project. She examines the use of symbolism around transgression and partial lives.

39. John Locke, *Two Treatises of Government*, edited with an introduction and notes

by Peter Laslett (Cambridge: Cambridge University Press, 1960), 269–70; emphasis is in the original.

40. Locke, *Two Treatises*, 289.

41. See Houston Baker Jr., "Critical Memory and the Black Public Sphere," *Public Culture* 7, no. 1 (fall 1994): 3–34.

42. A phrase he repeated in his withdrawal speech, 9 March 2000.

43. Joe Klein, "The Campaign: Authentic Is Out and the Race Will Only Get Uglier," *New Yorker*, 20 March 2000, 50. But of course this was only the beginning.

44. A strong example of Foucauldian analysis as discourse analysis occurs in Bellingham and Mathis's careful study of southern midwifery, in which the authors show a connection between the social construction of race and the institutionalization of a national health-care bureaucracy. In their analysis the "southern midwife" is more a creation of changes in the administration of public health than the systematization of a "native" form. Bruce Bellingham and Mary Pugh Mathis, "Race, Citizenship and the Biopolitics of the Maternalist Welfare State: Cultural and Political Economic Analysis of the Sheppard-Towner Act the 'Traditional Midwifery in the South,'" paper presented at the 10th Anniversary Conference of Theory, Culture, and Society, 16–19 August 1992, Champion, Pa.

45. Rachel Carnel has shown me several examples where the French of Foucault's work is more open and less static than the English translation. In *Birth of a Clinic*, for example, terms we identify with empirical research appear frequently. *Jeu* (play), which is used in the French phrase meaning "put into play," is rendered in the English as *system*. Michel Foucault, *Birth of a Clinic: An Archaeology of Medical Perception* (New York: Random House, 1975).

46. Foucault, *The Archaeology of Knowledge*; and Rajchman, *Philosophical Events*.

47. Habermas as a silent partner can provide the basis for political activism, particularly in a political culture such as ours, which is rooted in the ideal of a universal rationality and citizen rule. See, for example, Baker Jr., "Critical Memory and the Black Public Sphere." Baker shows how the idea of a public sphere played a role in the tactics of Martin Luther King Jr. in building one.

48. Rajchman, "Foucault's Art of Seeing," 69.

49. Ibid., 70.

50. John Rajchman, "What's New in Architecture?" chapter 8 in *Philosophical Events*, 152–63.

51. Jacques Derrida and Peter Eisenman, *Chora L Works*, ed. Jeffrey Kepnis and Thomas Leeser (New York: Monacelli Press, 1996); Ernest Pascussi, "Review of *Chora L Works*," *Bookforum* (winter 1996/spring 1997): 22–23.

52. Pascucci, "Review of *Chora L Works*," 22–23.

53. Rajchman, "Foucault's Art of Seeing," 73.

54. Ibid., 85.

55. Ibid., 93.

56. Ibid., 97. Rajchman is quoting David Hoy, ed., *A Critical Reader* (London: Basil Blackwell, 1986), 46.

57. See John Friedman and Clyde Weaver's classic study of how hope for American regional planning was transformed into river-basin planning based on a single urban industrial model of development during the 1930s. *Territory and Function: The Evolution of Regional Planning* (Berkeley: University of California Press, 1979). As mentioned above in connection with Tom Bier's work, promoting regional governance is a current movement in urban policy circles. In addition, there is ongoing debate about how to characterize the relationship among central cities and suburbs in regional urban processes.

58. "Arenas of social activity" is a modification of the phrase Allucquere Stone uses to introduce the notion that cyberspace not only expands the tools available in the society but also differs in kind from older self-contained computers. "They view computers not only as tools but also as arenas for social experience." *The War of Desire and Technology at the Close of the Mechanical Age* (Cambridge, Mass.: MIT Press, 1995), 15.

59. Michel de Certeau, "Spatial Stories," chapter 9 in *The Practice of Everyday Life*, 130.

60. Other discussions of *Las Meninas* are legion. A few useful to the present discussion include the Museo del Prado Web site; W. J. T. Mitchell, *Picture Theory: Essays on Verbal and Visual Representation* (Chicago: University of Chicago Press, 1994); Hubert L. Dreyfus and Paul Rabinow, *Michel Foucault: Beyond Structuralism and Hermeneutics* (Chicago: University of Chicago Press, 1983); and Gary Gutting, *Michel Foucault's Archaeology of Scientific Reason* (Cambridge: Cambridge University Press, 1989). The last three concentrate on Foucault's commentary as a representation of classical representation. They do not dwell on how he makes that presentation. The Museo del Prado's remarks are somewhat more informative about space. Among other things they praise the painting's "remarkable treatment of spatial perspective. Velázquez, like no other, knew how to capture atmosphere, the air itself in a sense, between figures and, above all, between the foreground and the background. In this way he was able to create the illusion of the space in his studio." That is akin to how Foucault makes space that illuminates the illusions that run lives in modernity.

61. Michel Foucault, *Les Mots et les choses* (Paris: Gallimard, 1990).

62. Foucault, *The Order of Things*, 9. Rachel Carnell pointed out to me (in conversation) that the French wording for "sequential elements of syntax" can also be translated as "succession of syntax," which goes nicely with the image of royal succession.

63. Dreyfus and Rabinow, *Michel Foucault*, 72.

64. "Like a donor in prayer, like an angel greeting the Virgin, a maid of honor on her knees is stretching out her hands towards the princess." This is to emphasize the Infanta Margarita, who at one level is "the very object of the painting." Foucault, *The Order of Things*, 12.

65. Ibid., 12–13.

66. Ibid., 13.

67. I am grateful to Joe Fusco for discussions of this aspect of *Las Meninas*.

68. Foucault, *The Order of Things*, 4–5; emphasis added.

69. W. J. T. Mitchell, *Picture Theory: Essays on Verbal and Visual Representation* (Chicago: University of Chicago Press, 1994), 62.

70. Foucault, *The Order of Things*, 95.

71. Ibid., 116.

72. Ibid., 117.

73. Ibid., 118.

74. Ibid., 120.

75. W. E. B. Du Bois, "Of the Sorrow Songs," in *The Souls of Black Folks* (New York: Vintage Books, 1990), 164–73, 166.

76. Du Bois "Of the Sorrow Songs," 168.

77. As Michel de Certeau puts it: ". . . because there corresponds to the constitution of a scientific space, the precondition of any analysis, the necessity of being able to transfer the objects of study into it. Only what can be transported can be treated. What cannot be uprooted remains by definition outside the field of research." From "Popular Culture: Ordinary Language," chapter 2 in *The Practice of Everyday Life*, 15–28, 20.

78. Du Bois, "Of the Sorrow Songs," 172–73.

79. Ibid., 173.

80. De Certeau, "Spatial Stories," 115–30.

81. Michel Foucault, ed., *I, Pierre Rivière, having slaughtered my mother, my sister, and my brother . . . : A Case of Parricide in the 19th Century* (New York: Pantheon Books, 1974).

82. Foucault, *I, Pierre Rivière*, 183.

83. "Their acts were discourses." Ibid., 183.

84. An exhibit at the Jacobs Gallery in Eugene, Oregon, a year after the event maintained this openness to an admirable degree. It was called "Life out of Balance."

85. Foucault, *The Order of Things*, 346–47.

86. Ibid., 353.

87. Ibid., 366.

88. Ibid., 364.

89. Michel de Certeau, "The Black Sun of Language," chapter 12 in *Heterologies: Discourse on the Other* (Minneapolis: University of Minnesota Press, 1986), 171–84.

City

1. The distinction is sometimes made between Foucault's "early" and "late" work. But his writing on systems of thought, his political activism, and the attention he gave near the end of his life to "the care of the self" can be seen as interwoven—questions about experience and involvement in the spaces in which we find ourselves.

2. This should include the technologies of war and their effects on cities.

3. In addition there has been a lag in translation, so that much of his writing has been available only to French readers until recently.

4. Consider, for example, the work of Bernard Tschumi, especially his development of *Event-Cities* (Cambridge, Mass.: MIT Press, 1994), or Herbert Muschamp's architectural commentary in the *New Yorker* and the *New York Times* for explicit commitments to urban life and the promise of the city. "The New Urbanism" is somewhat problematic in the context of the city, because its projects are at a "village" scale and are primarily residential settlements, but they too articulate a preference for urban life.

5. Henri Lefebvre was born in 1901. There is much debate about when modernity begins. See Raymond Williams for an explanation of why the beginning of the twentieth century is so often used, although he feels that it makes more sense to connect modernity to industrialization in England and Europe in the middle decades of the nineteenth century. Raymond Williams, *The Politics of Modernity* (London: Verso, 1989).

6. Two sources that put Lefebvre in the context of this time include: Eleonore Kofman and Elizabeth Lebas, "Lost in Transposition—Time, Space and the City," ed. Eleonore Kofman and Elizabeth Lebas, *Writings on Cities: Henri Lefebvre* (Oxford: Basil Blackwell, 1996), 3–60; David Harvey, afterword, in Henri Lefebvre, *The Production of Space* (Oxford: Basil Blackwell, 1991), 425–34. See also *October* 79, a special issue on Guy Debord; and the *International Situationniste* (winter 1997).

7. Lefebvre, *The Production of Space*, 25.

8. Ibid., 174.

9. Michael J. Shapiro, "The Political Rhetoric of Photography," in *The Politics of Representation* (Madison: University of Wisconsin Press, 1988), 124–78.

10. My interpretation differs slightly from that of Rob Shields, who says, "Lefebvre's real object of study is the process of the production of cultural notions and practices of space (i.e. the process of social spatialization), not space itself." Rob Shields, *Places on the Margin* (London: Routledge, 1991), 56.

11. This recalls Heidegger's sense of the spatial.

12. Deborah Bright, "Of Mother Nature and Marlboro Men: An Inquiry into the Cultural Meanings of Landscape Photography," in *The Contest of Meaning: Critical Histories of Photography* (Cambridge, Mass.: MIT Press, 1992), 128.

13. Lefebvre is not well served by interpretations of his work that oppose space to time as if this were similar to the opposition between diachronic and synchronic approaches in linguistics. Since space needs activity, time is necessarily involved. Lefebvre uses space to understand time and vice versa. In his thought, space is layered, carrying memory into contemporary life. Edward Soja, *Postmodern Geographies: The Reassertion of Space in Critical Social Theory* (London: Verso, 1989).

14. For further discussion, see Helen Liggett and David Perry, "Spatial Practices: An Introduction"; and Helen Liggett, "City Sights/Sites of Memories and Dreams"; both in *Spatial Practices*, ed. Liggett and Perry, 1–12, 243–73, respectively.

15. Lefebvre, *The Production of Space*, 33.

16. De Certeau builds a similar category system. He promotes the participatory potential of "operations of everyday life," which include both spatial practices and spaces of representation. De Certeau, *The Practice of Everyday Life*.

17. This is not my good idea. It was suggested during a special on hip-hop on *NewsHour with Jim Lehrer*, 24 February 1999.

18. John Allen and Michael Pryke, "The Production of Service Space," *Environment and Planning D: Society and Space* 12 (1994): 453–75.

19. See, for example, Raphael Fischler's analysis of how neighborhood planning in Boston was defined in terms of economic development. He illuminates how, by using both visual and textual codes, problems are constructed and solved within the discursive conventions of professional planning. Raphael Fischler, "Strategy and History in Professional Practice: Planning as World Making," in *Spatial Practices*, ed. Liggett and Perry, 13–58.

20. See, for example, "Robert Moses at Work: City Building and the Master Builder," in *Geography and Identity: Living and Exploring Geopolitics of Identity*, ed. Dennis Crow (Washington, D.C.: Maisonneuve Press, 1996), 193–210.

21. For further discussion of this case and of spatial analysis of city events using Lefebvre's three modes of assembly, see Liggett, "City Sights/Sites of Memories and Dreams," 243–73.

22. In Henri Lefebvre, "Notes Written One Sunday in the French Countryside," in *Critique of Everyday Life*, vol. 1 (London: Verso, 1991), 205–27.

23. Lefebvre says in "Notes Written One Sunday": "The 'pure' nature that some writers applaud is in fact this peasant life at a highly evolved state, and in point of fact at only very rare moments and places in history has it achieved a successful, happy, balanced form" (207). For a contemporary example, see Elizabeth Royte, photographs by Reza, "The Outcasts," *New York Times Magazine*, 19 January 1997, 37: "Among Rwanda's living, no one is more shunned than a Tutsi woman who has been raped by the enemy." As Lefebvre himself puts it: "In most cases, the continuation of a nomadic, bellicose way of life, or poor soil, or a bad climate, or furthermore, and especially, social crises and rapid formation of brutally dominant castes, have dragged social life down dead ends, nearly always precipitating its decline" ("Notes Written One Sunday," 207).

24. Lefebvre, "Notes Written One Sunday," 209.

25. Lefebvre, "Theses on the City," in *Writings on Cities*, 177–81, 179. This piece was written in 1967, which, as Lefebvre notes, was the "centenary of Capital" (181).

26. Harvey, Afterword, in Lefebvre, *The Production of Space*, 431.

27. Ibid., 429.

28. Lefebvre, "Notes Written One Sunday," 227.

29. The term *consumer society* originated with Lefebvre.

30. I've paraphrased this notion of engagement from Angela Miller. She argues from art that seeks not "to transcend history, but to engage it in a deep way" in a letter to the editor of *Art in America.* The purpose of the letter was to praise Peter Balakian's interpretation of Arshile Gorky's painting. "Such readings do full justice to the proposition that art does not transcend history but engages it on the deepest level." Balakian's article shows how Gorky's most famous paintings are not just part of the movement towards abstract expressionism in modern art but are connected to his own and his family's persecution as Armenians by the Turks in the late nineteenth and early twentieth centuries. Balakian's position is that the lionization of Gorky as an abstract painter misses seeing how "collective family sorrow" shaped him and his work. Angela Miller, "Arshile Gorky and the Armenian Genocide," *Art in America* (February 1996): 58–67, 108–9, 62.

31. See, for example, Cleveland City Planning Commission, *Cleveland Civic Vision 2000: Citywide Plan* (Cleveland: Cleveland City Planning Commission, 1991).

32. Jonathan Culler, "The Semiotics of Tourism," chapter 9 in *Framing the Sign: Criticism and Its Institutions* (Norman: University of Oklahoma Press, 1988), 153–67, 155.

33. Ibid., 148, 149. At the end of *The Order of Things*, Foucault presents "man" as a temporal construction. His analysis of the human sciences is illustrative. They construct "man" (as we understand him to be) at the center, but "the order of things" could and has been differently organized.

34. Fyodor Dostoevsky, *Crime and Punishment*, trans. Richard Pevear and Larissa Volokhonshy (New York: Random House, 1993).

35. Lefebvre, *The Production of Space*, 174.

36. Ibid., 423.

37. Lefebvre, "The Right to the City," 158, 150.

38. See M. Christine Boyer, "The Art of Collective Memory," chapter 4 in *The City of Collective Memory*, 129–201.

39. Karl Marx, "Critique of the Hegelian Dialectic and Philosophy as a Whole," in *Economic and Philosophic Manuscripts of 1844*, reprinted in *The Marx Engels Reader*, ed. Robert C. Tucker (New York: W. W. Norton, 1978), 106–25, 125.

40. Ibid., 119.

41. Ibid., 120–21.

42. Ibid., 121.

43. Jacques Derrida, *Specters of Marx: The State of the Debt, the Work of Mourning and the New International* (London: Routledge, 1994), 91.

44. Ibid.

45. Ibid.

46. Walter Benjamin, "On the Program of the Coming Philosophy," in *Walter Benjamin: Selected Writings*, vol. 1: *1913–1926*, ed. Marcus Bullock and Michael W. Jennings (Cambridge, Mass.: Harvard University Press, 1996), 100–110.

47. Walter Benjamin, "Theses on the Philosophy of History," in *Illuminations*, ed. Arendt, 253–64, 254.

48. Ibid., 255.

49. Ibid., 256.

50. Ibid., 262.

51. Karl Marx, "The Power of Money in Bourgeois Society," in *Economic and Philosophic Manuscripts of 1844*, reprinted in *The Marx Engels Reader*, ed. Robert C. Tucker (New York: W. W. Norton, 1978), 101–5, 105.

52. The late mayor Harold Washington of Chicago is particularly outstanding in this regard because of how he fought against policies that were purely accumulative.

53. Marx, "The Power of Money in Bourgeois Society," 105.

54. Ibid., 105.

55. Victor Burgin, "The City in Pieces," in *Different Spaces: Places and Memory in Visual Culture* (Berkeley: University of California Press, 1996), 139–58.

56. For Henri Lefebvre, as discussed below, space itself is porous. Much of our societal energy is devoted to making it possible to assume otherwise. See chapter 3, "Spatial Architectonics," in *The Production of Space*. Chambers's photo-text essay appears in "Naples: The Emergent Archaic," in *Strangely Familiar: Narratives of Architecture in the City*, ed. Iain Borden, Joe Kerr, Alicia Pivaro, and Jane Rendell (London: Routledge, 1996), 56.

57. Susan Buck-Morss, *The Dialectics of Seeing: Walter Benjamin and the Arcades Project* (Cambridge, Mass.: MIT Press, 1989), 27.

58. Ibid., 27.

59. Ibid., 27; emphasis added.

60. Leo Charney and Vanessa R. Schwarts, eds., *Cinema and the Invention of Modern Life* (Berkeley: University of California Press, 1995), 288.

61. Michael Taussig, *Mimesis and Alterity: A Particular History of the Senses* (London: Routledge, 1993).

62. Victor Burgin, *Some Cities* (Berkeley: University of California Press, 1996).

63. Walter Benjamin, "The Currently Effective Messianic Elements," in *Walter Benjamin: Selected Writings*, vol. I, 213.

64. Recent summer fashions have decreed a certain amount of unclothing in public for women, similar to what has always been the norm in tropical areas such as Hawaii. However, these fashions look like underwear, prompting a great deal of commentary of the predictable sort. Feminist: Women have a right to wear what they want. Psycho-economic: The hemlines are short; the economy will continue to be good. Political theory: At the same time as the United States and Germany are getting involved in custody suits, and intimate conversation is taking place on the street and everywhere else on cell phones, wearing slips in public is an indicator of the reorientation of public and private space. On the street: Such fashion provides opportunities for giving and receiving pleasure.

65. Benjamin as discussed in chapter 4, "Mythic History: Fetish," in Buck-Morss, *The Dialectics of Seeing*, 78–109. See also Marc Shell's interpretation of *The Merchant of Venice* as an overlapping series of economic and domestic presentations around problems of generation. Marc Shell, "The Whether and the Ewe: Verbal Usury in *The Merchant of Venice*," in *Money, Language, and Thought: Literary and Philosophical Economies from the Medieval to Modern Era* (Berkeley: University of California Press, 1982), 47–83.

66. This is complicated by the fact that mannequins are neither exactly inanimate nor real. Friends of mine who worked in display tell stories about this uncanny quality. For example, they may have a favorite mannequin who has a name and whom they treat in special ways. And it is distressing to see mannequin parts. See also Sara K. Schneider, *Vital Mummies/Performance Design for the Show-Window Mannequin* (New Haven: Yale University Press, 1995).

67. Georg Simmel, "The Metropolis and Modern Life," reprinted in *Metropolis: Center and Symbol of Our Times*, ed. Philip Kasinitz (New York: New York University Press, 1995), 30–45, 45.

68. Walter Benjamin, "Construction Site," in *One Way Street*, in *Walter Benjamin: Selected Writings*, vol. I, 449–50.

69. Look at the format of *One Way Street*, 444–88.

70. As far as I know the perfect phrase "literary snapshots" was invented by Anmarie McDonald. See "An African Glance: Penned Photographs from Zimbabwe," master's project, Department of Urban Studies, Cleveland State University, spring 1999.

71. Gilles Deleuze, *Negotiations* (New York: Columbia University Press, 1995).

72. Ibid., 44.

73. Edward Said, *Orientalism* (New York: Random House, 1979), 3.

74. Ibid., 247. The absence of the Oriental except in the colonializers' term is a point that postcolonial theorists such as Homi Bhabha pay particular attention to. See, for example, Homi Bhabha, "Signs Taken for Wonders: Questions of Ambivalence and Authority under a Tree Outside Deli, May 1817," in *The Location of Culture* (London: Routledge, 1994), 103, in which Homi Bhabha explores "the sudden fortuitous discovery of the English book," that is, a gift of the Bible. It is telling that he titles the essay spatially. The reader can easily formulate an image of the discussion to which he refers (men gathered under a large banyan tree). For the ambiguous positions of current writers, see Amitav Ghosh's *In an Antique Land* (New York: Vintage, 1994); and Ghosh's reflections on the role of the Indian intellectual in "The Ghosts of Mrs. Gandhi," *New Yorker*, 17 July 1995.

75. Said, *Orientalism*, 239.

76. Ibid., 325.

77. Ibid., 221.

78. Said does introduce the topic of the Orient as a liminal space for the European. See his discussion of Flaubert's oriental experiences mentioned above (ibid., 184 ff.). For an analysis of liminality in Western places, see Rob Shields, *Places on the Margin: Alternative Geographies of Modernity* (London: Routledge, 1991).

79. He is also heavily influenced by Foucault's *Birth of the Clinic* and *Discipline and Punish*.

80. Edward Said, photographs by Jean Mohr, *After the Last Sky: Palestinian Lives* (New York: Pantheon Books, 1986).

81. Derrida uses the figure of the ghost and an extended discussion of Hamlet in *Specters of Marx*.

82. Said and Mohr, *After the Last Sky*, 84.

83. Ibid., 78.

84. Ibid., 150.

85. Ibid., 164.

86. W. J. T. Mitchell, "The Photographic Essay: Four Case Studies," chapter 9 in *Picture Theory* (Chicago: University of Chicago Press, 1994), 281–322, 322.

Streets

1. I am grateful to Frank Serrao for vivid descriptions of behaviors of hungry executives at airport feeding stations.

2. The concept is Marc Augé's and appears in *non-places: introduction to an anthropology of supermodernity*, trans. John Howe (London: Verso, 1995): 77–78, 94. "If place can be defined as relational, historical and concerned with identity, then a space which cannot be defined as relational, or historical, or concerned with identity will be a non-place" (77–78). "*Non-place* designates two complementary but distinct realities: spaces formed in relation to certain ends (transport, transit, commerce, leisure), and the relations that individuals have with these spaces."

3. Michel de Certeau, "The Laugh of Michel Foucault," in *Heterologies: Discourse on the Other* (Minneapolis: University of Minnesota Press, 1989), 193–98, 194.

4. Montier and Henri Cartier-Bresson, *Henri Cartier-Bresson and the Artless Art*, 77–78.

5. Henri Cartier-Bresson, *Henri-Cartier-Bresson: Aperture Masters of Photography, Number Two* (New York: Aperture, 1976), 8.

6. Montier and Cartier-Bresson, *Henri Cartier-Bresson and the Artless Art*, 79.

7. John Szarkowski, *Winogrand: Figments from the Real World* (New York: Museum of Modern Art, 1988), 25.

8. Walker Evans, *The Hungry Eye*, ed. Gilles Mora and John T. Hill (New York: Abrams, 1993), 15.

9. See, for example, the clip of the tenth anniversary of the building of the Vietnam Veterans Memorial in the documentary *Maya Lin*; public statements make by Maya Lin on the occasion of the reopening of the Garden of the Cleveland Public Library, September 1998; and Veterans' Day interview of Maya Lin, by Susan Stanberg, on National Public Radio, 11 November 2000.

10. The difference between digitally manipulated photography and dark-room manipulated photography is a matter of the time it takes to execute certain operations and unanswered questions about how artists will use the digital technology in the future. Robbert Flick credits John Szarkowski with saying that when photography was invented, everybody knew what it could do, but nobody knew what it was for. Robbert Flick, "Representing Los Angeles," in *Rethinking Los Angeles*, ed. Michael J. Dear, H. Eric Schockman, and Greg Hise (Thousand Oaks, Calif.: Sage Publications, 1996), 21. In this context, Nathan Lyons argues that one of the reasons it is so important that artists use the new technology is to prevent it from being totally appropriated and developed by corporate capitalism. For examples of what artists are using computers to make, see not only the work of Robbert Flick but also the digitally created photomontages of Pedro Meyer, *Truths and Fictions: A Journey from Documentary to Digital Photography* (New York: Aperture, 1995); and the work of Martina Lopez and other artists presented in *Metamorphoses: Photography in the Electronic Age* (New York: Aperture, 1994). Also *Iterations: The New Image*, ed. Timothy Druckrey (Cambridge, Mass.: MIT Press, 1994); Peter Lunenfeld, *Snap to Grid* (Cambridge, Mass.: MIT Press, 2000); and current issues of *Artforum*.

11. The notion of the photograph as an instrument constructing the middle-class family led me to imagine an alternative family calendar accompanied by legends like the pointer lines used to connect captions to drawings in biology texts. The captions would tell something of the people, "outside" the pious notion of the happy family. "Deceased, doing hard time, unemployed" were the kind of things I had in mind—to give credit to the experiences a family may endure as the prerequisite for the production of the family calendar.

12. John Szarkowski, *Looking at Photographs: 100 Pictures from the Collection of the Museum of Modern Art* (New York: Museum of Modern Art, 1988), 196.

13. W. Eugene Smith, *W. Eugene Smith: His Photographs and Notes* (1969; New York: Aperture, 1993), unpaginated. The text in this book is identified only as "from Eugene Smith's notebooks and writings." The phrases quoted here accompany excerpts from his "Pittsburgh: A Labyrinthine Walk," 1955.

14. Selections of the Pittsburgh pictures appear in Smith, *W. Eugene Smith*, including the cover. More images appear in Sam Stephenson, "W. Eugene Smith's Unfinished Symphony: Previously Unpublished Photographs from the Pittsburgh Project," *Doubletake* (spring 1998): 81–97. A book-length version was published on the occasion of a touring exhibition by the same name. *Dream Street: W. Eugene Smith's Pittsburgh Project*, ed. Sam Stephenson (New York: W. W. Norton, 2001).

15. Lincoln Kirstein, "W. Eugene Smith, Success or Failure: Art of History," foreword to *W. Eugene Smith*, unpaginated.

16. Szarkowski, *Looking at Photographs*, 138. I am grateful to Janet Smith for bringing these comments to my attention.

17. Edward Agee, introductory essay, in Helen Levitt, *A Way of Seeing* (Durham: Duke University Press, 1992), xiii. The book is a reprinted collection of Helen Levitt's street photography.

18. André Bazin, "The Ontology of the Photographic Image," reprinted in *Classic Essays on Photography*, ed. Alan Trachtenberg (New Haven, Conn.: Leete's Island Books, 1980), 237–44, 242.

19. Walter Benjamin, "A Short History of Photography," reprinted in *Classic Essays on Photography*, ed. Trachtenberg, 199–216, 202. A newer translation appears with the more subtle title "Little History of Photography," in *Walter Benjamin Selected Writings*, vol. 2 (Cambridge, Mass.: Harvard University Press, 1999), 507–30.

20. Two current camera-based projects come to mind in this regard. The first is the publication in various venues and an exhibition in 1999 of recently uncovered photographs of Cambodians who had been put in prison by the Khmer Rouge and later killed, many after being tortured. These are quite difficult to look at, and I think the decision to treat them as objects for display is morally suspect for a number of reasons. At the same time there is an urgency to the project of witnessing a genocide that the Western countries had chosen to diminish in importance. The world is not so simple that "the next new thing" can be clearly separated from enlarging the common consciousness. So this project remains ambiguous.

In another recent project, about which there has been much less publicity, a small number of photographers working in Rwanda have taken photographs of lost children and posted them in the refugee camps. Approximately two thousand children have been found and reunited with their families because of this project. A couple of things are striking about this work: what a "simple" use of the camera it is and what a great deal of good it does. The Rwanda photographs are exactly the same kind of shots that compose the Cambodian collection.

21. Barthes, *Camera Lucida*, 27, 38, 40.

22. Ibid., 42.

23. Ibid., 73.

24. John Berger, *About Looking* (New York: Pantheon Books, 1980).

25. Angela Davis, "Afro Images: Politics, Fashion, and Nostalgia," *Critical Inquiry* 21 (autumn 1994): 37–45.

26. Barthes, *Camera Lucida*, 76.

27. Ibid., 85, 89; emphasis added.

28. Janet Malcolm, "Aristocrats," in *Diana and Nikon: Essays on Photography* (New York: Aperture, 1997), 179–89, 188–89.

29. Barthes, *Camera Lucida*, 91.

30. Ibid., 113.

31. Ibid., 119.

32. Ibid., 116–17.

33. Roland Barthes, "The Third Meaning," in *Image, Music, Text* (New York: Hill and Wang, 1977), 52–68, 59.

34. Eduardo Cadava, *Words of Light: Theses on the Photography of History* (Princeton: Princeton University Press, 1997), xxix.

35. Benjamin, "Little History of Photography," 527. It was Laszlo Moholy-Nagy.

36. "What in the end, makes advertisements so superior to criticism? Not what the moving red neon sign says—but the fiery pool reflecting it in the asphalt." Benjamin, "One Way Street," 426.

37. Ibid.

38. Walter Benjamin, sections 5, 6, and 7, "Thesis on the Philosophy of History," reprinted in *Illuminations* (New York: Schocken Books, 1978), 253–64, especially 255–56.

39. See Barbara Maria Stafford, *Good Looking: Essays on the Virtue of Images* (Cambridge, Mass.: MIT Press, 1996).

40. Ian Chambers, "Naples: The Emergent Archaic," in *Strangely Familiar*, ed. Borden et al., 52–56, 56.

41. Quoted in Leo Charney, "In a Moment: Film and the Philosophy of Modernity," chapter 10 in *Cinema and the Invention of Modern Life*, ed. by Leo Charney and Vanessa R. Schwartz (Berkeley: University of California Press, 1995), 279–94, 282.

42. Taussig, *Mimesis and Alterity*, 37.

43. The phrase "strangely familiar," is taken from *Strangely Familiar*, ed. Borden et al., a book put together by a group of planners and designers in England who operate with the sensible goal of including the city in urban architecture.

44. Taussig, *Mimesis and Alterity*, 57.

45. Ibid., 37.

46. Ibid., 191.

47. Lincoln Kirstein, "Photographs of America: Walker Evans," in Walker Evans, *American Photographs* (1938; New York: Museum of Modern Art, 1988), 189–98, 191.

48. Charney and Schwartz, *Cinema and the Invention of Modern Life*, 1.

49. Alan Trachtenberg, "A Book Nearly Anonymous," chapter 5 in *Reading American Photographs* (New York: Noonday Press, 1990), 231–84.

50. The photographs for *The Americans* were taken by Robert Frank in 1955 and 1956 on a grant from the John Simon Guggenheim Foundation. Frank had difficulty publishing the work in this country. *The Americans* was originally published by Robert Delpire, Paris, 1958, and by Grove Press, New York, 1959.

51. This tradition continues and is developed further in the work of Nathan Lyons, founder of the Visual Studies Workshop in Rochester, New York, and Jim Gibson. Nathan Lyons, *Verbal Landscapes/Dinosaur Sat Down* (Buffalo: Albright-Knox Gallery and CEPA Gallery, 1987); Nathan Lyons, *Notations in Passing* (Cambridge, Mass.: MIT Press, 1974); Jim Gibson, *False Evidence Appearing Real* (Ottawa: Canadian Museum of Contemporary Photography, 1993). See also Balázs Czeizel, *This Is Not America Either*, Montage 91: International Festival of the Image (Rochester, N.Y.: Visual Studied Workshop, 1993). Current heirs to the tradition include Philip Brookman and Jim Goldberg. See their *Raised by Wolves* (Zurich: SCALO, 1995).

52. See Robert Frank, *Moving Out*, with text by Sarah Greenough, Philip Brookman, W. S. DiPiero, Martin Gasser, and John Hanhardt (Washington, D.C.: National Gallery of Art and SCALO, 1994); and Robert Frank, *Thank You* (Zurich: SCALO, 1996).

53. For an overview of Smith's work, see *W. Eugene Smith*.

54. For excerpts of the photo essays "Country Doctor" and "Nurse Midwife," see ibid. As noted above, selections from the Pittsburgh work appear in *W. Eugene Smith*; in Sam Stephenson, "W. Eugene Smith's Unfinished Symphony"; and in *Dream Street*, ed. Stephenson. His images of jazz musicians appear in W. Eugene Smith, "Nights of Incandescence" (previously unpublished study prints by W. Eugene Smith), *Doubletake* 18 (fall 1999): 46–51.

55. Stephenson, "W. Eugene Smith's Unfinished Symphony," 81.

56. Colin Westerbeck and Joel Meyerowitz, *Bystander: A History of Street Photography* (Boston: Little, Brown, 1994), 198.

57. See the section titled "Situation," in Theodor W. Adorno's *Aesthetic Theory* ([Minneapolis: University of Minnesota Press 1997], 16–45) for a discussion of these issues that is still timely.

58. John Goodman, "A Few Rounds of Photography" (A Conversation with John Paul Caponigro), *Camera Arts* (August/September 1999): 10–22, 18.

59. Ibid., 18.

60. "Martine Franck," in *Magnum's Women Photographers* (Munich: Prestel Verlag, 1999), 58–97, 58.

61. Michel Foucault and Gilles Deleuze, "Intellectuals and Power," *Discourses: Conversations in Postmodern Art and Culture*, ed. R. Ferguson, W. Olander, M. Tucker, and D. Fiss (Cambridge, Mass.: MIT Press, 1990), 9–16, 9.

62. Rajchman, "Foucault's Art of Seeing," 93.

63. Levitt, *A Way of Seeing*. Also Westerbeck and Meyerowitz, "Collective Vision," chapter 13 in *Bystander*, 253–66; and Helen Levitt, *Crosstown* (New York: Power House Books, 2001).

64. See Keith Davis, *Dorothea Lange: American Photographs* (New York: Chronicle Books; 1994); *The Photographs of Dorothea Lange* (Kansas City: Hallmark Cards in association with Abrams, 1995); and Westerbeck and Meyerowitz, "Collective Vision."

65. Sources on Roy DeCarava's work include: Roy DeCarava and Langston Hughes, *The Sweet Flypaper of Life* (1955; reprinted, Washington, D.C.: Howard University Press, 1984); Roy DeCarava, *Roy DeCarava: A Retrospective* (New York: Museum of Modern Art, 1996); Vicki Goldberg, "Quiet, Tender Moments of Urban Melancholy," *New York Times*, 11 February 1996, Arts and Leisure section, 37; Andy Grundberg, "Command and Control," *See* 2, no. 2 (1996): 72; Maren Stange, "Shadow and Substance," *Art in America* (March 1996): 35–39; Max Kozloff, "Time Stands Still," *Artforum* (May 1996): 78–83; and Roy DeCarava, *The Sound I Saw: Improvisation on a Jazz Theme* (London: Phaidon, 2001). Sources on W. Eugene Smith include: Smith, *W. Eugene Smith*; Stephenson, "W. Eugene Smith's Unfinished Symphony"; Smith, "Nights of Incandescence"; and Shephenson, *Dream Street*.

66. DeCarava first worked as a commercial artist and then as a freelance photographer. In 1954 he founded the Photographer's Gallery on the Upper West Side. He exhibited photographers whose work he admired. These included Chicago photographer Harry Callahan and Minor White, a founder and the first editor of *Aperture*.

67. DeCarava and Hughes, *The Sweet Flypaper of Life*, 48.

68. Sources on Winogrand include: Szarkowski, *Winogrand*; Garry Winogrand, *The Man in the Crowd: The Uneasy Streets of Garry Winogrand*, introduction by Fran Lebowitz, essay by Ben Lifson (San Francisco: Fraenkel Gallery in association with DAP, 1999). See also Westerbeck and Meyerowitz, *Bystander*.

69. Sources on Sally Mann include: Sally Mann, *At Twelve: Portraits of Young Women* (New York: Aperture, 1988); Sally Mann, *Immediate Family* (New York: Aperture, 1992); Alfred Corn, "Photography Degree Zero," *Art in America* (January 1998): 88–91; Hilton Als, "The Unvanquished: Sally Mann's Portrait of the South," *New Yorker*, 27 September 1999, 98–102; and Lyle Rexer, "Marriage under Glass: Intimate Exposures," *New York Times*, Sunday, 19 November 2000, Arts and Leisure section, 1, 41.

70. Simmel, "The Metropolis and Mental Life."

71. Alexander Alberro, "Between the Tides: The Photographs of Roy Arden," *Artforum* (January 1997): 70–73, 70.

72. Jim Lewis, "No Place Like Home: The Photographs of Richard Billingham," *Artforum* (January 1997): 62–67, 62; Richard Billingham, *Ray's a Laugh* (New York: SCALO, 1996).

73. Charles A. Hartman, "In Print" *See* 2, no. 3 (1996): 62–63, 62.

74. Lewis, "No Place Like Home," 67.

Index

abstract space: dominance in the present of, 79–80

abstract thought: as barrier to experience, 40

advertising, 1–2, 106–7, 137; "City Tales" series, 23–24; representational spaces appropriated by, 85

aesthetics of distinction, 17, 19, 35, 38; social and democratic relations fostered by, 24; urban development and, 22, 26

aesthetics of existence, 35, 38, 59, 77, 169n.72

African Americans: De Carava's photographs of, 149–51; identity construction by, 66–67; Little Rock, Arkansas, school-children, civil rights era photograph of, 68; migration to northern cities, 12; Smith's images of black America, 148. *See also* race

After the Last Sky (Said), 111–15

Agee, James, 124–25, 144

Aguililla, Mexico, 30

Alberro, Alexander, 155–56

Ali, Muhammad: Winogrand's photograph of, 152

alienation, 97

Allen, John, 85

American Photographs (Evans), 138

Americans, The (Frank), 138, 180n.50

American urban theory: basic tenets of, 7–9

antiurbanism, 3, 12

Arbus, Diane, 128–29

Arcades Project (Benjamin), 25, 135

Archaeology of Knowledge, The (Foucault), 110, 111

architecture: neoclassical, 20–21; Rajchman's analysis of, 58–59

Arden, Roy, 155–56

arrest, 127–28; arrested development, 128; Barthes's use of term, 127, 128, 129, 130; photographs reacquiring a living context, 127–28; space for witnessing, 131

art, engaged, 90, 107
Artforum: January 1997 issue, 155–58
articulable: Foucault's notion of, 83
articulation: photograph as space of, 126;
    spaces of visibility interwoven with
    spaces of, 47–48
artist's book, 109
assembly: complex political valence of three
    modes of, 86–87; Lefebvre's notion of,
    78, 80–88; three modes of assembly,
    82–88
assimilation, politics of, xii
Athens, Greece: restoration as collective
    memory of birthplace of democracy,
    19–22, 32
Augé, Marc, 177n.2
authentication: power of, 128, 130, 131, 153
Avalon (movie), 167n.23

Balakian, Peter, 175n.30
Ball, Edward: interview on National Public
    Radio with, 51–52
Barthes, Roland, 125, 126–32, 137, 141, 158
Battery Park City (New York), 16, 23
Bazin, André, 126
bearing witness: photography as faithful
    witness, 122–32; potential for love as
    opportunity for, 100; responsibility for,
    97–98
Beauregard, Robert, 10–16, 29, 91
Bellamy, Edward, 43
Bellingham, Bruce, 171n.44
Benjamin, Walter, xi, xiii, 21, 22, 26, 40,
    77–78, 95, 97–104, 115, 141, 155, 158,
    165n.2, 169n.1; Arcades Project, 25, 135;
    conceptualization of moment, 97, 134–35;
    flash of insight/recognition, notion of,
    97, 133, 135, 136; fragments recontextual-
    ized into new constellations, 26, 27, 29;
    on photography and camera, 122, 126–27,
    132–33; on responsibility of heirs to
    Western philosophical tradition, 98–99;
    use of montage, 78, 104–10
Berger, John, 127–28
Bhabha, Homi, 177n.74
biases, antiurban, 3, 12
BIDs. *See* business improvement districts
Bier, Thomas, 7, 9, 10, 28–29, 90

Billingham, Richard, 156–58
*Birth of a Clinic: An Archaeology of Medical
    Perception* (Foucault), 171n.45
blacks. *See* African Americans
body: gesturing, 107; Lefebvre on, 92
border life in Tijuana, 29–35
border maintenance functions, xii
Borges, Jorge, 41–42
Boyer, M. Christine, 29, 30, 91, 95; on city
    of collective memory, 16–17, 19–26; on
    figured vs. disfigured city, 22–26
Bradley, Bill, 55
Buck-Morss, Susan, 25, 101, 102–3, 169n.1
Burgin, Victor, 101, 105–6
Bush, George W., 55
business improvement districts (BIDs),
    25–26

Cadava, Eduardo, 131
Callahan, Harry, 142
Cambodians imprisoned by Khmer Rouge,
    exhibition of photographs of, 179n.20
camera: as active tool of presentation, 120;
    approaches to, 119–20; facility for decon-
    textualization and recontextualization,
    122; pinhole, 136; relationship to time,
    120. *See also* photography
Camera Lucida (Barthes), 126–27, 131, 155
capital: reorganization of identity of middle
    class by, 12
capitalism: alienation and, 97; contradic-
    tions between democracy and, 11–12, 14;
    reduced identities for labor and for
    owners in industrial, 89
Cartier-Bresson, Henri, 118–19, 144, 154,
    166n.4
category of the moment, 134, 155
central business districts (CBDs), 8, 9
central place: marginalization of city and
    notions of, 4
Chambers, Ian, 101, 134
Charney, Leo, 104, 134, 135, 138
Chicago School, 7–9, 14, 83, 167n.17
Chinese encyclopedia: categorization of
    animals by, 41–42
chiropractors: as example of spatial practices,
    83–84
Chora L Works (Derrida and Eisenman), 58

"circuit and border": notions of, 30–35

citizenship in America: barriers to full, implemented by racialization, 52; notions of, 54–57. *See also* membership

city(ies), 75–115; of collective memory, 16–17, 19–26; "comeback," 2; coming to terms with "responsibility of an heir," 94–104; as composite of "gestures," 92–93; defining not-city by, xii; disfigured, 22, 26; figured (nodes of development), 22–26; institutionalized rejection of, 145; Lefebvre's use of, 76; marginalization of, 4, 45; material and experience combined in, xv; in modernist theory, xi; occupied space and occasion for urban encounters, 78–94; participatory reading and means to testify, 77, 78, 104–15, 118; as places of life, ix, 34–35; as sites of layered history, 90; societal disinclination to tend to, 13; as subset of contemporary urban practices, xi–xii; types, in European context, 3–4

city, common presentations of, 2–26; objects to be interpreted, 4, 10–16, 29; raw material for production, 5, 16–26, 29; urban decline and city as particular place, 2, 4, 6–10, 15–16

City of Collective Memory: Its Historical Imagery and Architectural Entertainments, The (Boyer), 16–17, 19–26

"City Tales" (advertisement series), 23–24

civility, politics of, 51–52

classical systems of knowledge, 64–66

classical theory of language, 64–65

Cleanthes, Stamatis, 20

Cleveland, 28; as "comeback" city, 2; commuter corridors leading into, 84; "Enhancing the Public Realm" lecture series, 75–76; indicators of urban decline in, 7; tax bases of Greater Cleveland region, report on, 6–7, 9

Cleveland Public Library: garden of, 121–22

cognition and emotion: distinction between, 134

Cohen, Leonard, 75

collective memory: Athens restoration based on, 19–22, 32; city of, 16–17, 19–26; museum as "deliberate" instrument of,

95; redevelopment in New York during 1980s and, 22–24; role in constructing urban space, 22–24; selectivity of, 19

"comeback" cities, 2

commodity: Marx's notion of, 82, 87

completeness and closure: cultural preferences for, 27, 28

concentric zone theory, 83

"concrete abstractions," 82

Condition of the Working Class in England (Engels), 17–20

connectiveness with existence, 142–44

consumer society, 89–90

consumption: festive market places, 16, 90–91; newly made urban nodes as spaces of, 22–24; as required recreational activity, 107; themed spaces about, 87

"Country Doctor" photo essay (Smith), 148

Crime and Punishment (Dostoevsky), 92

"Critique of the Hegelian Dialectic and Philosophy as a Whole" (Marx), 95–97

Culler, Jonathan, 90–91

cultural analysis, European, xi: *See also* Benjamin, Walter; Foucault, Michel; Lefebvre, Henri

cultural conventions: expectation of urban space and, ix

cultural critique, xii–xiii

cultural dreamwork, 103, 106

cultural studies, 133

culture: high, 30; popular, 30; urban, 3–4, 30–35, 57–58; urban decline as component of, 4, 10–16; visual, of modernity, 132–33

Cunningham, Merce, 132

Dahl, Robert, 167n.29

dailiness of creating urban life, 31–32

dangers of discourse, 27, 29, 32, 35

Davis, Angela, 128

Death and Labyrinth: The World of Raymond Roussel (Foucault), 56

debates: as opportunities to show political order as complete, 55

DeCarava, Roy, 147, 149–51, 181n.66

de Certeau, Michel, 39, 69, 72, 118, 172n.77

decontextualization, 122

deeply feminine, the, 152–54

Deleuze, Gilles, 39, 40, 42, 44, 47, 48, 109–10, 143, 169n.1
delinquent father, 51, 52
democracy: contradictions between capitalism and, 11–12, 14; neoclassical architecture as markers for, 20–21; restoration of Athens, as collective memory of birthplace of, 19–22, 32
Derrida, Jacques, 58, 97–98
desire: function of, xi
deterritorialization, 31, 34
Deuteronomy: dietary rules in, 48–51
"dialectics of seeing," 104
dietary rules: in Leviticus and Deuteronomy, 48–51
digital technology, 178n.10
Discipline and Punish (Foucault), 110
discourse: dangers of, 27, 29, 32, 35
discourse analysis, 110, 111, 171n.44
discursive and nondiscursive elements of social order: relationship between, 42–48
disfigured city, 22, 26
Disney Corporation, 43
Disneyland: critique of American culture as all, 86–87
distance: in Winogrand's photography, 152
distinction: aesthetics of, 17, 19, 22, 24, 26, 35, 38
Dostoevsky, F., 92
Douglas, Mary, 48–52
Dreyfus, Hubert C., 62
Du Bois, W. E. B., 66, 67

economic development: festive market places, 16, 90–91; role of images of city in, 16
economic restructuring in 1970s and 1980s, 12
Eisenman, Peter, 58
electoral process: difference between governing process and, 100
emotion and cognition: distinction between, 134
empirical research: interpretative work woven into, 10; place-based approach as, 2, 4, 6–10
engaged art, 90, 107

engagement, x; book as site of, 109–10; camera as tool of, xiv, 118, 120; as generative, 103, 108; testifying by linking montage principle to physical, 104–10
Engels, Friedrich, 17–20, 22, 26
"Enhancing the Public Realm" lecture series, 75–76
equality: boundaries of citizenship shaped by notions of, 54–57; Locke on, 53
ethics, 165n.3; of participation, xiv–xv; of photography, 141
ethnology, 72, 73
European cultural analysis, xi
European idealization of ancient Greek civilization, 19–22, 32
European photography: parallel developments in American and, 138–39
Evans, Walker, xiv, 121, 138, 139, 144, 156
Event-Cities (Tschumi), 173n.4
events: Foucault on, 142, 155; photography and construction of, 129–30
everyday approach to photography, 138, 139
everyday life: spatial practices as patterns of, 83–84
exchange value, 82
exclusion, politics of, 48, 51–59; citizenship in America and, 54–57; connection between membership and righteousness, 49–51, 52; Foucault and exposure of, 52
executive suites, 117–18; as paradigmatic "non-places," 118
existence: aesthetics of, 35, 38, 59, 77, 169n.72; connectiveness with, 142–44; heterotopic space and terms of, 44–48
experience: abstract thought as barrier to, 40; images as instrument of human, 133; memory and, 39, 40, 90–91, 93; provoked by photograph, 130

faithful witness: instruments of the moment used as, 134; photography as, 122–32; testifying as, 104–15; witnessing as generative relationship, 130
fashion, 107, 176n.64
father, delinquent, 51, 52
feeding station: executive suites with, 117–18
female-headed households: urban decline and percentage of, 52

feminine, the deeply, 152–54
festive market places, 16, 90–91
figured city (nodes of development), 22–26
Fischler, Raphael, 174n.19
flash of insight/recognition: Benjamin's
    notion of, 97, 133, 135, 136
Flaubert, Gustave, 110
Flick, Robbert, 178n.10
Forester, C. S., 11
Foucault, Michel, xi, 27, 32, 38–48, 92, 95,
    110, 143, 171n.45; aesthetics of existence,
    35, 38, 59, 77, 169n.72; American profile
    of, 56; bouts of surprise of, 118; on events,
    142, 155; "flash of light," 44; heterotopic
    space, xiii, 38, 40–48, 57, 77, 94, 115, 122;
    on human sciences, 71–72, 175n.33;
    interpretation of Velázquez's *Las Meninas*,
    61–73; similarities to Lefebvre, 76, 80;
    spatial approach, 39, 40–48
Franck, Martine, 142–43
Frank, Robert, 138, 139, 180n.50
Fulton Fish Market (New York), 23

García Canclini, Néstor, 29–35, 45, 90
generative relationship: between labor and
    humanity, 97; with material world, 103,
    108; witnessing as, 130
gestures, 92–93, 135; of occupation, 115
gesturing body, 107
Getty Museum: photography at, 94–95
globalization: economic and cultural, 57–58
Goodman, John, 142
Gore, Al, 55
Gorky, Arshile, 175n.30
governing process: difference between
    electoral process and, 100
Graham, Dan, 156
Greece: European idealization of ancient,
    19–22, 32
Grosz, George, 139
growth, urban: as inevitable and positive,
    8–9; legacy of belief in long-term benefits
    of, 9

Habermas, Jürgen, 75
Harlem Project photographs of DeCarava,
    150
Harry and David's advertisement, 1–2

Hartman, Charles A., 156
Harvey, David, 88
Hausman, Raoul, 139
Heartfield, John, xiv, 139
Hegel, Georg Wilhelm Friedrich, 95–97, 104
Hellenism: symbols of, 20–21
Hemiciclo Juárez in Alameda of Mexico
    City, 33–34
Herculine Barbin (Foucault), 56
heterotopic space, xiii, 38, 40–48, 57, 77,
    94, 115, 122; as active component of
    modernity, 73; cohabitation of larger
    normalizing spatial order and, xi; retire-
    ment homes as, 45–47; terms of existence
    and, 44–48
high culture, 30
Hill, John T., 121
hip-hop: as street form appropriated by big
    business, 85
Hoch, Hannah, 139
Hughes, Langston, 150, 151
humanism, positive, 96–97
human sciences: knowledge of Man at
    center of modern, 71, 175n.33; normative
    perspectives, 72; volatile intellectual space
    producing, 71–72
"Hybrid Cultures, Oblique Powers" (García
    Canclini), 29–35

*I, Pierre Rivière, having slaughtered my
    mother, my sister, and my brother. . . :
    A Case of Parricide in the 19th Century*
    (Foucault), 56, 69
identity and sociality: play between, 146–47
indebtedness: spaces of, 143, 154–58
individual: Lange's images of singular,
    145–46
internal combustion society: reification into
    abstract knowledge of political economy
    of, 83
interpretation: cities as objects for, 4, 10–16,
    29
intimacy of Mann's photography, 152–54

jazz series: of DeCarava, 150; of Smith, 149
Jewish culture: dietary rules of ancient,
    48–52
juxtaposition, 108, 139

Kennedy, John F.: Winogrand's photograph of, 152
Kirstein, Lincoln, 124, 138
knowledge: classical systems of, 64–66

labor as generative of humanity: Marx and Hegel on, 97
Lacis, Asja, 100, 101, 102, 103
Lange, Dorothea, 118, 145–47
language: classical theory of, 64–65
Laslett, Peter, 53
Las Meninas (Velázquez): Foucault's interpretation of, 61–73
Le Corbusier, 43
Lefebvre, Henri, xi, xiii, 38–39, 59, 73, 77, 78–94, 95, 104, 107, 115, 122, 134, 158, 165n.1; concerns about modernity, 78–80; gestures, 92–93, 115, 135; as Marxist, 81–82, 89; on moments, 88, 89; notion of assembly, 78, 80–88; origin myth of, 79; "right to the city," 76, 89, 90, 91, 93–94, 120, 144, 155; similarities to Foucault, 76, 80; "spatial practices," 83–84, 88–89; spatial theory of, 76–77; three-part model of spatial processes, 82–88
Leviticus: dietary rules in, 48–51
Levitt, Helen, 124–25, 144–47
Lewis, Jim, 156–58
liberal ethic: single-minded attention to exclusions essentializing, 56–57
liminal urban places of modernity, 13–14, 15
Lin, Maya, 121–22
literacy, visual, 132
literary montage, xiii
"Little History of Photography" (Benjamin), 132–33
Locke, John, 52–54, 57, 58
London's financial district: "production of service space" in, 85
love: art as acts of, 154; Cartier-Bresson's notion of, 119; image making in terms of, 141, 142; Marx on, 100; photography as form of, 157–58; provoked by photograph, 130, 131
Lyons, Nathan, 178n.10

McCain, John, 55
Malcolm, Janet, 128–29

Manchester, England: Engels's book on condition of working class in, 17–20, 22
Mann, Sally, 152–54
mannequins, 107, 133, 176n.66
Marcus, Steven, 17–18
marginalization of city, 4, 45
market places, festive, 16, 90–91
Marx, Karl, 40, 81, 82, 99–100, 104
Marxist opposition in American urban studies, x–xi
Mathis, Mary Pugh, 171n.44
mayors: difficulty pursuing redistributive policies, 100
meaning, construction of, 2
medieval murals: photography compared to, 139–40
membership: citizenship in America as, 54–57; political and moral space organized by aspiration to, 48–51; and righteousness, connection between, 49–51, 52
memory: as bringing into the present, 39; continual construction of, in context of daily experience, 29–35; experience and, 39, 40, 90–91, 93
Mexico: border life in Tijuana, 29–35; monuments in, 30, 32–34
Mexico City: Hemiciclo Juárez in Alameda of, 33–34
middle class, 90; disengagement from urban life, conditions legitimating, 12; identity reorganized by capital, 12; of suburbs, 12, 167n.23
migrant farm workers: Lange's work on, 146
Miller, Angela, 175n.30
Mitchell, W. J. T., 64, 114
modernist theory, xi
modernity: beginnings of, debate about, 173n.5; challenges to reason in, 132–41; heterotopic space as active component of, 73; Lefebvre's concerns about, 78–80; liminal urban places of, 13–14, 15; photography and, 126; search for life worth living in, 141–44; as source of tools, xii, xiii; visual culture of, 132–33
Mohr, Jean, 111, 112, 113
moment(s): Benjamin's conceptualization of,

97, 134–35; category of the, 134, 155; Lefebvre's discussion of, 88, 89; manufactured, 89; as spatial circumstances generative of engaged life experience, 89

money, 99–100; homogeneous forms of valuation imposed by, 100

montage: Benjamin's use of, 78, 104–10; literary, xiii; as mode of testifying, 104–10; photographic, xiv, 138–39

Montier, Jean-Pierre, 118

monuments: in Mexico, 30, 32–34; recoding of, as part of everyday flow of urban culture, 34, 169n.71; role in supporting state power, 32–33

Mora, Gilles, 121

More, Thomas, 43

Moscow, Russia, 105

Mots et les choses, Les (Gallimard), 61

movement through images, 139

Muschamp, Herbert, 173n.4

museum as "deliberate" instrument of "collective memory," 95

naming: representation as, 65–66

Naples, Italy, 101–4

"Naples" (Benjamin), 102

National Endowment for the Arts, 134

National Public Radio: interview about southern writers, 60; interview with Edward Ball, 51–52

nativism: Progressive Era antiurban, 12

neighborhood change: traditional theories of, 167n.17

neoclassical architecture: as markers of democracy, 20–21

NewsHour with Jim Lehrer (TV): interview with Merce Cunningham on, 132

"New Urbanism, The," 173n.4

New York: business improvement districts in, 25–26; "City Tales" advertisement series celebrating, 23–24; Levitt's photography of 1930s and 1940s in, 145–47; redevelopment during 1980s in, 22–24; South Street Seaport, 16, 22–23, 91

"non-places," 118, 177n.2

"Notes Written One Sunday in the French Countryside" (Lefebvre), 87, 174n.23

"Nurse Midwife" photo essay (Smith), 148

oblique power: exercising, 31, 32, 44, 47

obtuse meaning, 130

occupation: gestures of, 115

occupied space, 39, 78–94, 115; gesture as fundamental to, 92–93; Lefebvre's assembly of space presupposing, 80; occasion for urban encounters and, 78–94

"Of Other Spaces" (Foucault), 48

One Way Street (Benjamin), 100–101, 104, 107–9

"On the Program of the Coming Philosophy" (Benjamin), 98–99

Order of Things, The (Foucault), 41, 56, 61, 64, 158, 175n.33

Orientalism (Said), 110–11, 112, 114

Palestinian space, 111–15

participatory reading, 77, 78, 104–15, 118

Pascucci, Ernest, 58

peace: photographers in search of, 147–51

pensive photography, 127

performative aspects of interpretative work, 16

photographic montage, xiv, 138–39

photographic sequence, 138, 139

photographic space: viewers' participation in making, 126

photography: approaches to camera, 119–20; as arena of social activity, 67–69; commodity and collector subcultures of, 136; as connecting light between subject and image viewer experiences, 136; construction of events by, 129–30; digitally manipulated vs. dark-room manipulated, 178n.10; direct engagement of city through, 118, 120; ethics of, 141; as faithful witness, 122–32; history of, 135; images as instrument of human experience, 133; modernity and, 126; as modern storyteller, 137; parallel developments in American and European, 138–39; pensive, 127; photographs as sites of participatory reading provoking urban encounters, 118; as productive part of city life, 120; radical openness of, 120–21

Photography as Art, 155–56

photojournalism: Cartier-Bresson's definition of, 166n.4

pinhole camera, 136

pity provoked by photograph, 130, 131

place-based approach to city, 2, 4, 6–10, 15–16

politics: of civility, 51–52; of exclusion, 48, 51–59; involved in ongoing deployment of image, 137–38; of presentation, 11; of representation, 2, 3

popular culture, 30

porousness of spaces, 107; Naples, 101, 102–3; reasons for recognizing, 70–71. *See also* heterotopic space

positive humanism, 96–97

postcolonial theory, 110

power: of authentication, 128, 130, 131, 153; oblique, exercising, 31, 32, 44, 47

"Power of Money in Bourgeois Society, The" (Marx), 99–100

prejudices, x

presentation: politics of, 11; professional space of, 86

presidential campaigns of 2000, 55

"Producing the Show" (Boyer), 22–23

Production of Space, The (Lefebvre), 84, 92

professional practices: spaces of, 83

professional space of presentation, 86

Progressive Era antiurban nativism, 12

Pryke, Michael, 85

psychoanalysis, 72, 73

public policy: role in promoting outlying growth, 9

public space: photographer-photograph-viewer relationship as, 125

punctum, 127

Rabinow, Paul, 62

race: barriers to full membership and citizenship implemented by racialization, 52; De Carava's photographs of black America, 149–51; identity construction by African Americas, 66–67; in rhetoric of urban decline, use of, 12; Smith's images of black America, 148; spatial approach to interpreting, 67; urban themes linked to, 13

racism, 149–50, 151

Rajchman, John, 58–59, 143

Ralph Lauren, 129

rationality, 56

raw material for production, city as, 5, 16–26, 29; Athens restoration, 19–22, 32; business improvement districts (BIDs), 25–26; Engels on Manchester, England, 17–20, 22; redevelopment in New York during 1980s, 22–24

Ray's a Laugh (Billingham), 156–58

real and representational: inconsistencies contained in notions of, 1–2

realized abstraction: State as, 87

reason: challenges to, 132–41

recognition/insight: experience of, 97, 133, 135, 136

recontextualization, 122

redemption narrative, 14

regionalism, 28–29, 60, 69, 90, 171n.57

reification into abstract knowledge of political economy of internal combustion society, 83

relativism: specter of, 28

relays, 2

representation: in classical age, 64–66; inconsistencies contained in notions of real and representational, 1–2; as naming, 65–66; politics of, 2, 3

"representational space": as active "spaces of presentation," 85; Lefebvre on, 84–85; potential, as accomplices of representations of space, 86

representations of space, 83, 86

resemblance, 66

responsibility of heir: coming to terms with, 94–104, 115

reterritorialization, 31, 34

retirement homes: as heterotopic spaces of deviation in contemporary life, 45–47; multiple contradictions and interlocking spatial practices in, 45–47; political economy of, 46

Rexer, Lyle, 152, 154

righteousness and membership: connection between, 49–51, 52

"Right to the City, The" (Lefebvre), 89, 90, 91, 93–94

Rivière, Pierre, 70

Rouse, J., 30
Ruscha, Edward, 156
Rwanda: photographs of lost children in, 179n.20
Rybczynski, Witold, 3

Sade, Marquis de, 69, 158
safe urban space: business improvement districts and, 25–26
Said, Edward, 13, 110–15
scenic lookout points in wilderness: designation of, 81
Schauber, Eduard, 20
Schwartz, Vanessa R., 138
Second Treatise on Government (Locke), 52–53, 57
Second World War: Smith's photos of, 147–48, 149
See (journal), 156
self and space: connections between, 92; gesture linking, 115
Semper, Gottfried, 20–21
Shapiro, Michael, 80
Shell, Marc, 176n.65
Shields, Rob, 173n.10
shock, 142
Simmel, Georg, 107, 134, 154
situation awareness, ix, xv
situationists, 89, 90
Smith, Janet L., 167n.17
Smith, W. Eugene, 123–24, 140, 141, 144, 147–49, 151; images of black America, 148; war photos, 147–48, 149
sociality and identity: play between, 146–47
social movements expanding boundaries of citizenship: political rhetoric of, 54–57
social sciences: perpetual reform notion in, 56–57
Some Cities (Burgin), 105–6
sorrow songs: spirituals as, 66, 67
Sound I Saw, The (DeCarava), 150
southern writers: American tradition of, 60
South Street Seaport (New York), 16, 22–23, 91
space(s), 37–73; as "arena of activity," 61; conceptualized as productive activity, 80; as instrument of thought, 67–69; local politics and development of American

Foucault, 48–59; notions of, 42; occupied, 39, 78–94, 115; as practiced place, 61, 69; self and, 92, 115; spatial presentation from *Las Meninas* to afterimage of modernity, 59–73; themed, 86–87, 92; as unitary process, 81. *See also* heterotopic space
spaces of indebtedness, 143, 154–58
spaces of presentation: in opposition to themed existences, 92
"spatial practices": Lefebvre on, 83–84, 88–89
Specters of Marx (Derrida), 97–98
spirituality, 66–67
Springfield, Oregon: 1998 school shooting in, 70
Stallybrass, P., 13–14
"state of nature," Locke's, 53, 54
Stieglitz, Alfred, 156
Stone, A. R., 107
Stone, Allucquere, 172n.58
street photography, 117–58; challenges to reason in modernity, 132–41; connection between photographic testimony and search in modernity for life worth living, 141–44; connections between self and space in, 92; the deeply feminine and reach for existence, 151–54; as faithful witness, 122–32; of Lange, 118, 145–47; of Levitt, 124–25, 144–47; in search of peace, 147–51; spaces of indebtedness, 154–58; of W. Eugene Smith, 123–24, 140, 141, 144, 147–49, 151
studium type of witness, 127, 130, 156
suburbs, suburban life style, xii–xiii, 3, 12, 167n.23
surrealism, 42–43
Sweet Flypaper of Life, The, 150
Szarkowski, John, 117, 120, 122–23, 131, 135, 178n.10

Taussig, Michael, 104, 135, 136–37
Tax Base Disparity: Development of Greater Cleveland's Sapphire Necklace, 6–7, 9
Taylor, Paul, 146
testimony: on behalf of urban life, 26–35; connection between photographic, and search in modernity for life worth living, 141–44; means to testifying as faithful

witness, 104–15; montage as mode of, 104–10; photography as faithful witness, 122–32

themed spaces, 86–87, 92

"Theses on the Philosophy of History" (Benjamin), 98–99

"Third Meaning, The" (Barthes), 130

Tijuana: case study of border life in, 29–35

time: camera's relationship to, 120

"Times Square Gym" series (Goodman), 142

Tocqueville, Alexis de, 3

tourist places, 90–91

town meetings: as opportunities to show political order as complete, 55

Trachtenberg, Alan, 138

transportation planning, 83

Tschumi, Bernard, 173n.4

Two Treatises of Government (Locke), 53

unpredictability of use, 27, 28

urban culture: García Canclini's studies of, 30–35; spread of, 3–4; universal, development of, 57–58

urban decline: 91; city as particular kind of place and, 2, 4, 6–10, 15–16; as component of culture, 4, 10–16; importance of interrogating notions of, 11; percentage of female-headed households as measure of, 52; public policy debate about, 2; race in rhetoric of, use of, 12

urban design: role of images of city in, 16

urban development: Boyer's analysis of contemporary, 22–26

urban encounters: occupied space and occasion for, 78–94

urban life: dailiness of creating, 31– 32; testimony on behalf of, 26–35

urban planning, 86

urban space: collective memory and construction of, 22–24; misleading aspects to current representations of, 91; as raw material for production, 5, 16–26, 29; shifts in notion of what constitutes, 11. *See also* city(ies)

urban studies and planning education: American, x–xi: basic tenets of American urban theory, 7–9

utopias (no spaces), 43

Vancouver, British Columbia: Arden's photographs of, 155–56

Velázquez, Diego Rodriguez de Silva y, 61

Vietnam Veterans Memorial, 87, 121

violence: acts of containment in response to, 70; as acts of discourse, 69–70; encountered in unprotected way, 70–71

visibilities, 58; Deleuze on, 40, 47, 48; related to dietary laws of Leviticus, 49–51; spaces of articulation interwoven with spaces of, 47–48

visual culture of modernity, 132–33

visual literacy, 132

Voices of Decline: The Postwar Fate of U.S. Cities (Beauregard), 10–16

voting: citizenship and, 54

War on Poverty, 14

Washington, Harold, 176n.52

Westerbeck, Colin, 142

Weston, Edward, 120

White, A., 13–14

White, Minor, 141

Who Governs? (Dahl), 14, 167n.29

wilderness areas: assembly of, 80–81

wildness of Levitt's photographs, 124–25, 144

Winogrand, Garry, 120, 144, 151–52, 153, 154

witness: types of, 127, 130, 156. *See also* bearing witness; faithful witness

working class, 89; in Manchester, England, Engels on, 17–20, 22

World Trade Organization: protests in 1999 against, 57–58

Zapata, Emiliano, 33

zones, city, 8

Helen Liggett works in theory and photography, with a special interest in the art and politics of presentation. Her photographs have been exhibited at the Cleveland Center for Contemporary Art and the Here Here Gallery in Cleveland, and she participates in the Arts in the Embassies Program. She created public art for the Harare International Festival for the Arts in Zimbabwe and the Urban Design Collaborative of Northeast Ohio. Her writing has been published in *Theory and Event, Urban Affairs Review, Whiskey Island Magazine,* and *Planning Theory.* She is professor of urban studies at Cleveland State University.